ASPEN PUBLISHERS

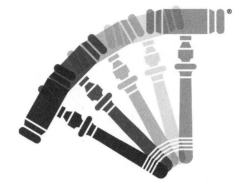

Casenote™ Legal Briefs

INTERNATIONAL LAW

Keyed to Courses Using

Damrosch, Henkin, Murphy, and Smit's
International Law

Fifth Edition

Wolters Kluwer
Law & Business

AUSTIN   BOSTON   CHICAGO   NEW YORK   THE NETHERLANDS

This publication is designed to provide accurate and authoritative information in regard to the subject matter covered. It is sold with the understanding that the publisher is not engaged in rendering legal, accounting, or other professional services. If legal advice or other expert assistance is required, the services of a competent professional person should be sought.

— From a Declaration of Principles adopted jointly
by a Committee of the American Bar Association
and a Committee of Publishers and Associates

Format for the Casenote Legal Brief

Nature of Case: This section identifies the form of action (e.g., breach of contract, negligence, battery), the type of proceeding (e.g., demurrer, appeal from trial court's jury instructions), or the relief sought (e.g., damages, injunction, criminal sanctions).

Fact Summary: This is included to refresh your memory and can be used as a quick reminder of the facts.

Rule of Law: Summarizes the general principle of law that the case illustrates. It may be used for instant recall of the court's holding and for classroom discussion or home review.

Facts: This section contains all relevant facts of the case, including the contentions of the parties and the lower court holdings. It is written in a logical order to give the student a clear understanding of the case. The plaintiff and defendant are identified by their proper names throughout and are always labeled with a (P) or (D).

Palsgraf v. Long Island R.R. Co.

Injured bystander (P) v. Railroad company (D)

N.Y. Ct. App., 248 N.Y. 339, 162 N.E. 99 (1928).

NATURE OF CASE: Appeal from judgment affirming verdict for plaintiff seeking damages for personal injury.

FACT SUMMARY: Helen Palsgraf (P) was injured on R.R.'s (D) train platform when R.R.'s (D) guard helped a passenger aboard a moving train, causing his package to fall on the tracks. The package contained fireworks which exploded, creating a shock that tipped a scale onto Palsgraf (P).

🏛 RULE OF LAW
The risk reasonably to be perceived defines the duty to be obeyed.

FACTS: Helen Palsgraf (P) purchased a ticket to Rockaway Beach from R.R. (D) and was waiting on the train platform. As she waited, two men ran to catch a train that was pulling out from the platform. The first man jumped aboard, but the second man, who appeared as if he might fall, was helped aboard by the guard on the train who had kept the door open so they could jump aboard. A guard on the platform also helped by pushing him onto the train. The man was carrying a package wrapped in newspaper. In the process, the man dropped his package, which fell on the tracks. The package contained fireworks and exploded. The shock of the explosion was apparently of great enough strength to tip over some scales at the other end of the platform, which fell on Palsgraf (P) and injured her. A jury awarded her damages, and R.R. (D) appealed.

ISSUE: Does the risk reasonably to be perceived define the duty to be obeyed?

HOLDING AND DECISION: (Cardozo, C.J.) Yes. The risk reasonably to be perceived defines the duty to be obeyed. If there is no foreseeable hazard to the injured party as the result of a seemingly innocent act, the act does not become a tort because it happened to be a wrong as to another. If the wrong was not willful, the plaintiff must show that the act as to her had such great and apparent possibilities of danger as to entitle her to protection. Negligence in the abstract is not enough upon which to base liability. Negligence is a relative concept, evolving out of the common law doctrine of trespass on the case. To establish liability, the defendant must owe a legal duty of reasonable care to the injured party. A cause of action in tort will lie where harm,

though unintended, could have been averted or avoided by observance of such a duty. The scope of the duty is limited by the range of danger that a reasonable person could foresee. In this case, there was nothing to suggest from the appearance of the parcel or otherwise that the parcel contained fireworks. The guard could not reasonably have had any warning of a threat to Palsgraf (P), and R.R. (D) therefore cannot be held liable. Judgment is reversed in favor of R.R. (D).

DISSENT: (Andrews, J.) The concept that there is no negligence unless R.R. (D) owes a legal duty to take care as to Palsgraf (P) herself is too narrow. Everyone owes to the world at large the duty of refraining from those acts that may unreasonably threaten the safety of others. If the guard's action was negligent as to those nearby, it was also negligent as to those outside what might be termed the "danger zone." For Palsgraf (P) to recover, R.R.'s (D) negligence must have been the proximate cause of her injury, a question of fact for the jury.

▶ ANALYSIS
The majority defined the limit of the defendant's liability in terms of the danger that a reasonable person in defendant's situation would have perceived. The dissent argued that the limitation should not be placed on liability, but rather on damages. Judge Andrews suggested that only injuries that would not have happened but for R.R.'s (D) negligence should be compensable. Both the majority and dissent recognized the policy-driven need to limit liability for negligent acts, seeking, in the words of Judge Andrews, to define a framework "that will be practical and in keeping with the general understanding of mankind." The Restatement (Second) of Torts has accepted Judge Cardozo's view.

Quicknotes

FORESEEABILITY A reasonable expectation that change is the probable result of certain acts or omissions.

NEGLIGENCE Conduct falling below the standard of care that a reasonable person would demonstrate under similar conditions.

PROXIMATE CAUSE The natural sequence of events without which an injury would not have been sustained.

Party ID: Quick identification of the relationship between the parties.

Concurrence/Dissent: All concurrences and dissents are briefed whenever they are included by the casebook editor.

Analysis: This last paragraph gives you a broad understanding of where the case "fits in" with other cases in the section of the book and with the entire course. It is a hornbook-style discussion indicating whether the case is a majority or minority opinion and comparing the principal case with other cases in the casebook. It may also provide analysis from restatements, uniform codes, and law review articles. The analysis will prove to be invaluable to classroom discussion.

Issue: The issue is a concise question that brings out the essence of the opinion as it relates to the section of the casebook in which the case appears. Both substantive and procedural issues are included if relevant to the decision.

Holding and Decision: This section offers a clear and in-depth discussion of the rule of the case and the court's rationale. It is written in easy-to-understand language and answers the issue presented by applying the law to the facts of the case. When relevant, it includes a thorough discussion of the exceptions to the case as listed by the court, any major cites to the other cases on point, and the names of the judges who wrote the decisions.

Quicknotes: Conveniently defines legal terms found in the case and summarizes the nature of any statutes, codes, or rules referred to in the text.

Aspen Publishers is proud to offer *Casenote Legal Briefs*—continuing thirty years of publishing America's best-selling legal briefs.

Casenote Legal Briefs are designed to help you save time when briefing assigned cases. Organized under convenient headings, they show you how to abstract the basic facts and holdings from the text of the actual opinions handed down by the courts. Used as part of a rigorous study regimen, they can help you spend more time analyzing and critiquing points of law than on copying bits and pieces of judicial opinions into your notebook or outline.

Casenote Legal Briefs should never be used as a substitute for assigned casebook readings. They work best when read as a follow-up to reviewing the underlying opinions themselves. Students who try to avoid reading and digesting the judicial opinions in their casebooks or online sources will end up shortchanging themselves in the long run. The ability to absorb, critique, and restate the dynamic and complex elements of case law decisions is crucial to your success in law school and beyond. It cannot be developed vicariously.

Casenote Legal Briefs represents but one of the many offerings in Aspen's Study Aid Timeline, which includes:

- *Casenote Legal Briefs*
- *Emanuel Law Outlines*
- *Examples & Explanations* Series
- *Introduction to Law* Series
- Emanuel *Law in a Flash* Flashcards
- Emanuel *CrunchTime* Series

Each of these series is designed to provide you with easy-to-understand explanations of complex points of law. Each volume offers guidance on the principles of legal analysis and, consulted regularly, will hone your ability to spot relevant issues. We have titles that will help you prepare for class, prepare for your exams, and enhance your general comprehension of the law along the way.

To find out more about Aspen Study Aid publications, visit us online at *http://lawschool.aspenpublishers.com* or email us at *legaledu@wolterskluwer.com*. We'll be happy to assist you.

Get this Casenote Legal Brief as an AspenLaw Studydesk eBook today!

By returning this form to Aspen Publishers, you will receive a complimentary eBook download of this Casenote Legal Brief in the AspenLaw Studydesk digital format.* Learn more about AspenLaw Studydesk today at *www.AspenLaw.com*.

Name	Phone ( )
Address	**Apt. No.**
City	**State**	**ZIP Code**

Law School	Year (check one) ☐ 1st ☐ 2nd ☐ 3rd

Cut out the UPC found on the lower left corner of the back cover of this book. Staple the UPC inside this box. Only the original UPC from the book cover will be accepted. (No photocopies or store stickers are allowed.)

Attach UPC inside this box.

Email (Print legibly or you may not get access!)

Title of this book (course subject)

ISBN of this book (10- or 13-digit number on the UPC)

Used with which casebook (provide author's name)

Mail the completed form to: Aspen Publishers, Inc.
Legal Education Division
130 Turner Street, Bldg 3, 4th Floor
Waltham, MA 02453-8901

* Upon receipt of this completed form, you will be emailed a code for the digital download of this book in AspenLaw Studydesk format. The AspenLaw Studydesk application is available as a 60-day free trial at *www.AspenLaw.com*.

For a full list of print titles by Aspen Publishers, visit *lawschool.aspenpublishers.com*.
For a full list of digital eBook titles by Aspen Publishers, visit *www.AspenLaw.com*.

Make a photocopy of this form and your UPC for your records.

For detailed information on the use of the information you provide on this form, please see the PRIVACY POLICY at www.aspenpublishers.com.

How to Brief a Case

A. Decide on a Format and Stick to It

Structure is essential to a good brief. It enables you to arrange systematically the related parts that are scattered throughout most cases, thus making manageable and understandable what might otherwise seem to be an endless and unfathomable sea of information. There are, of course, an unlimited number of formats that can be utilized. However, it is best to find one that suits your needs and stick to it. Consistency breeds both efficiency and the security that when called upon you will know where to look in your brief for the information you are asked to give.

Any format, as long as it presents the essential elements of a case in an organized fashion, can be used. Experience, however, has led *Casenotes* to develop and utilize the following format because of its logical flow and universal applicability.

NATURE OF CASE: This is a brief statement of the legal character and procedural status of the case (e.g., "Appeal of a burglary conviction").

There are many different alternatives open to a litigant dissatisfied with a court ruling. The key to determining which one has been used is to discover *who is asking this court for what.*

This first entry in the brief should be kept as *short as possible.* Use the court's terminology if you understand it. But since jurisdictions vary as to the titles of pleadings, the best entry is the one that addresses who wants what in this proceeding, not the one that sounds most like the court's language.

RULE OF LAW: A statement of the general principle of law that the case illustrates (e.g., "An acceptance that varies any term of the offer is considered a rejection and counteroffer").

Determining the rule of law of a case is a procedure similar to determining the issue of the case. Avoid being fooled by red herrings; there may be a few rules of law mentioned in the case excerpt, but usually only one is *the* rule with which the casebook editor is concerned. The techniques used to locate the issue, described below, may also be utilized to find the rule of law. Generally, your best guide is simply the chapter heading. It is a clue to the point the casebook editor seeks to make and should be kept in mind when reading every case in the respective section.

FACTS: A synopsis of only the essential facts of the case, i.e., those bearing upon or leading up to the issue.

The facts entry should be a short statement of the events and transactions that led one party to initiate legal proceedings against another in the first place. While some cases conveniently state the salient facts at the beginning of the decision, in other instances they will have to be culled from hiding places throughout the text, even from concurring and dissenting opinions. Some of the "facts" will often be in dispute and should be so noted. Conflicting evidence may be briefly pointed up. "Hard" facts must be included. Both must be *relevant* in order to be listed in the facts entry. It is impossible to tell what is relevant until the entire case is read, as the ultimate determination of the rights and liabilities of the parties may turn on something buried deep in the opinion.

Generally, the facts entry should not be longer than three to five *short* sentences.

It is often helpful to identify the role played by a party in a given context. For example, in a construction contract case the identification of a party as the "contractor" or "builder" alleviates the need to tell that that party was the one who was supposed to have built the house.

It is always helpful, and a good general practice, to identify the "plaintiff" and the "defendant." This may seem elementary and uncomplicated, but, especially in view of the creative editing practiced by some casebook editors, it is sometimes a difficult or even impossible task. Bear in mind that the *party presently* seeking something from this court may not be the plaintiff, and that sometimes only the cross-claim of a defendant is treated in the excerpt. Confusing or misaligning the parties can ruin your analysis and understanding of the case.

ISSUE: A statement of the general legal question answered by or illustrated in the case. For clarity, the issue is best put in the form of a question capable of a "yes" or "no" answer. In reality, the issue is simply the Rule of Law put in the form of a question (e.g., "May an offer be accepted by performance?").

The major problem presented in discerning what is *the* issue in the case is that an opinion usually purports to raise and answer several questions. However, except for rare cases, only one such question is really the issue in the case. Collateral issues not necessary to the resolution of the matter in controversy are handled by the court by language known as *"obiter dictum"* or merely *"dictum."* While dicta may be included later in the brief, they have no place under the issue heading.

To find the issue, ask *who wants what* and then go on to ask *why did that party succeed or fail in getting it.* Once this is determined, the "why" should be turned into a question.

The complexity of the issues in the cases will vary, but in all cases a single-sentence question should sum up the issue. *In a few cases,* there will be two, or even more rarely, three issues of equal importance to the resolution of the case. Each should be expressed in a single-sentence question.

Since many issues are resolved by a court in coming to a final disposition of a case, the casebook editor will reproduce the portion of the opinion containing the issue or issues most relevant to the area of law under scrutiny. A noted law professor gave this advice: "Close the book; look at the title on the cover." Chances are, if it is Property, you need not concern yourself with whether, for example, the federal government's treatment of the plaintiff's land really raises a federal question sufficient to support jurisdiction on this ground in federal court.

The same rule applies to chapter headings designating sub-areas within the subjects. They tip you off as to what the text is designed to teach. The cases are arranged in a casebook to show a progression or development of the law, so that the preceding cases may also help.

It is also most important to remember to *read the notes and questions* at the end of a case to determine what the editors wanted you to have gleaned from it.

HOLDING AND DECISION: This section should succinctly explain the rationale of the court in arriving at its decision. In capsulizing the "reasoning" of the court, it should always include an application of the general rule or rules of law to the specific facts of the case. Hidden justifications come to light in this entry; the reasons for the state of the law, the public policies, the biases and prejudices, those considerations that influence the justices' thinking and, ultimately, the outcome of the case. At the end, there should be a short indication of the disposition or procedural resolution of the case (e.g., "Decision of the trial court for Mr. Smith (P) reversed").

The foregoing format is designed to help you "digest" the reams of case material with which you will be faced in your law school career. Once mastered by practice, it will place at your fingertips the information the authors of your casebooks have sought to impart to you in case-by-case illustration and analysis.

B. Be as Economical as Possible in Briefing Cases

Once armed with a format that encourages succinctness, it is as important to be economical with regard to the time spent on the actual reading of the case as it is to be economical in the writing of the brief itself. This does not mean "skimming" a case. Rather, it means reading the case with an "eye" trained to recognize into which "section" of your brief a particular passage or line fits and having a system for quickly and precisely marking the case so that the passages fitting any one particular part of the brief can be easily identified and brought together in a concise and accurate manner when the brief is actually written.

It is of no use to simply repeat everything in the opinion of the court; record only enough information to trigger your recollection of what the court said. Nevertheless, an accurate statement of the "law of the case," i.e., the legal principle applied to the facts, is absolutely essential to class preparation and to learning the law under the case method.

To that end, it is important to develop a "shorthand" that you can use to make margin notations. These notations will tell you at a glance in which section of the brief you will be placing that particular passage or portion of the opinion.

Some students prefer to underline all the salient portions of the opinion (with a pencil or colored underliner marker), making marginal notations as they go along. Others prefer the color-coded method of underlining, utilizing different colors of markers to underline the salient portions of the case, each separate color being used to represent a different section of the brief. For example, blue underlining could be used for passages relating to the rule of law, yellow for those relating to the issue, and green for those relating to the holding and decision, etc. While it has its advocates, the color-coded method can be confusing and time-consuming (all that time spent on changing colored markers). Furthermore, it can interfere with the continuity and concentration many students deem essential to the reading of a case for maximum comprehension. In the end, however, it is a matter of personal preference and style. Just remember, whatever method you use, underlining must be used sparingly or its value is lost.

If you take the marginal notation route, an efficient and easy method is to go along underlining the key portions of the case and placing in the margin alongside them the following "markers" to indicate where a particular passage or line "belongs" in the brief you will write:

N (NATURE OF CASE)
RL (RULE OF LAW)
I (ISSUE)
HL (HOLDING AND DECISION, relates to the RULE OF LAW behind the decision)
HR (HOLDING AND DECISION, gives the RATIONALE or reasoning behind the decision)
HA (HOLDING AND DECISION, APPLIES the general principle(s) of law to the facts of the case to arrive at the decision)

Remember that a particular passage may well contain information necessary to more than one part of your brief, in which case you simply note that in the margin. If you are using the color-coded underlining method instead of margin notation, simply make asterisks or checks in the margin next to the passage in question in the colors that indicate the additional sections of the brief where it might be utilized.

The economy of utilizing "shorthand" in marking cases for briefing can be maintained in the actual brief writing process itself by utilizing "law student shorthand" within the brief. There are many commonly used words and phrases for which abbreviations can be substituted in your briefs (and in your class notes also). You can develop abbreviations that are personal to you and which will save you a lot of time. A reference list of briefing abbreviations can be found on page xii of this book.

C. Use Both the Briefing Process and the Brief as a Learning Tool

Now that you have a format and the tools for briefing cases efficiently, the most important thing is to make the time spent in briefing profitable to you and to make the most advantageous use of the briefs you create. Of course, the briefs are invaluable for classroom reference when you are called upon to explain or analyze a particular case. However, they are also useful in reviewing for exams. A quick glance at the fact summary should bring the case to mind, and a rereading of the rule of law should enable you to go over the underlying legal concept in your mind, how it was applied in that particular case, and how it might apply in other factual settings.

As to the value to be derived from engaging in the briefing process itself, there is an immediate benefit that arises from being forced to sift through the essential facts and reasoning from the court's opinion and to succinctly express them in your own words in your brief. The process ensures that you understand the case and the point that it illustrates, and that means you will be ready to absorb further analysis and information brought forth in class. It also ensures you will have something to say when called upon in class. The briefing process helps develop a mental agility for getting to the *gist* of a case and for identifying, expounding on, and applying the legal concepts and issues found there. The briefing process is the mental process on which you must rely in taking law school examinations; it is also the mental process upon which a lawyer relies in serving his clients and in making his living.

Abbreviations for Briefs

Table of Cases

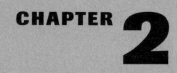

CHAPTER 2

Sources: Customary International Law

Quick Reference Rules of Law

The Paquete Habana

Country at war (P) v. Fishermen (D)

175 U.S. 677 (1900).

NATURE OF CASE: Appeal from judgment condemning two fishing vessels and their cargoes as prizes of war.

FACT SUMMARY: The owners (D) of fishing vessels seized by officials of the United States (P) argued that international law exempted coastal fishermen from capture as prizes of war.

 RULE OF LAW
Coastal fishing vessels, with their cargoes and crews, are exempt from capture as prizes of war.

FACTS: The owners (D) of two separate fishing vessels brought this appeal of a district court decree condemning two fishing vessels and their cargoes as prizes of war. Each vessel was a fishing smack, running in and out of Havana, sailing under the Spanish flag, and regularly engaged in fishing on the coast of Cuba. The cargoes of both vessels consisted of fresh fish that had been caught by their respective crews. Until stopped by the blockading United States squadron (P), the owners (D) had no knowledge of the existence of a war or of any blockage. The owners (D) had no arms or ammunition on board the vessels and had made no attempt to run the blockade after learning of its existence. The owners (D) did not offer any resistance at the time of capture. On appeal, the owners (D) argued that both customary international law and the writings of leading international scholars recognized an exemption from seizure at wartime of coastal fishing vessels.

ISSUE: Are coastal fishing vessels, with their cargoes and crews, exempt from capture as prizes of war?

HOLDING AND DECISION: (Gray, J.) Yes. Coastal fishing vessels, pursuing their vocation of catching and bringing in fresh fish, have been recognized as exempt, with their cargoes and crews, from capture as prizes of war. The doctrine that exempts coastal fishermen, with their vessels and cargoes, from capture as prizes of war, has been familiar to the United States from the time of the War of Independence, and has been recognized explicitly by the French and British governments. Where there are no treaties and no controlling executive or legislative acts or judicial decisions, as is the case here, resort must be had to the customs and usages of civilized nations, and, as evidence of these, to the works of jurists and commentators, who are well acquainted with the field. Such works are resorted to by judicial tribunals, not for the speculations of their authors concerning what the law ought to be, but for trustworthy evidence of what the law really is. At the present time, by the general consent of the civilized nations of the world, and independently of any express treaty or other public act, it is an established rule of international law that coastal fishing vessels, with their implements and supplies, cargoes, and crews, unarmed and honestly pursuing their peaceful calling of catching and bringing in fresh fish, are exempt from capture as prizes of war. Reversed.

ANALYSIS

In a dissenting opinion, which was not published in the main body of this casebook, Chief Justice Fuller argued that the captured vessels were of such a size and range as to not fall within the exemption. The Chief Justice also contended that the exemption in any case had not become a customary rule of international law, but was only an "act of grace" that had not been authorized by the President.

■■■

Quicknotes

BLOCKADE When one country prevents materials or persons from entering or leaving another.

CUSTOM Generally any habitual practice or course of action that is repeated under like circumstances.

INTERNATIONAL LAW The body of law applicable to dealings between nations.

■■■

The Case of the S.S. Lotus
(France v. Turkey)

Country of citizen (P) v. Country claiming jurisdiction (D)

Permanent Court of Int'l Justice, P.C.I.J. (ser. A) No. 10 (1927).

NATURE OF CASE: Action to determine validity of exercise of criminal jurisdiction.

FACT SUMMARY: France (P) contended that Turkey (D) violated international law by asserting jurisdiction over a French citizen who had been the first officer of a ship that collided with a Turkish ship on the high seas.

🏛 RULE OF LAW
There is no rule of international law prohibiting a state from exercising criminal jurisdiction over a foreign national who commits acts outside of the state's national jurisdiction.

FACTS: On August 2, 1926, just before midnight, a collision occurred between the French (P) mail steamer Lotus, which was captained by Demons, a French citizen, and the Turkish (D) collier Boz-Kourt, captained by Hassan Bey. The Boz-Kourt, which was cut in two, sank, and eight Turkish (D) nationals who were on board perished. After having done everything possible to help the ship-wrecked persons, the Lotus continued on its course to Constantinople, where it arrived on August 3. On August 5, Lieutenant Demons was requested by the Turkish (D) authorities to go ashore to give evidence. The examination led to the placing under arrest of Lieutenant Demons, without previous notice being given to the French (P) Consul-General, and Hassan Bey. Although Demons argued that the Turkish (D) courts lacked jurisdiction over him, Demons was convicted of negligent conduct in allowing the accident to occur. France (P) and Turkey (D) then agreed to submit to the Permanent Court of International Justice the question of whether the exercise of Turkish (D) criminal jurisdiction over Demons for an incident that occurred on the high seas violated international law.

ISSUE: Is there a rule of international law prohibiting a state from exercising criminal jurisdiction over a foreign national who commits acts outside of the state's national jurisdiction?

HOLDING AND DECISION: (Per curiam) No. There is no rule of international law prohibiting a state from exercising criminal jurisdiction over a foreign national who commits acts outside of the state's national jurisdiction. The first and foremost restriction imposed by international law upon a state is that, failing the existence of a permissive rule to the contrary, it may not exercise its power in any form in the territory of another state. It does not, however, follow that international law prohibits a state from exercising jurisdiction in its own territory, in respect of any case that relates to acts that have taken place abroad, and in which it cannot rely on some permissive rule of international law. The territoriality of criminal law is not an absolute principle of international law, and by no means coincides with territorial sovereignty. Here, because the effects of the alleged offense occurred on a Turkish (D) vessel, it is impossible to hold that there is a rule of international law that prohibits Turkey (D) from prosecuting Lieutenant Demons simply because he was aboard a French (P) ship at the time of the incident. Because there is no rule of international law in regard to collision cases to the effect that criminal proceedings are exclusively within the jurisdiction of the state whose flag is flown, both states here may exercise concurrent jurisdiction over this matter.

▶ ANALYSIS

In conformity with the holding of this case, France in 1975 enacted a law regarding its criminal jurisdiction over aliens. That law, cited in 102 *Journal Du Droit International* 962 (Clunet 1975), provides that aliens who commit a crime outside the territory of the Republic may be prosecuted and judged pursuant to French law, when the victim is of French nationality. The holding in this case has been criticized by several eminent scholars for seeming to imply that international law permits all that it does not forbid.

■■■

Quicknotes

FOREIGN NATIONAL A person owing allegiance to a foreign state.

JURISDICTION The authority of a court to hear and declare judgment in respect to a particular matter.

■■■

Legality of the Threat or Use of Nuclear Weapons (Advisory Opinion)

[Parties not identified.]

I.C.J., Advisory Opinion, 1996 I.C.J. 226.

NATURE OF CASE: Advisory opinion examining whether the threat or use of nuclear weapons is permitted under international law.

FACT SUMMARY: [The International Court of Justice was asked by the U.N. General Assembly for an advisory opinion as to whether states are permitted to use nuclear weapons under international law.]

 RULE OF LAW
The threat or use of nuclear weapons in certain circumstances is permitted under international law.

FACTS: [The International Court of Justice was asked by the U.N. General Assembly for an advisory opinion as to whether states are permitted to use nuclear weapons under international law.]

ISSUE: Is the threat or use of nuclear weapons in certain circumstances permitted under international law?

HOLDING AND DECISION: [Judge not stated in casebook excerpt.] Yes. The threat or use of nuclear weapons in certain circumstances is permitted under international law. Customary and conventional international law neither authorizes nor prohibits the threat or use of nuclear weapons in all circumstances. A threat or use of nuclear weapons would be considered legal under the U.N. Charter if it met all requirements of Article 51, which deals with states' rights to self-defense. Such a threat or use should also be compatible with the requirements of international law applicable in armed combat, particularly those principles and rules of international humanitarian law, as well as with specific obligations under treaties and other undertakings that expressly deal with nuclear weapons and their proliferation. In any case, a state obligation exists to pursue in good faith and bring to a conclusion negotiations leading to nuclear disarmament in all its aspects under strict and effective international control.

▶ ANALYSIS

This case illustrates the idea that despite steps taken by a very large part of the international community toward complete nuclear disarmament, no customary rule specifically proscribing the threat or use of nuclear weapons entirely exists. Too many dissenters express reservations about the notion that there are no imaginable circumstances warranting their use.

Quicknotes

ADVISORY OPINION A decision rendered at the request of an interested party as to how the court would rule should the particular issue arise.

North Sea Continental Shelf Cases
(Federal Republic of Germany v. Denmark;
Federal Republic of Germany v. Netherlands)

State not a party (D) v. Parties to Geneva Convention (P)

I.C.J., 1969 I.C.J. 3.

NATURE OF CASE: Action to determine national boundaries.

FACT SUMMARY: Denmark (P) and the Netherlands (P) contended that customary rules of international law determined the boundaries of areas located on the continental shelf between those countries and the Federal Republic of Germany (D).

RULE OF LAW
A custom, to be binding as international law, must amount to a settled practice and must be rendered obligatory by a rule of law requiring it.

FACTS: Denmark (P) and the Netherlands (P) contended that the boundaries between their respective areas of the continental shelf in the North Sea, and the area claimed by the Federal Republic of Germany (D), should be determined by the application of the principle of equidistance set forth in Article 6 of the Geneva Convention of 1958 on the Continental Shelf, which by January 1, 1969, had been ratified or acceded to by 39 states, but to which Germany (D) was not a party. Denmark (P) and the Netherlands (P) contended that Germany (D) was bound to accept delimitation on an equidistance basis because the use of this method was not merely a conventional obligation, but was a rule that was part of the corpus of general international law and like other rules of general or customary international law was binding automatically on Germany (D), independent of any specific assent, direct or indirect, given by Germany (D).

ISSUE: Must delimitation be the object of an equitable agreement between the states involved?

HOLDING AND DECISION: [Judge not stated in casebook excerpt.] Yes. Delimitation must be the object of an equitable agreement between the states involved. The equidistance principle, as stated in Article 6 of the Geneva Convention, is not part of customary international law. Article 6 is of the type of articles under which reservations may be made by any state on signing or ratifying the Convention, so that the state is not necessarily bound in all instances by that article. A general or customary law has equal force for all members of the international community and cannot be unilaterally abrogated. Article 6 has not been accepted as part of the general corpus of international law by the *opinio juris,* so as to have become binding even for countries that have never and do not become parties to the Convention. Rather than giving the principle of equidistance a fundamental norm-creating character, which is necessary to the formation of a general rule of law, Article 6 makes the obligation to use the equidistance method a secondary one, which comes into play only in the absence of an agreement between the parties. The delimitation here is to be executed by equitable agreement, taking into account the relevant circumstances.

DISSENT: (Lachs, J.) The principles and rules enshrined in the Convention, including the equidistance rule, have been accepted not only by those states that are parties to the Convention on the Continental Shelf, but also by those that have subsequently followed it in agreements, or in their legislation, or have acquiesced in it when faced with legislative acts of other states affecting them. This can be viewed as evidence of a practice widespread enough to satisfy the criteria for a general rule of law.

ANALYSIS

The dissent's analysis of the concept of *opinio juris* is in accord with the position taken by some legal scholars who maintain that *opinio juris* may be presumed from uniformities of practice regarding matters viewed normally as involving legal rights and obligations. A contrary position maintains that the practice of states must be accompanied by or consist of statements that something is law before it can become law.

Quicknotes

GENEVA CONVENTION International agreement that governs the conduct of warring nations.

OPINIO JURIS An "opinion of law," or belief that certain conduct must occur due to legal obligation.

Military and Paramilitary Activities in and Against Nicaragua
(Nicaragua v. United States)

Complaining nation (P) v. Alleged wrongdoer (D)

I.C.J., 1986 I.C.J. 14.

NATURE OF CASE: Proceeding before the International Court of Justice.

FACT SUMMARY: Nicaragua (P) complained that the United States (D) was conducting military operations in its territory. The United States (D) claimed that the International Court of Justice did not have jurisdiction over the matter.

RULE OF LAW
The International Court of Justice has jurisdiction to hear a case involving a provision of an international treaty, despite one party's refusal to concede jurisdiction over disputes under the treaty, if the provision represents the codification of customary international law.

FACTS: Nicaragua (P) claimed the United States (D) was conducting military and paramilitary activities in and against Nicaragua (P). The case is multifaceted, and the United States (D) accepted the jurisdiction of the International Court of Justice for some matters in dispute, but had made a reservation that I.C.J. jurisdiction would not apply to certain disputes covered by the U.N. Charter or the Organization of American States. The United States (D) claimed the I.C.J. lacked jurisdiction over the matter in dispute in this case because it centered on a provision of the U.N. Charter, while Nicaragua (P) claimed that its case was based on rules of customary law, and both parties agreed that the relevant provision in the U.N. Charter was very similar to the customary international law on the subject.

ISSUE: Does the International Court of Justice have jurisdiction to hear a case involving a provision of an international treaty, despite one party's refusal to concede jurisdiction over disputes under the treaty, if the provision represents the codification of customary international law?

HOLDING AND DECISION: [Judge not stated in casebook excerpt.] Yes. The International Court of Justice has jurisdiction to hear a case involving a provision of an international treaty, despite one party's refusal to concede jurisdiction over disputes under the treaty, if the provision represents the codification of customary international law.

The first step in resolving this dispute is to name the rules of customary international law that apply to the dispute. To do so, the U.N. Charter may be considered, despite a lack of jurisdiction over disputes arising under it, for the limited purpose of identifying customary international law. In addition, the views of the parties may be considered, though even where there is agreement between the parties as to the customary international law, their views do not free the Court from ascertaining for itself what rules are applicable. The Court must satisfy itself that the rule exists in the *opinio juris* of states as confirmed by practice.

In this case, the parties agree that on the central question of the lawfulness of the use of force in interstate relations, the rules of general and customary international law and those of the U.N. Charter are identical. Their consent to the text of the resolutions can be understood not only as acquiescence to be bound to the treaty as a whole, but as an acceptance of the validity of the individual rules included in the resolution, as discreet and separate from the other provisions of the charter. Thus the parties to the Charter expressed an *opinio juris* respecting the prohibition of the use of force, indicating that the rule is considered to be a principle of customary international law. Practice confirms that it is valid as a customary international law: It is frequently referred to in statements by state representatives as being not only a principle of customary international law, but also a fundamental or cardinal principle of such law. Even the United States (D) argued, albeit for a different conclusion, that the rule contained in the Charter was an expression of customary international law. [Judgment for Nicaragua (P).]

ANALYSIS

In parts of the opinion not covered by the casebook excerpt, the I.C.J. found that the United States (D) was "in breach of its obligations under customary international law not to use force against another State," and "not to violate its sovereignty," among other things. The United States (D) refused to participate after the I.C.J. rejected its argument that the I.C.J. lacked jurisdiction to hear the case, and later blocked enforcement by the Security Council, making Nicaraguan (P) attempts at obtaining compliance futile. The Nicaraguan government (P) finally withdrew the complaint from the Court in September 1991.

Note also that an important aspect of the case as covered by the excerpt is that *opinio juris* was not disputed by the parties. The United States (D) argued that because *opinio juris* was codified in the U.N. Charter, and disputes under the Charter were outside I.C.J. jurisdiction, the I.C.J. lacked jurisdiction, despite *opinio juris*. The I.C.J. looked to the parties' practice after noting the existence of the law.

Continued on next page.

In this case, practice matters less than in the *Lotus* and *North Sea* cases.

■■■■

Quicknotes

JURISDICTION The authority of a court to hear and declare judgment in respect to a particular matter.

OPINIO JURIS An "opinion of law," or belief that certain conduct must occur due to legal obligation.

■■■■

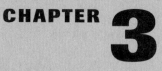
The Law of Treaties

Quick Reference Rules of Law

Maritime Delimitation and Territorial Questions (Qatar v. Bahrain)

Sovereign (P) v. Sovereign (D)

I.C.J., 1994 I.C.J. 112.

NATURE OF CASE: Territorial dispute between sovereigns.

FACT SUMMARY: Qatar (P) filed a claim in the International Court of Justice against Bahrain (D) to settle a dispute involving sovereignty over certain islands, sovereign rights over certain shoals, and delimitation of a maritime boundary. Bahrain (D) disputed the Court's jurisdiction.

🏛 RULE OF LAW
Meeting minutes and exchanges of letters can constitute an international agreement creating rights and obligations for the signatories.

FACTS: Qatar (P) and Bahrain (D) sought for over 20 years to resolve a dispute concerning sovereignty over certain islands and shoals, and delimitation of a maritime boundary. In the process, they exchanged some letters, which were accepted by the respective parties' heads of state. A Tripartite Committee was created, consisting of representatives from Qatar (P), Bahrain (D), and Saudi Arabia "for the purpose of approaching the International Court of Justice. . . ." The committee met several times but failed to produce an agreement on the specific terms for submitting the dispute to the Court. Eventually, the meetings culminated in "Minutes," which reaffirmed the process and stipulated that the parties "may" submit the dispute to the I.C.J. after giving the Saudi King six months to resolve the dispute. Qatar (P) filed a claim in the I.C.J., and Bahrain (D) disputed the Court's jurisdiction.

ISSUE: Can meeting minutes and exchanges of letters constitute an international agreement creating rights and obligations for the signatories?

HOLDING AND DECISION: [Judge not stated in casebook excerpt.] Yes. Meeting minutes and exchanges of letters can constitute an international agreement creating rights and obligations for the signatories. The parties agree that the letters constitute an international agreement with binding force, but Bahrain (D) argues that the Minutes were only a record of negotiations, and therefore could not serve as a basis for the I.C.J.'s jurisdiction. International agreements can take many forms under the Vienna Convention on the Law of Treaties, and the I.C.J. has enforced that rule in the past. The Minutes in this case are not only a record of the meetings; they contain reaffirmation of obligations previously agreed to, agreement to allow the King of Saudi Arabia to try to find a solution to the dispute during a six-month period, and indication of the possibility of the involvement of the I.C.J. The Minutes set forth

commitments to which the parties agreed, thereby creating rights and obligations in international law. They are therefore an international agreement. The Foreign Minister of Bahrain's (D) argument that no agreement exists because he never intended to enter an agreement fails, because he signed the document creating rights and obligations for his country. And Qatar's (P) six-month delay in applying to the United Nations Secretariat does not indicate that Qatar (P) never considered the Minutes to be an international agreement, as Bahrain (D) argues. In any event, registration or non-registration with the Secretariat does not have any effect on the validity of the agreement.

▶ *ANALYSIS*

No doubt the language used in various writings will influence a court's decision as to whether an agreement has been entered into, and in this case, the language was the main focus of the I.C.J., and it was the contents of the Minutes that persuaded the I.C.J. to reject the Bahrain foreign minister's (D) claim that he did not intend to enter into an agreement. Compare this to general U.S. contract law, where a claim by one of the parties that no contract existed because there was no meeting of the minds might cause a U.S. court to consider whether a contract existed with more care and thought than the I.C.J. gave the foreign minister of Bahrain's (D) claim.

■═■

Quicknotes

INTERNATIONAL LAW The body of law applicable to dealings between nations.

JURISDICTION The authority of a court to hear and declare judgment in respect to a particular matter.

SOVEREIGN A state or entity with independent authority to govern its affairs.

■═■

Reservations to the Convention on Genocide

I.C.J., Advisory Opinion, 1951 I.C.J. 15.

NATURE OF CASE: Advisory opinion regarding the effect of reservations to the U.N. Convention on Genocide.

FACT SUMMARY: Several signatory states to the U.N. Convention on Genocide effected reservations to various provisions therein.

🏛 RULE OF LAW

A state may effect a reservation to the U.N. Convention on Genocide and still be considered a signatory thereto.

FACTS: In 1951, the United Nations unanimously adopted the Convention on Genocide. Several states made reservations to one or more of its provisions. The International Court of Justice was asked to render an opinion as to whether a party could express reservations and still be considered a signatory.

ISSUE: May a state effect a reservation to the U.N. Convention on Genocide and still be considered a signatory thereto?

HOLDING AND DECISION: (Per curiam) Yes. A state may effect a reservation to the U.N. Convention on Genocide and still be considered a signatory thereto. A reservation is permitted in a multilateral treaty as long as the reservation does not defeat the purpose of the treaty. It has been argued that any state may effect any reservation by virtue of its sovereignty. Such a rule would lead to a complete disregard for the object and purpose of a convention. Here, since numerous reservations were made by different states, the validity of each must be examined on a case-by-case basis. [The Court also held that a state objecting to a reservation could, if it desired, consider the reserving state not to be a party to the Convention.]

▶ ANALYSIS

As is often the case, politics played a role in the decision here. Historically, international law usually held that reservations to a multilateral treaty had to be accepted by all other parties. Such a rule here would have made unanimous acceptance of the Convention impossible. The Court was undoubtedly determined to facilitate such unanimity.

■═■

Quicknotes

ADVISORY OPINION A decision rendered at the request of an interested party of how the court would rule should the particular issue arise.

INTERNATIONAL LAW The body of law applicable to dealings between nations.

■═■

Application of the Convention on the Prevention and Punishment of the Crime of Genocide
(Bosnia and Herzegovina v. Serbia and Montenegro)

State (P) v. State (D)

I.C.J., 2007 I.C.J. 191.

NATURE OF CASE: Action brought in the International Court of Justice to determine whether a state committed a criminal violation of international law.

FACT SUMMARY: Bosnia and Herzegovina (P) filed suit against Serbia and Montenegro (D) following the genocide of Bosnian Muslims.

🏛 RULE OF LAW
The contracting parties to the Genocide Convention are bound by the obligation under the Convention not to commit, through their organs or persons or groups whose conduct is attributable to them, genocide and the other acts enumerated in Article III.

FACTS: Bosnia and Herzegovina (P) brought suit in 1993 against the Federal Republic of Yugoslavia (Serbia and Montenegro) (D) under the Genocide Convention. The suit claimed that Serbia (D) breached the Convention by committing genocide against Bosnia's (P) Muslim population. In this, the first part of the case, the International Court of Justice interpreted provisions of the Genocide Convention, including the undertaking to "prevent and punish" genocide in Article I, the definition of genocide in Article II, and the phrase "responsibility of a State for genocide" in Article IX. [For additional facts in the case, see Chapter 8, pages 54-55.]

ISSUE: Are the contracting parties to the Genocide Convention bound by the obligation under the Convention not to commit, through their organs or persons or groups whose conduct is attributable to them, genocide and the other acts enumerated in Article III?

HOLDING AND DECISION: [Judge not stated in casebook excerpt.] Yes. The contracting parties to the Genocide Convention are bound by the obligation under the Convention not to commit, through their organs or persons or groups whose conduct is attributable to them, genocide and the other acts enumerated in Article III. Serbia (D) violated its responsibility under the Genocide Convention to prevent and punish genocide. What obligations the Convention imposes on the parties depends on the ordinary meaning of the terms of the Convention, read in context and in light of the Convention's object and purpose. Confusion as to terms, context, or purpose can be resolved by resorting to supplementary means of interpretation, including the Convention's preparatory work and the circumstances of its conclusion.

Article I contains two propositions. The first states that genocide is a crime under international law, a statement that recognizes existing requirements of customary international law on the subject. The second is the undertaking by the parties to prevent and punish the crime of genocide. The ordinary meaning of the word "undertake" is to give a formal promise, to bind or engage oneself, and to give a pledge or promise. Thus, Article I, particularly its undertaking to prevent, creates obligations distinct from those that appear in the subsequent Articles. This conclusion is supported by the humanitarian and civilizing purpose of the Convention. Preparatory work of the Convention supports this conclusion as well, because the U.N. General has said that genocide is an international crime entailing national and international responsibility on the part of individuals and states. In addition, during drafting, several states proposed to move from the preamble to Article I of the Convention the language with the undertaking to prevent and punish, in order to make it more effective.

The parties are also under an obligation under the Convention not to commit genocide themselves. The Convention does not expressly impose the obligation, but the effect of Article II is to prohibit states from themselves committing genocide. The prohibition follows from the fact that the Article categorizes genocide as an international law crime, and by agreeing to such a categorization, the parties must logically undertake not to commit the act described. It also follows from the expressly stated obligation to prevent the commission of acts of genocide.

Serbia (D) argued that the drafting history of the Convention shows that states are not directly responsible under the Convention for acts of genocide, but that states have a civil responsibility to prevent and punish genocide committed by individuals. But the drafting history also makes clear that the Chairman of the Sixth Committee believed that Article IX as modified provided for state responsibility for genocide.

▶ ANALYSIS

Serbia's (D) violations of its obligations derived not only from the Genocide Convention, but also from two protective measures issued by the I.C.J. in April and September 1993, under which the then-Federal Republic of Yugoslavia was ordered explicitly to prevent the crimes of genocide and to make sure that such crimes were not committed

Continued on next page.

by military or paramilitary formations operating under its control or with its support. Despite the order, Serbia (D) did nothing to prevent the July 1995 Srebrenica massacre, although, according to the I.C.J., it should have "been aware of the serious danger that acts of genocide would be committed."

■■■■■

Quicknotes

GENOCIDE The systematic killing of a particular group.

INTERNATIONAL LAW The body of law applicable to dealings between nations.

■■■■■

Jesse Lewis (The David J. Adams) Claim
(United States v. Great Britain)

Claimant (P) v. Condemnor (D)

Clms. Arbitration under Special Agreement of August 18, 1910, 1921, Nielsen Rep. 526, 6 U.N.R.I.A.A. 85.

NATURE OF CASE: Arbitration of claims concerning terms of an international treaty.

FACT SUMMARY: The United States (P) claimed that the interpretation of the Treaty of London of 1818 by the Canadian government (D) was incorrect.

RULE OF LAW
The duty of an international tribunal is to determine, from an international perspective, how the provisions of a treaty are to be interpreted and applied to the facts.

FACTS: The United States (P) agreed in the Treaty of London of 1818 that its nationals would not fish in Canadian (D) waters. In 1886, an American fishing schooner was seized by Canadian (D) authorities for alleged violations of the Treaty. A Canadian (D) court condemned the vessel after finding it had violated both the Treaty and Canadian legislation. The U.S. government (P) then sought damages from the British government (D) on the grounds that the seizure of the schooner was wrongful based on an erroneous interpretation of the Treaty. Britain (D) argued that the Arbitral Tribunal was not competent to re-examine the Canadian (D) court's interpretation.

ISSUE: Is it the duty of an international tribunal to determine, from an international perspective, how the provisions of a treaty are to be interpreted and applied to the facts?

HOLDING AND DECISION: [No judge listed.] Yes. The duty of an international tribunal is to determine, from an international perspective, how the provisions of a treaty are to be interpreted and applied to the facts. The unilateral interpretation of a bilateral contract by one party is not binding on the other party. The fact that the interpretation was given by legislative or judicial authority does not make it binding on the other party.

ANALYSIS

The Tribunal ultimately found that the Canadian (D) court's interpretation was not erroneous. Some courts have held that unilateral interpretations of treaties have only an advisory effect. Others claim such interpretations are to be regarded as amendments to the treaty.

Quicknotes

BILATERAL CONTRACT An agreement pursuant to which each party promises to undertake an obligation, or to forbear from acting, at some time in the future.

TREATY An agreement between two or more nations for the benefit of the general public.

Advisory Opinion on Namibia

I.C.J., Advisory Opinion, 1971, I.C.J. Rep. 16.

NATURE OF CASE: Advisory opinion as to legality of occupation.

FACT SUMMARY: South Africa (D) occupied Namibia under a claim of right to annex that territory, but in violation of a United Nations (U.N.) Security Council Mandate which, though later terminated due to South Africa's breach, empowered the Security Council to enforce its terms.

🏛 RULE OF LAW

Mandates adopted by the United Nations are binding upon all Member States, and violations or breaches result in a legal obligation on the part of the violator to rectify the violation and upon the other Member States to recognize the conduct as a violation and to refuse to aid in such violation.

FACTS: South Africa (D) began occupation of Namibia under a claim of right to annex that territory and under a claim that the people of Namibia desired South African (D) rule. South Africa (D) was a Member State of the United Nations and was subject to a U.N. Mandate prohibiting Member States from taking physical control of other territories. The U.N. General Assembly adopted Resolution 2145 (XXI) terminating the Mandate for South Africa (D), and the Security Council adopted Resolution 276 (1970) declaring South Africa's (D) continued presence in Namibia to be illegal and calling upon the other Member States to act accordingly. The International Court of Justice was called upon to render an advisory opinion.

ISSUE: Are mandates adopted by the United Nations binding upon all Member States so as to make breaches or violations thereof result in a legal obligation on the part of the violator to rectify the violation and upon other Member States to recognize the conduct as a violation and to refuse to aid in such violation?

HOLDING AND DECISION: Yes. Mandates adopted by the United Nations are binding upon all Member States, and violations or breaches result in a legal obligation on the part of the violator to rectify the violation and upon the other Member States to recognize the conduct as a violation and to refuse to aid in such violation. The Member States have assumed an obligation to keep intact and preserve the rights of other States and the people in them. When a party to the Mandate giving rise to this obligation fails to fulfill its own obligations under it, that party cannot be recognized as retaining the rights that it claims to derive from the relationship. The General Assembly found that South Africa (D) was in material breach of the Mandate because of deliberate and persistent violations of it by occupying Namibia. The Assembly has the right to terminate the Mandate with respect to a violating Member State, which was accomplished by resolution 2145 (XXI) in this case. The decisions and resolutions of the Security Council in enforcing such termination are binding upon all Member States, regardless of how they voted on the measure when adopted. South Africa (D) is thus subject to the Mandate, the resolution terminating it as to South Africa (D), and the enforcement procedures of the Security Council. South Africa's (D) illegal action gives rise to an obligation to put the violative conduct to an end. Mandates adopted by the United Nations are binding upon all Member States and violations or breaches result in legal obligations on the part of the violator to rectify the violation, and upon the other Member States to recognize the conduct as a violation and to refuse to aid in such violation.

▶ ANALYSIS

South Africa (D) did not restore independence to Namibia despite agreeing to do so with the United Nations The General Assembly adopted a number of resolutions imposing mandatory sanctions for enforcement. South Africa (D) was "strongly condemned" for its actions.

▪️▬▪️

Quicknotes

ADVISORY OPINION A decision rendered at the request of an interested party of how the court would rule should the particular issue arise.

BREACH The violation of an obligation imposed pursuant to contract or law, by acting or failing to act.

▪️▬▪️

Appeal Relating to the Jurisdiction of the ICAO Council (India v. Pakistan)

Petitioner (P) v. Alleged wrongdoer (D)

I.C.J., 1972 I.C.J. 46.

NATURE OF CASE: Proceeding before the International Court of Justice.

FACT SUMMARY: Pakistan (D) claimed that the I.C.J. did not have jurisdiction over a dispute regarding aviation treaties.

🏛 RULE OF LAW

A merely unilateral suspension does not per se render jurisdictional clauses inoperative.

FACTS: Pakistan (D) brought a complaint against India (P) before the Council of the International Civil Aviation Organization (ICAO) for violation of treaty provisions after India (P) unilaterally suspended flights of Pakistan (D) aircraft over Indian (P) territory. India (P) appealed to the I.C.J., asserting that the treaties had been suspended by India (P) on grounds of a breach by Pakistan (D) when it hijacked an Indian (P) plane. Pakistan (D) objected to the I.C.J.'s jurisdiction, claiming India's (P) unilateral suspension had made the jurisdictional clauses inoperative.

ISSUE: Does a merely unilateral suspension per se render jurisdictional clauses inoperative?

HOLDING AND DECISION: [Judge not stated in casebook excerpt.] No. A merely unilateral suspension does not per se render jurisdictional clauses inoperative. If a mere allegation that a treaty was no longer operative could be used to defeat its jurisdictional clauses, all such clauses would become potentially a dead letter. The Court has jurisdiction.

▶ ANALYSIS

The Court reasoned that any treaty could be destroyed by one party's assertion that the treaty was no longer operative. The main purpose of the treaty would thus be compromised. It may precisely be one of the objects of jurisdictional clauses of a treaty to enable that matter to be adjudicated upon.

■═■

Quicknotes

JURISDICTION The authority of a court to hear and declare judgment in respect to a particular matter.

TREATY An agreement between two or more nations for the benefit of the general public.

UNILATERAL One-sided; involving only one person.

■═■

Fisheries Jurisdiction
(United Kingdom v. Iceland)

Applicant (P) v. Alleged treaty violator (D)

I.C.J., 1973 I.C.J. 3.

NATURE OF CASE: Proceeding before the International Court of Justice.

FACT SUMMARY: Iceland (D) claimed that a fishing treaty with the United Kingdom (P) was no longer applicable because of changed circumstances.

🏛 RULE OF LAW
In order that a change of circumstances may give rise to a ground for invoking the termination of a treaty it is necessary that it has resulted in a radical transformation of the extent of the obligations still to be performed.

FACTS: In 1961, the United Kingdom (P) recognized Iceland's (D) claim to a 12-mile fisheries limit in return for Iceland's (D) agreement that any dispute concerning Icelandic fisheries jurisdiction beyond the 12-mile limit be referred to the International Court of Justice (I.C.J.). When Iceland (D) in 1972 proposed to extend its exclusive fisheries jurisdiction from 12 to 50 miles around its shores, the United Kingdom (P) filed an application before the I.C.J. Iceland (D) claimed that the agreement was no longer valid because of changed circumstances since the 12-mile limit was now generally recognized and there would be a failure of consideration for the 1961 agreement.

ISSUE: In order that a change of circumstances may give rise to a ground for invoking the termination of a treaty is it necessary that it has resulted in a radical transformation of the extent of the obligations still to be performed?

HOLDING AND DECISION: [Judge not stated in casebook excerpt.] Yes. In order that a change of circumstances may give rise to a ground for invoking the termination of a treaty it is necessary that it has resulted in a radical transformation of the extent of the obligations still to be performed. The change must have increased the burden of the obligations yet to be executed to the extent of rendering the performance something essentially different from that initially undertaken. The change of circumstances alleged by Iceland (D) cannot be said to have transformed radically the extent of the jurisdictional obligation that was imposed in the 1961 Exchange of Notes.

▶ ANALYSIS

The original agreement between the parties provided for recourse to the I.C.J. in the event of a dispute. Iceland's (D) economy is very dependent on fishing. The Court did not reach the merits of Iceland's (D) argument here, however, but rather dealt with the jurisdictional issues.

■═■

Quicknotes

JURISDICTION The authority of a court to hear and declare judgment in respect to a particular matter.

TREATY An agreement between two or more nations for the benefit of the general public.

■═■

Gabčíkovo-Nagymaros Project
(Hungary/Slovakia)

Treaty partner (D) v. Treaty partner (P)

I.C.J., 1997 I.C.J. 7 (1997).

NATURE OF CASE: Proceeding before the International Court of Justice.

FACT SUMMARY: Hungary (D) claimed that changed circumstances made enforcement of a treaty with Slovakia (P) impossible.

🏛 RULE OF LAW
A fundamental change of circumstances must have been unforeseen and the existence of the circumstances at the time of the treaty's conclusion must have constituted an essential basis of the consent of the parties to be bound.

FACTS: Hungary (D) and Slovakia (P) had agreed in 1977 to build and operate a system of locks along the Danube River comprising a dam, reservoir, hydroelectric power plant, and flood control improvements. This project was never completed and both countries underwent changes in their political and economic systems beginning in 1989. Hungary (D) first suspended and then abandoned its part of the works and later gave notice of termination of the treaty. In 1992, Hungary (D) and Slovakia (P) asked the I.C.J. to decide on the basis of international law whether Hungary (D) was entitled to suspend, and subsequently abandon, its part of the works, on the basis of the doctrine of impossibility of performance.

ISSUE: Must a fundamental change of circumstances have been unforeseen and must the existence of the circumstances at the time of the treaty's conclusion have constituted an essential basis of the consent of the parties to be bound?

HOLDING AND DECISION: [Judge not stated in casebook excerpt.] Yes. A fundamental change of circumstances must have been unforeseen and the existence of the circumstances at the time of the treaty's conclusion must have constituted an essential basis of the consent of the parties to be bound. Where the prevalent political and economic conditions were not so closely linked to the object and purpose of the treaty as to constitute an essential basis of the consent of the parties, there was no fundamental change of circumstances. The plea of fundamental change of circumstances may only be applied in exceptional cases.

▶ ANALYSIS

The Court relied on the Vienna Convention. The Vienna Convention may be seen as a codification of existing customary law on the subject of termination of a treaty on the basis of change in circumstances. New developments in environmental law were not completely unforeseen.

■■■

Quicknotes

DOCTRINE OF IMPOSSIBILITY A doctrine relieving the parties to a contract from liability for nonperformance of their duties thereunder, if the subject matter of the contract ceases to exist, a person essential to the performance of the contract is deceased, or the service or goods contracted for has become illegal.

ENVIRONMENTAL LAW A body of federal law passed in 1970 that protects the environment against public and private actions that harm the ecosystem.

TREATY An agreement between two or more nations for the benefit of the general public.

■■■

Techt v. Hughes

Non-citizen sister (D) v. Citizen sister (P)

N.Y. Ct. App., 229 N.Y. 222, 128 N.E. 185, *cert. denied,* 254 U.S. 643 (1920).

NATURE OF CASE: Appeal from inheritance dispute decided in favor of non-citizen.

FACT SUMMARY: Techt (D) claimed that she was entitled to take property in New York on the basis of the Treaty of 1848 between the United States and Austria, despite the fact that the U.S. and Austria were at war at the time.

🏛 RULE OF LAW
Where a treaty between belligerents at war has not been denounced, the court must decide whether the provision involved in a controversy is inconsistent with national policy or safety.

FACTS: Techt's (D) father, an American citizen, died intestate in New York. Techt (D) had married an Austro-Hungarian citizen and, under federal law at that time, had lost her United States citizenship as a result. Under New York law, Techt (D) could take property as inheritance if she were found to be an alien friend. When the court found that Techt (D) was an alien friend and that she could claim half the inheritance, her sister (P) appealed, claiming she was entitled to the whole property because Techt (D) was an alien enemy. Since the U.S. was at war with Austria-Hungary in 1919, the appeals court found Techt (D) was not an alien friend under the statute. Techt (D) then argued that under the terms of the Treaty of 1848 between the U.S. and Austria, nationals of either state could take real property by descent.

ISSUE: Where a treaty between belligerents at war has not been denounced, must the court decide whether the provision involved in a controversy is inconsistent with national policy or safety?

HOLDING AND DECISION: (Cardozo, J.) Yes. Where a treaty between belligerents at war has not been denounced, the court must decide whether the provision involved in a controversy is inconsistent with national policy or safety. A treaty, if in force, is the supreme law of the land. There is nothing incompatible with the policy of the government, the safety of the nation, or the maintenance of the war in the enforcement of this treaty, so as to sustain Techt's (D) title. Affirmed.

▶ *ANALYSIS*

The court noted that the effect of war on the existing treaties of belligerents is an unsettled area of the law. Some have said that treaties end ipso facto at time of war. The court here found that treaties end only to the extent that their execution is incompatible with the war.

Quicknotes

ALIEN ENEMY An alien who is the resident of a foreign nation that is an enemy of the United States.

IPSO FACTO By the fact itself.

NATIONALITY The country in which a person is born or naturalized.

TREATY An agreement between two or more nations for the benefit of the general public.

WAR Hostilities between nations.

CHAPTER 4

Other Sources of Law

Quick Reference Rules of Law

Prosecutor v. Tadić

Prosecutor (P) v. War criminal (D)

Int'l Crim. Tribunal for the Former Yugoslavia, Decision on Interlocutory Appeal on Jurisdiction, 1995. Appeals Chamber, Case No. IT-94-1-AR72, 35 I.L.M. 32 (1996).

NATURE OF CASE: War crimes trial.

FACT SUMMARY: Tadić (D) was prosecuted for alleged war crimes committed at a Serb-run concentration camp in Bosnia-Herzegovina.

🏛 RULE OF LAW
The International Tribunal has jurisdiction to examine the plea against its jurisdiction based on the invalidity of its establishment by the Security Council.

FACTS: Tadić (D) was prosecuted for alleged war crimes committed at a Serb-run concentration camp in Bosnia-Herzegovina. Tadić (D) challenged the tribunal's jurisdiction as exceeding the authority of the U.N. Security Council. The trial court dismissed the challenge and Tadić (D) appealed.

ISSUE: Does the International Tribunal have jurisdiction to examine the plea against its jurisdiction based on the invalidity of its establishment by the Security Council?

HOLDING AND DECISION: (Judge Cassese, Presiding; Judges Li, Deschenes, Abi-Saab, and Sidhwa) Yes. The International Tribunal has jurisdiction to examine the plea against its jurisdiction based on the invalidity of its establishment by the Security Council. For an international tribunal to be established according to rule of law, it must be established in accordance with the proper international standards; it must provide all guarantees of fairness, justice, and evenhandedness, in full conformity with internationally recognized human rights instruments. When a tribunal such as the present one is created, it necessarily must be endowed with primacy over national courts.

▶ ANALYSIS

Tadić (D) attacked the authority of the Security Council to establish a tribunal for the determination of a criminal charge. The tribunal is authorized to be established for the determination of such charges so long as it is "established by law." The Council requires that it be "set up by a competent organ in keeping with relevant legal procedures, and that it observes the requirements of procedural fairness."

■■■■

Quicknotes

JURISDICTION The authority of a court to hear and declare judgment in respect to a particular matter.

■■■■

The Diversion of Water from the Meuse (Netherlands v. Belgium)

Country (P) v. Country (D)

Permanent Court of Int'l Justice, P.C.I.J. (ser. A/B) No. 70, 76–78.

NATURE OF CASE: Proceeding before the International Court of Justice.

FACT SUMMARY: The Netherlands (P) claimed that Belgium (D) violated an agreement by building certain canals.

🏛 RULE OF LAW
Principles of equity form a part of international law.

FACTS: The Netherlands (P) objected to the construction of certain canals by Belgium (D) that would alter the water level of the Meuse River in violation of an earlier agreement. Belgium (D) counterclaimed based on the construction of a lock by Netherlands (P) at an earlier time. The Court rejected both claims.

ISSUE: Do principles of equity form a part of international law?

HOLDING AND DECISION: [Holding and decision not stated in casebook excerpt.]

CONCURRENCE: (Hudson, J.) Yes. Principles of equity form a part of international law. Under Article 38, and independently of that statute, this Court has some freedom to consider principles of equity. The maxim, "He who seeks equity must do equity," is derived from Anglo-American law.

▌ ANALYSIS

The Court also referred to Roman Law. A similar principle in Roman Law made the obligations of a vendor and a vendee concurrent. Neither could compel the other to perform unless he had done, or tendered, his own part.

■═■

Quicknotes

EQUITY Fairness; justice; the determination of a matter consistent with principles of fairness and not in strict compliance with rules of law.

MAXIMS Rules of law.

■═■

Corfu Channel Case
(United Kingdom v. Albania)

Warships (D) v. Mined waters (P)

I.C.J., 1949 I.C.J. 4, 22.

NATURE OF CASE: Proceeding before the International Court of Justice.

FACT SUMMARY: The United Kingdom (D) claimed that Albanian (P) authorities should have warned of the presence of mines in Albanian (P) waters.

🏛 **RULE OF LAW**
Elementary considerations of humanity create international obligations in peace time.

FACTS: British naval personnel died as a result of the explosion of mines in Albanian (P) waters. The U.K. (D) claimed Albania (P) was internationally responsible for damages.

ISSUE: Do elementary considerations of humanity create international obligations in peace time?

HOLDING AND DECISION: [Judge not stated in casebook excerpt.] Yes. Elementary considerations of humanity create international obligations in peace time. Every state has an obligation not to knowingly allow its territory to be used for acts contrary to the rights of other states.

▶ *ANALYSIS*

The Court found that the Hague Convention of 1907 did not apply. The Hague Convention only applies in times of war. This case was decided on the basis of the principle of freedom of maritime communication.

∎≡∎

Quicknotes

HAGUE CONVENTION Multilateral treaty governing service of process in foreign jurisdictions.

∎≡∎

Filartiga v. Pena-Irala

Relatives of decedent (P) v. Police officer (D)

630 F.2d 876 (2d Cir. 1980).

NATURE OF CASE: Appeal of dismissal of wrongful death action.

FACT SUMMARY: Filartiga (P) filed an action against Pena-Irala (D), contending he had tortured to death Filartiga's (P) decedent.

🏛 RULE OF LAW
Torture may be considered to violate the law of nations for purposes of the Alien Tort Statute.

FACTS: Filartiga (P) brought an action against Pena-Irala (D), claiming that he had tortured to death Filartiga's (P) decedent while Pena-Irala (D) was police Inspector-General. All parties were Paraguayan citizens. Jurisdiction was based on the Alien Tort Statute, 28 U.S.C. § 1350, which provided jurisdiction for torts committed in violation of "the law of nations." The district court dismissed for lack of jurisdiction. Filartiga (P) appealed.

ISSUE: May torture be considered to violate the law of nations for purposes of the Alien Tort Statute?

HOLDING AND DECISION: [Judge not stated in casebook excerpt.] Yes. Torture may be considered to violate the law of nations for purposes of the Alien Tort Statute. The prohibition against torture has become part of customary international law. This is particularly evidenced by various United Nations declarations, such as the Universal Declaration of Human Rights and the 1975 Declaration on the Protection of All Persons from Torture. A declaration from the United Nations is a formal and solemn instrument, and can be considered an authoritative statement from the international community. Beyond that, torture has been officially renounced in the vast majority of nations. For these reasons, this court concludes that torture violates the law of nations.

▶ ANALYSIS

It is no great secret that what many members of the United Nations say in their pronouncements and what they do in practice are not quite the same things. Torture is still widely practiced if not in a majority of countries then in a significant number. Commentators have argued that actual practice, not U.N. declarations, constitutes customary international law.

Quicknotes

INTERNATIONAL LAW The body of law applicable to dealings between nations.

JURISDICTION The authority of a court to hear and declare judgment in respect to a particular matter.

WRONGFUL DEATH An action brought by the beneficiaries of a deceased person, claiming that the deceased's death was the result of wrongful conduct by the defendant.

Sosa v. Alvarez-Machain

[Parties not identified.]

542 U.S. 692 (2004).

NATURE OF CASE: Appeal of judgment awarding damages to foreign national.

FACT SUMMARY: [Alvarez-Machain (P) claimed he was involuntarily detained by bounty hunters and brought to the United States.]

⚖ RULE OF LAW
The abduction of a foreign national does not amount to an "arbitrary arrest" within the meaning of the Universal Declaration of Human Rights and the International Covenant on Civil and Political Rights.

FACTS: [Alvarez-Machain (P) claimed he was involuntarily detained by bounty hunters and brought to the United States.]

ISSUE: Does the abduction of a foreign national amount to an "arbitrary arrest" within the meaning of the Universal Declaration of Human Rights and the International Covenant on Civil and Political Rights?

HOLDING AND DECISION: [Judge not stated in casebook excerpt.] No. The abduction of a foreign national does not amount to an "arbitrary arrest" within the meaning of the Universal Declaration of Human Rights and the International Covenant on Civil and Political Rights. The Declaration does not impose obligations as a matter of international law, and while the Covenant binds the United States as a matter of international law, the United States ratified it on the express understanding that it was not self-executing, and therefore did not itself create obligations that were enforceable in the federal courts.

▶ ANALYSIS

This short case excerpt illustrates the concept of self-determination under international law. No document can give rise to obligations as a matter of international law that does not expressly purport to do so, and no state can be bound to any international pact without its consent.

■≡■

Quicknotes

COVENANT A written promise to do, or to refrain from doing, a particular activity.

INTERNATIONAL LAW The body of law applicable to dealings between nations.

■≡■

Legal Status of Eastern Greenland
(Norway v. Denmark)

Occupier (D) v. Sovereign (P)

Perm. Court of Int'l Justice, 1933 P.C.I.J. (ser. A/B) No. 53 at 71.

NATURE OF CASE: Proceeding before the International Court of Justice.

FACT SUMMARY: Denmark (P) claimed that a statement made by a Norwegian Minister was binding on Norway (D).

🏛 RULE OF LAW
A reply given by the Minister of Foreign Affairs on behalf of his government is binding upon the country to which the Minister belongs.

FACTS: Denmark (P) wanted to obtain from Norway (D) its agreement not to obstruct Danish (P) plans with regard to Greenland. The Minister for Foreign Affairs made a declaration on behalf of the Norwegian government (D) that the Norwegian government (D) would not make any difficulty in the settlement of the question.

ISSUE: Is a reply given by the Minister of Foreign Affairs on behalf of his government binding upon the country to which the Minister belongs?

HOLDING AND DECISION: [Judge not stated in casebook excerpt.] Yes. A reply given by the Minister of Foreign Affairs on behalf of his government is binding upon the country to which the Minister belongs. It is beyond dispute that a reply of the nature given here in response to a request by the diplomatic representative of a foreign power is binding upon the country the Minister represents.

▶ *ANALYSIS*

The Vienna Convention on the Law of Treaties is the main source of international law on treaties. The Convention was ratified by 35 countries but not by the United States. Unilateral statements may also be binding on states.

■══■

Quicknotes

TREATY An agreement between two or more nations for the benefit of the general public.

UNILATERAL One-sided; involving only one person.

■══■

Nuclear Tests Case
(Australia & New Zealand v. France)

Neighboring countries (P) v. Nuclear testing country (D)

I.C.J., 1974 I.C.J. 253, 457.

NATURE OF CASE: Proceeding before the International Court of Justice.

FACT SUMMARY: Australia and New Zealand (P) demanded that France (D) cease atmospheric nuclear tests in the South Pacific.

🏛 RULE OF LAW
Declarations made by way of unilateral acts may have the effect of creating legal obligations.

FACTS: France (D) completed a series of nuclear tests in the South Pacific. Australia and New Zealand (P) applied to the I.C.J. demanding that France (D) cease testing immediately. While the case was pending, France (D) announced the series of tests was complete and that it did not plan any further such tests. France (D) moved to dismiss the applications.

ISSUE: May declarations made by way of unilateral acts have the effect of creating legal obligations?

HOLDING AND DECISION: [Judge not stated in casebook excerpt.] Yes. Declarations made by way of unilateral acts may have the effect of creating legal obligations. The sole relevant question is whether the language employed in any given declaration reveals a clear intention. One of the basic principles governing the creation and performance of legal obligations is the principle of good faith. The statements made by the President of the French Republic must be held to constitute an engagement of the State in regard to the circumstances and intention with which they were made. The statements made by the French authorities are therefore relevant and legally binding. Applications dismissed.

▶ ANALYSIS

The unilateral statements made by French authorities were first communicated to the government of Australia. To have legal effect there was no need for the statements to be directed to any particular state. The general nature and characteristics of the statements alone were relevant for evaluation of their legal implications.

■══■

Quicknotes

RELEVANCE The admissibility of evidence based on whether it has any tendency to prove or disprove a matter at issue to the case.

UNILATERAL One-sided; involving only one person.

■══■

Frontier Dispute Case
(Burkina Faso/Mali)

[Parties not identified.]

I.C.J., 1986 I.C.J. 554.

NATURE OF CASE: Interpretation of a statement made by the head of state.

FACT SUMMARY: The Mali Head of State made a declaration that was interpreted to be a unilateral act.

🏛 RULE OF LAW
Unilateral declarations made by heads of state bind the state to its terms only when the intention confers on the declaration the character of a legal undertaking.

FACTS: [Facts not stated in casebook excerpt.]

ISSUE: Do unilateral declarations made by heads of state bind the state to its terms only when the intention confers on the declaration the character of a legal undertaking?

HOLDING AND DECISION: [Judge not stated in casebook excerpt.] Yes. Unilateral declarations made by heads of state bind the state to its terms only when the intention confers on the declaration the character of a legal undertaking. It is for the court to "form its own view of the meaning and scope intended by the author of a unilateral declaration which might create a legal obligation." In order to assess the intentions of the author of a unilateral act, account must be taken of all the factual circumstances in which the act occurred. Here, there was nothing to hinder the parties from entering a formal agreement. Since no such agreement was entered, there are no grounds to interpret the Mali Head of State's declaration as a unilateral act with legal implications.

▶ ANALYSIS

In the *Nuclear Tests* cases, the Court interpreted the French government's unilateral declarations as effectively communicating the intent to terminate atmospheric testing. In that case, the French government had no alternative but to express its intentions by unilateral declarations. This case is distinguished since the parties had the normal method of formal agreement available.

■══■

Quicknotes

LEGAL OBLIGATION A duty to act that is imposed by law.

UNILATERAL ACT One-sided; involving only one person.

■══■

States

Quick Reference Rules of Law

Reference Re Secession of Quebec

Sup. Ct. of Canada 2 S.C.R. 217, 37 I.L.M. 1340 (1998).

NATURE OF CASE: Advisory opinion regarding self-determination in relation to separatist movements.

FACT SUMMARY: Quebec attempted to secede from Canada.

🏛 RULE OF LAW
A people's right to self-determination cannot be said to ground a right to unilateral secession.

FACTS: [Facts not stated in casebook excerpt.]

ISSUE: Is there a right to self-determination under international law that would give the National Assembly, legislature, or government of Quebec the right to effect Quebec's unilateral secession from Canada?

HOLDING AND DECISION: [Judge not stated in casebook excerpt.] The international law principle of self-determination has evolved within a framework of respect for the territorial integrity of existing states. The right to external self-determination has only been granted to peoples under colonial rule or foreign occupation, based on the assumption that both are entities inherently distinct from the colonialist power and the occupant power. External self-determination has also been bestowed upon peoples totally frustrated in their efforts to exercise internally their rights to self-determinism. In this case, Quebec is neither a colony nor a foreign-occupied land. Further, the people of Quebec have not been victims of attacks on their physical existence or integrity or of massive human rights violations. Quebecers are equitably represented in legislative, executive, and judicial institutions; occupy prominent positions within the government of Canada; and enjoy the freedom to pursue their political, economic, social, and cultural development.

▶ ANALYSIS

The *Reference Re Secession of Quebec* leaves open the possibility that the international law right of self-determination could entail secession as a "last resort" in cases of especially severe oppression in which other channels for exercising internal self-determination had been "totally frustrated."

Quicknotes

ADVISORY OPINION A decision rendered at the request of an interested party of how the court would rule should the particular issue arise.

INTERNATIONAL LAW The body of law applicable to dealings between nations.

Tinoco Claims Arbitration
(Great Britain v. Costa Rica)

Contracting party (P) v. Restored regime (D)

1 U.N. Rep. Int'l Arb. Awards 369 (1923).

NATURE OF CASE: Arbitration of contract repudiation.

FACT SUMMARY: Great Britain (P) claimed that the former government of Costa Rica (D), the Tinoco regime, had granted oil concessions to a British company that had to be honored by the present regime.

🏛 RULE OF LAW
A government that establishes itself and maintains a peaceful de facto administration need not conform to a previous constitution and nonrecognition of the government by other governments does not destroy the de facto status of the government.

FACTS: The Tinoco regime had seized power in Costa Rica by coup. Great Britain (P) and the United States never recognized the Tinoco regime. When the Tinoco regime fell, the restored government nullified all Tinoco contracts, including an oil concession to a British company. Great Britain (P) claimed that the Tinoco government was the only government in existence at the time the contract was signed and its acts could not be repudiated. Costa Rica (D) claimed that Great Britain (P) was estopped from enforcing the contract by its nonrecognition of the Tinoco regime. The matter was sent for arbitration.

ISSUE: Does nonrecognition of a new government by other governments destroy the de facto status of the government?

HOLDING AND DECISION: (Taft, C.J., Arb.) No. A government that establishes itself and maintains a peaceful de facto administration need not conform to a previous constitution and nonrecognition of the government by other governments does not destroy the de facto status of the government. Great Britain's (P) nonrecognition of the Tinoco regime did not dispute the de facto existence of that regime. There was no estoppel since the successor government had not been led by British nonrecognition to change its position.

▶ ANALYSIS

The arbitrator found there was no estoppel. The evidence of nonrecognition did not outweigh the evidence of the de facto status of the Tinoco regime. Unrecognized governments thus may have the power to form valid contracts.

Quicknotes

DE FACTO STATUS In fact; something that is recognized by virtue of its existence in reality, but is illegal for failure to comply with statutory requirements.

ESTOPPEL An equitable doctrine precluding a party from asserting a right to the detriment of another who justifiably relied on the conduct.

Salimoff & Co. v. Standard Oil

Former owner (P) v. Purchaser (D)

N.Y. Ct. App., 262 N.Y. 220, 186 N.E. 679 (1933).

NATURE OF CASE: Appeal from dismissal of action for an accounting.

FACT SUMMARY: Salimoff (P) claimed that the Soviet government did not have good title to pass when it sold oil property confiscated from Russian nationals.

🏛 RULE OF LAW
When no right of action is created at the place of the wrong, no recovery in tort can be had in any other state.

FACTS: Salimoff (P) was the equitable owner of oil property that had been seized by a nationalization decree and confiscated by the Soviet government in Russia. When the Soviet government sold oil extracted from that property to Standard Oil (D), Salimoff (P) sought an accounting, alleging that the confiscatory decrees by the unrecognized Soviet government had no legal effect. The complaint was dismissed and Salimoff (P) appealed.

ISSUE: When no right of action is created at the place of the wrong, can recovery in tort be had in another state?

HOLDING AND DECISION: (Pound, C.J.) No. When no right of action is created at the place of the wrong, no recovery in tort can be had in any other state. The United States government recognizes that the Soviet government has functioned as a de facto government since 1917, ruling within its borders. The courts cannot refuse to recognize a de facto government merely because the State Department has not recognized the Soviet government as a de jure government. Affirmed.

▶ *ANALYSIS*

Salimoff (P) claimed the Soviet government was nothing more than a band of robbers and had no legitimacy. The court asked the rhetorical question whether Soviet Russia was a band of robbers or a government. Everyone knows it is a government, according to this court.

■■■

Quicknotes

CONFISCATORY DECREE A court order to condemn private property for public use.

DE FACTO GOVERNMENT A government that sustains its power against the lawful government by force.

DE JURE GOVERNMENT Government legally vested with the authority to govern.

NATIONALIZATION Government acquisition of a private enterprise.

■■■

National Petrochemical Co. of Iran v. M/T Stolt Sheaf

Iranian corporation (P) v. Unidentified party (D)

860 F.2d 551 (2d Cir. 1988).

NATURE OF CASE: Appeal of federal district court dismissal.

FACT SUMMARY: [An Iranian corporation (P) brought suit as a plaintiff in a U.S. federal court. The district court dismissed the claim because the United States had never extended recognition to the government of the Islamic Republic of Iran.]

🏛 RULE OF LAW
A foreign government is not necessarily barred from access to U.S. courts if it has not been formally recognized by the United States.

FACTS: [An Iranian corporation (P) brought suit as a plaintiff in a U.S. federal court. The district court dismissed the claim because the United States had never extended recognition to the government of the Islamic Republic of Iran. The U.S. government entered the case as amicus curiae, and argued that the Iranian corporation (P) ought to be granted access.]

ISSUE: Is a foreign government necessarily barred from access to U.S. courts if it has not been formally recognized by the United States?

HOLDING AND DECISION: [Judge not stated in casebook excerpt.] No. A foreign government is not necessarily barred from access to U.S. courts if it has not been formally recognized by the United States. Recognition can occur even where the U.S. government has withheld formal recognition, which it sometimes does where recognition can be misinterpreted as approval. In addition, the Executive Branch has the power to deal with foreign nations outside formal recognition. In this case, relations between the United States and Iran have been tumultuous. The Executive Branch must therefore have broad discretion involving matters of foreign relations.

▶ ANALYSIS

The case as excerpted does not illustrate the point as clearly as one might hope. But the thrust is that the intervention of the United States as amicus and its arguments in favor of allowing the case to proceed in the U.S. court system were exercises of the power of the executive branch over matters of foreign relations, to which the court deferred.

■══■

Quicknotes

AMICUS CURIAE A third party, not implicated in the suit, that seeks to file a brief containing information for the court's consideration in conformity with its position.

■══■

Island of Palmas Case
(United States v. The Netherlands)

Discovering country (P) v. Occupier (D)

Perm. Ct. of Arbitration, 2 U.N. Rep. Int'l Arb. Awards 829 (1928).

NATURE OF CASE: Arbitration of territorial dispute.

FACT SUMMARY: The United States (P) claimed that the Island of Palmas was part of the Philippines but the Netherlands (D) claimed title as well.

🏛 RULE OF LAW
An inchoate title cannot prevail over a definite title founded on continuous and peaceful display of sovereignty.

FACTS: The United States (P) claimed the Island of Palmas was part of the Philippines and had been ceded by Spain by the Treaty of Paris in 1898. The United States (P), as successor to the rights of Spain over the Philippines, based its claim of title in the first place on discovery. The Netherlands (D) claimed that it had possessed and exercised rights of sovereignty over the island from 1677 or earlier to the present.

ISSUE: Can an inchoate title prevail over a definite title founded on continuous and peaceful display of sovereignty?

HOLDING AND DECISION: (Huber, Arb.) No. An inchoate title cannot prevail over a definite title founded on continuous and peaceful display of sovereignty. The continuous and peaceful display of territorial sovereignty is as good as title. Discovery alone, without any subsequent act, cannot suffice to prove sovereignty over the island. There is no positive rule of international law that islands situated outside territorial waters should belong to a state whose territory forms the nearest continent or large island. No one contested the exercise of territorial rights by the Netherlands (D) from 1700 to 1906. The title of discovery, at best an inchoate title, does not prevail over the Netherlands, (D) claim of sovereignty.

▶ ANALYSIS

The arbitrator examined evidence of contracts made by the East India Company and the Netherlands (D). The Netherlands (D) also based its claims on conventions it had with the princes and native chieftains of the islands. Spain was found not to have had dominion over the island at the time of the Treaty of Paris in 1898.

Quicknotes

INCHOATE Impartial or incomplete.

SOVEREIGNTY The absolute power conferred to the state to govern and regulate all persons located and activities conducted therein.

Frontier Dispute Case
(Burkina Faso/Mali)

[Parties not identified.]

I.C.J., 1986 I.C.J. 554.

NATURE OF CASE: Petition to resolve a border dispute.

FACT SUMMARY: Burkina Faso and Mali submitted a question to the International Court of Justice regarding a border dispute.

🏛 RULE OF LAW
There exists an obligation to respect pre-existing international frontiers in the event of a state succession.

FACTS: [Facts not stated in casebook excerpt.]

ISSUE: Does there exist an obligation to respect pre-existing international frontiers in the event of a state succession?

HOLDING AND DECISION: (Judges Lachs, Ruda, Bedjaoui, Luchaire, and Abi-Saab) Yes. There exists an obligation to respect pre-existing international frontiers in the event of a state succession, whether or not the rule is expressed in the form of *uti possidetis*. Thus, the numerous declarations of the intangibility of the frontiers at the time of the declaration of independence of the African states are declaratory. The fact that the principle did not exist when the states declared such independence in 1960 does not foreclose its present application.

▶ ANALYSIS

The principle of *uti possidetis* developed with respect to the Spanish American colonies. In a similar dispute between El Salvador and Honduras, the Court described the principle as follows: "The general principle offered the advantage of establishing an absolute rule that there was not in law in the old Spanish America any *terra nullius;* while there might exist many regions that had never been occupied by the Spaniards . . . the regions were reputed to belonging in law to whichever of the republics succeeded to the Spanish province to which these territories attached by virtue of the old Royal ordinances of the Spanish mother country."

Quicknotes

SUCCESSION The scheme pursuant to which property is distributed in the absence of a valid will or of a disposition of particular property.

TERRA NULLIUS Land belonging to nobody.

UTI POSSIDETIS In civil law, the granting of a right of possession to one who was already in possession of a thing in order that he may be declared the legal possessor.

International and Non-Governmental Organizations

Quick Reference Rules of Law

Reparation for Injuries Suffered in the Service of the United Nations

[Parties not identified.]

I.C.J., Advisory Opinion, 1949 I.C.J. 174.

NATURE OF CASE: Advisory opinion.

FACT SUMMARY: [Facts not stated in casebook excerpt.]

🏛 RULE OF LAW
The United Nations has the capacity to bring an international claim against a country that causes an agent of the United Nations to suffer an injury in the performance of his duties with a view to obtaining the reparation due in respect of the damage caused to the United Nations or to the victim or persons entitled through him.

FACTS: [Facts not stated in casebook excerpt.]

ISSUE: Does the United Nations have the capacity to bring an international claim against a country that causes an agent of the United Nations to suffer an injury in the performance of his duties with a view to obtaining the reparation due in respect of the damage caused to the United Nations or to the victim or persons entitled through him?

HOLDING AND DECISION: [Judge not stated in casebook excerpt.] Yes. The United Nations has the capacity to bring an international claim against a country that causes an agent of the United Nations to suffer an injury in the performance of his duties with a view to obtaining the reparation due in respect of the damage caused to the United Nations or to the victim or persons entitled through him. The damage means exclusively damage caused to the interests of the organization itself, to its administrative machine, to its property and assets and to the interests of which it is guardian. With respect to damages caused the victim or persons entitled through him, the Charter does not expressly confer the capacity to include such claim for reparation. However, in order that its agents may perform their duties satisfactorily, they must feel that their protection is assured by the Organization. For that purpose it is necessary when an infringement occurs that the Organization should be able to call upon the responsible state to remedy its default, and to obtain reparation for the damage that it might have caused the agent.

▶ ANALYSIS

The Court states that the same conclusion applies whether or not the defendant state is a member of the United Nations. If competing interests arise between the defendant's national state and the United Nations, there is no rule assigning priority to one over the other, so the Court states that goodwill and common sense must apply.

■≡■

Quicknotes

ADVISORY OPINION A decision rendered at the request of an interested party of how the court would rule should the particular issue arise.

AGENT An individual who has the authority to act on behalf of another.

■≡■

Certain Expenses of the United Nations

[Parties not identified.]

I.C.J., 1962 I.C.J. 151.

NATURE OF CASE: Determination of classification of U.N. expenses.

FACT SUMMARY: [Facts not stated in casebook excerpt.]

🏛 RULE OF LAW

Expenditures made by the United Nations may be classified as authorized under the U.N. Charter if they are made to advance one of the organization's purposes as set forth in the Charter.

FACTS: [Facts not stated in casebook excerpt. The case involves U.N. peacekeeping efforts in Congo and Egypt.]

ISSUE: May expenditures made by the United Nations be classified as authorized under the U.N. Charter if they are made to advance one of the organization's purposes as set forth in the Charter?

HOLDING AND DECISION: [Judge not stated in casebook excerpt.] Yes. Expenditures made by the United Nations may be classified as authorized under the U.N. Charter if they are made to advance one of the organization's purposes as set forth in the Charter. The purposes as set forth in the Charter are to (1) promote international peace and security, (2) promote friendly relations, (3) achieve economic, social, cultural, and humanitarian goals and human rights, and (4) be a center for harmonizing the actions of nations in the pursuit of these goals. Where the United Nations acts in a way that does not conform to the division of functions among the several organs prescribed by the Charter, a conclusion that the expense incurred in taking the action was not an expense of the organization within the meaning of the Charter is not necessarily warranted, because the action of the organ may bind the United Nations as the act of an agent. [In this case, the peacekeeping efforts were agreed to by Congo and Egypt, and the measures fell within the scope of the U.N.'s purposes, and costs associated with the operations could be classified as expenses of the United Nations.]

▌ *ANALYSIS*

This case illustrates the I.C.J.'s process of analyzing whether expenses can properly be classified as "expenses of the United Nations" under the Charter. First, any expense incurred to further the U.N.'s express purposes is presumed to be a U.N. expense. Where the expense is for an action, such as the deployment of peacekeeping forces, and the action is carried out in a way that does not conform to the functions of the U.N.'s internal structure, such as by the wrong U.N. agency, the expenses incurred are not automatically considered by the I.C.J. to be unqualified expenses under the Charter. But in such a case, the I.C.J. will look at the internal structure and operation of the United Nations and determine whether the organization is responsible, through agency principles, for the actions of one of its agencies.

■═■

Prosecutor v. Tadić

State (P) v. Wrongdoer (D)

App. Chamber, Int'l Crim. Trib. for Former Yugoslavia, 1992 Case No. IT-94-1-AR72, 35 I.L.M. 32 (1996).

NATURE OF CASE: Interlocutory appeal from challenge of validity of International Tribunal.

FACT SUMMARY: Tadić (D) claimed that the Security Council was not authorized to establish an international criminal tribunal.

🏛 RULE OF LAW

Once the Security Council determines that a particular situation poses a threat to the peace, it enjoys a wide margin of discretion in choosing the course of action.

FACTS: The Charter of the United Nations provides that the Security Council shall determine the existence of any threat to the peace and decide what measures shall be taken to restore international peace and security. When the Security Council established an International Criminal Tribunal to deal with armed conflict in the former Yugoslavia, Tadić (D) claimed the Security Council lacked the power to do so.

ISSUE: Once the Security Council determines that a particular situation poses a threat to the peace, does it enjoy a wide margin of discretion in choosing the course of action?

HOLDING AND DECISION: [Judge not stated in casebook excerpt.] Yes. Once the Security Council determines that a particular situation poses a threat to the peace, it enjoys a wide margin of discretion in choosing the course of action. Where internal armed conflicts are determined to pose a threat to the peace, the Security Council may exercise its exceptional powers under Chapter VI or Chapter VII of the U.N. Charter. These powers are coercive and mandatory. Although the establishment of an international tribunal is not explicitly mandated, the measures described in the Charter are merely illustrative and not exhaustive.

▶ ANALYSIS

Tadić (D) had originally contested the Security Council's power to determine whether the situation in the former Yugoslavia constituted a threat to the peace. At this stage, Tadić (D) no longer raised that argument. Here, Tadić (D) was challenging the legality and appropriateness of the measures chosen by the Security Council.

■≡■

Quicknotes

INTERLOCUTORY APPEAL The appeal of an issue that does not resolve the disposition of the case, but is essential to a determination of the parties' legal rights.

■≡■

Legality of Use of Force
(Serbia & Montenegro v. United Kingdom)

Non-U.N. member (P) v. U.N. member (D)

I.C.J., 2004 I.C.J. 1307.

NATURE OF CASE: Claim of illegal use of force against various NATO states.

FACT SUMMARY: [The Federal Republic of Yugoslavia (Serbia and Montenegro) (F.R.Y.) (P) brought a claim in the International Court of Justice against various NATO states (D), including the United Kingdom (D), in 1999. The I.C.J. first considered the issue of jurisdiction.]

🏛 RULE OF LAW
The legal position of a state within the United Nations must be determined and clearly defined by the competent organs of the United Nations.

FACTS: [The Federal Republic of Yugoslavia (Serbia and Montenegro) (F.R.Y.) (P) brought a claim in the International Court of Justice against various NATO states (D), including the United Kingdom (D) in 1999. Before considering the claim, the I.C.J. had to determine if it had jurisdiction to hear the case, which would only be the case if the F.R.Y. (P) was at the time of the claim a U.N. member state. Its predecessor state, the Socialist Federal Republic of Yugoslavia, was a member state at the time.]

ISSUE: Must the legal position of a state within the United Nations be determined and clearly defined by the competent organs of the United Nations?

HOLDING AND DECISION: [Judge not stated in casebook excerpt.] Yes. The legal position of a state within the United Nations must be determined and clearly defined by the competent organs of the United Nations. The legal position of the F.R.Y. (P) remained ambiguous between 1992 and 2000, the period during which its claim against certain NATO states (D), including the United Kingdom (D), was filed. The U.N. Security Council and General Assembly both decided that the F.R.Y. (P) could not automatically continue the membership of the Socialist Federal Republic of Yugoslavia in the United Nations, and that the F.R.Y. (P) should reapply for membership. These resolutions were approved by a majority of member voters, but they cannot be construed as conveying an authoritative determination of the F.R.Y.'s (P) legal status in the United Nations, because certain events made the F.R.Y.'s (P) status seem ambiguous—the General Assembly assessed annual contributions to the United Nations, the F.R.Y. (P) maintained that it continued the legal personality of the S.F.R.Y., and the Secretariat of the United Nations kept up the practice of the status quo ante that was in place up to the dissolution of the S.F.R.Y. But the situation cleared when the elected president of the F.R.Y. (P) in 2000 requested admission to the United Nations from the Secretary-General, which then recommended the state's admission. F.R.Y. (P) was admitted in late 2000. In hindsight, then, the F.R.Y. (P) was not a member of the United Nations when it began this action in 1999. Therefore, there was no jurisdiction to hear its claim.

▶ ANALYSIS

The I.C.J.'s opinion focused on the F.R.Y.'s (P) status within the United Nations. But note that non-U.N. members may also become parties to the I.C.J.'s statute under Article 93(2). Remember also that while a state that is a party to the I.C.J.'s statute is entitled to participate in cases before the I.C.J., being a party to the statute does not automatically give the I.C.J. jurisdiction over disputes involving those parties.

Quicknotes

CLAIM The demand for a right to payment or equitable relief; the fact or facts giving rise to such demand.

JURISDICTION The authority of a court to hear and declare judgment in respect to a particular matter.

Individuals and Corporations

Quick Reference Rules of Law

LaGrand Case
(Germany v. United States)

State (P) v. State (D)

I.C.J., 2001 I.C.J. 466.

NATURE OF CASE: Multiple plaintiff action against a state for violation of the Vienna Convention.

FACT SUMMARY: Germany (P) filed suit in the International Court of Justice against the United States (D), claiming that U.S. law enforcement personnel failed to advise aliens upon their arrests of their rights under the Vienna Convention.

🏛 RULE OF LAW
A state that breaches its obligations to another under the Vienna Convention on Consular Relations by failing to inform an arrested alien of the right to consular notification and to provide judicial review of the alien's conviction and sentence also violates individual rights held by the alien under international law.

FACTS: Article 36(1)(b) of the Vienna Convention on Consular Relations provides that a state trying an alien in a death sentence case must inform the alien of his rights to have his consular authorities informed of the arrest. Paraguay (P), Germany (P), and Mexico (P) filed suit in the International Court of Justice against the United States (D), claiming that U.S. law enforcement personnel failed to advise aliens upon their arrest of their rights, and that as a remedy for violation of the Vienna Convention, state courts should review and reconsider the death sentences to determine if the lack of consular access prejudiced the aliens. Germany's (P) case involved LaGrand and his brother, who was executed before the matter came to the I.C.J. The I.C.J. found that the United States (D) breached its obligations to Germany (P) under the Convention by not immediately informing LaGrand and his brother of the right of consular notification, and by failing to provide judicial review of the conviction and sentence.

ISSUE: Does a state that breaches its obligations to another under the Vienna Convention on Consular Relations by failing to inform an arrested alien of the right to consular notification and to provide judicial review of the alien's conviction and sentence also violate individual rights held by the alien under international law?

HOLDING AND DECISION: [Judge not stated in casebook excerpt.] Yes. A state that breaches its obligations to another under the Vienna Convention on Consular Relations by failing to inform an arrested alien of the right to consular notification and to provide judicial review of the alien's conviction and sentence also violates individual rights held by the alien under international law. The ordinary meaning of the clause "said authorities shall inform the person concerned without delay of his rights under this subparagraph" of Article 36 suggests that the right to be informed of the rights under the Convention is an individual right of every national of a state that is party to the Convention.

▶ ANALYSIS

Diplomatic efforts by the German ambassador and German Members of Parliament and the recommendation of Arizona's clemency board, failed to change the mind of Arizona Governor Jane Dee Hull, who insisted that the executions of the LaGrand brothers be carried out. Karl LaGrand was executed on February 24, 1999, by lethal injection, and Walter LaGrand was executed March 3, 1999, by gas chamber. Compare this case to a ruling by the I.C.J. involving Mexican nationals, *Avena and other Mexican Nationals (Mexico v. United States)*, 2004 I.C.J. 12, and the U.S. Supreme Court's refusal to give effect to the I.C.J.'s *Avena* decision in *Medellin v. Texas*, 128 S. Ct. 1346 (2008).

▪━▪

Quicknotes

BREACH The violation of an obligation imposed pursuant to contract or law, by acting or failing to act.

INTERNATIONAL LAW The body of law applicable to dealings between nations.

JUDICIAL REVIEW The authority of the courts to review decisions, actions, or omissions committed by another agency or branch of government.

▪━▪

Nottebohm Case
(Liechtenstein v. Guatemala)

Country of citizenship (P) v. Country of residence (D)

I.C.J., 1955, I.C.J. 4 (1955).

NATURE OF CASE: Appeal by a state from the refusal of another state to admit one of its nationals.

FACT SUMMARY: Nottebohm (P), a German citizen, lived in Guatemala (D) for 34 years and applied for Liechtenstein (P) citizenship one month after the start of World War II.

 RULE OF LAW
While nationality conferred on a party is normally only the concern of that nation, such nationality may be disregarded by other states where it is clear that it was a mere device/subterfuge.

FACTS: Nottebohm (P) was a German by birth. Nottebohm (P) lived in Guatemala (D) for 34 years, retaining his German citizenship and family and business ties with it. One month after the outbreak of World War II, Nottebohm (P) applied for citizenship with Liechtenstein (P), a neutral country. Nottebohm (P) had no ties with Liechtenstein (P) and intended to remain in Guatemala (D). Liechtenstein (P) approved the naturalization application and impliedly waived its three-year residency requirement. Nottebohm (P) briefly visited Liechtenstein (P) and, on his return to Guatemala (D), was refused admittance, being deemed a German national. Nottebohm's (P) Liechtenstein (P) citizenship was not honored. Liechtenstein (P) brought an action before the International Court to compel Guatemala (D) to recognize Nottebohm (P) as one of its nationals. Guatemala (D) challenged the validity of Nottebohm's (P) citizenship, the right of Liechtenstein (P) to bring the action and alleged its belief that Nottebohm (P) remained a German national.

ISSUE: Must a nation automatically recognize the citizenship conferred on a party by another nation?

HOLDING AND DECISION: [Judge not stated in casebook excerpt.] No. As a general rule, matters concerning citizenship are solely the concern of the granting nation. It alone will normally bear the burdens or attain the benefits from the conferral of citizenship on a party. However, the conferring state may not require other states to automatically accept its designation unless it has acted in conformity with the general aim of forging a genuine bond between it and its national. Here, no relationship exists between Liechtenstein (P) and Nottebohm (P). There was never an intent to reside in Liechtenstein (P), no business or family connections, no acceptance of traditions and the severing of old ties, etc. The change in nationality was a more convenience/subterfuge mandated by the war. Under such circumstances, Guatemala (D) was not forced to recognize it. Dismissed.

▶ *ANALYSIS*

A state putting forth a claim must establish a *locus standi* for that purpose. This is almost exclusively a showing of nationality of the claimant. The real claimant must have continuously and without interruption from the time of the injury to the making of an award been a national of the state making the claim and must not have been a national of the state against whom the claim has been filed. International Law 347 (8th Ed. 1955) Vol. 1.

Quicknotes

LOCUS STANDI Standing to bring suit in court.

NATIONALITY The country in which a person is born or naturalized.

Iran-United States Claims Tribunal, Case No. A/18

Dual citizens (P) v. Iran (D)

Dec. No. 32-A/18-FT, 5 Iran-U.S. Cl. Trib. Rep. 251 (1984-I).

NATURE OF CASE: Jurisdictional consideration by arbitral tribunal.

FACT SUMMARY: People with dual Iranian-U.S. citizenship (P) filed claims against Iran (D) in an arbitral tribunal in The Hague under a Claims Settlement Declaration, which was part of the Algiers Accords reached in the aftermath of the 1979 Iranian seizure of U.S. diplomatic and consular personnel in Iran (D) as hostages. Iran (D) challenged the jurisdiction of the tribunal.

🏛 RULE OF LAW
The Claims Settlement Declaration arbitral tribunal has jurisdiction over claims against Iran by dual Iran-United States nationals if the dominant and effective nationality of the claimant is that of the United States.

FACTS: Iranian militants seized U.S. diplomatic and consular personnel in Iran (D) as hostages after the 1979 Iranian revolution. The United States seized Iranian assets in the United States, and people and companies with claims against Iran (D) filed suit in U.S. courts, levying attachments against blocked Iranian assets. Algeria mediated a solution in January 1981, and the Algiers Accords was adopted by both states. The Algiers Accords included a Claims Settlement Declaration, and created an arbitral tribunal in The Hague to hear claims by the nationals of either state against the government of the other state. Certain people with dual Iranian-U.S. citizenship (P) filed claims against Iran (D) in the tribunal, and Iran (D) challenged its jurisdiction.

ISSUE: Does the Claims Settlement Declaration arbitral tribunal have jurisdiction over claims against Iran (D) by dual Iran-United States nationals (P) if the dominant and effective nationality of the claimant is that of the United States?

HOLDING AND DECISION: [Judge not stated in casebook excerpt.] Yes. The Claims Settlement Declaration arbitral tribunal has jurisdiction over claims against Iran (D) by dual Iran-United States nationals (P) if the dominant and effective nationality of the claimant is that of the United States. The text of the Claims Settlement Declaration is not completely unambiguous on the issue, but the 1930 Hague Convention as modified by recent developments in international law, precedent, and legal literature suggest a person's dominant and effective nationality is determined by the stronger factual ties between the person concerned and one of the states whose nationality is involved. Factors to consider when determining the stronger factual ties include residence, center of interests, family ties, and participation in public life. Use of the word "national" or "nationals" in the Algiers Accords must be understood in a way that is consistent with this rule of international law, and jurisdiction under the Claims Settlement Agreement in these cases involving persons with dual citizenship against Iran (D) when the dominant and effective nationality of the person during the relevant period was that of the United States.

▶ ANALYSIS

In 1982, the tribunal closed to new claims by private individuals. In total, it received approximately 4,700 private U.S. claims, ordered payments by Iran (D) to U.S. nationals totaling over $2.5 billion.

■=■

Quicknotes

JURISDICTION The authority of a court to hear and declare judgment in respect to a particular matter.

NATIONALITY The country in which a person is born or naturalized.

■=■

Eritrea Ethiopia Claims Commission, Partial Award, Civilian Claims, Eritrea's Claims 15, 16, 23 & 27-32

Eritrea (P) v. Ethiopia (D)

44 I.L.M. 601 (2005).

NATURE OF CASE: Review of denationalization procedures.

FACT SUMMARY: Ethiopia (D) denationalized nationals that voted for the creation of an independent state of Eritrea (P). Eritrea (P) challenged the action.

🏛 RULE OF LAW
In time of war, a state may denationalize persons whose second nationality is that of an enemy state, provided denationalization is not arbitrary.

FACTS: A new state of Eritrea (P) was admitted to the United Nations in May 1993 after persons of Eritrean origin voted overwhelmingly in favor of establishing the new state from a portion of Ethiopia (D). Persons who obtained an Eritrean "national identity card" were allowed to vote. After the 1998-2000 border war between Eritrea (P) and Ethiopia (D), approximately 66,000 people who voted were still living in Ethiopia (D). Ethiopia (D) claimed that because they voted, they were Eritrean nationals, and could therefore be expelled to Eritrea (P) under international law as enemy nationals. Eritrea (P) argued that they never relinquished their Ethiopian nationality and were being unlawfully denationalized and expelled. A bilateral claims commission that was established by Eritrea (P) and Ethiopia (D) concluded that persons still living in Ethiopia (D), who also voted to create Eritrea (P), were dual nationals—they acquired Eritrean nationality by voting in the referendum, and retained Ethiopian nationality by continuing to live in Ethiopia (D) and receive the benefits of Ethiopian nationality.

ISSUE: In time of war, may a state denationalize persons whose second nationality is that of an enemy state, provided denationalization is not arbitrary?

HOLDING AND DECISION: [Judge not stated in casebook excerpt.] Yes. In time of war, a state may denationalize persons whose second nationality is that of an enemy state, provided denationalization is not arbitrary. International law does not prohibit states from permitting nationals to possess another nationality, but also does not prohibit states from prohibiting the possession of another nationality. Ethiopia (D) allowed Ethiopians who had also acquired Eritrean nationality to continue to exercise their Ethiopian nationality, while agreeing with Eritrea (P) that these people would have to choose one nationality or the other at some future time.

The war then came, and Ethiopia (D) denationalized dual nationals falling in six groups: (1) those who Ethiopia (D) believed posed a security risk; (2) those who chose to leave Ethiopia (D) during the war and go to Eritrea (P); (3) those who remained in Ethiopia (D); (4) those who were in third countries or who left Ethiopia (D) to go to third countries; (5) those who were in Eritrea (P); and (6) those who were expelled for other reasons.

International law limits states' power to deprive persons of their nationality through the Universal Declaration of Human Rights, Article 15 of which states that "no one shall be arbitrarily deprived of his nationality." Because deprivation of nationality is serious, with lasting consequences to those affected, those affected must be given adequate notice of the proceedings, the opportunity to present a case against denationalization before an objective decision maker, and the opportunity for outside review.

With respect to the first group, Ethiopia's (D) complex process of identifying and denationalizing security risks fell short of this standard. But given the wartime circumstances, the loss of Ethiopian nationality after being identified through the security process was not arbitrary or contrary to international law.

As to the second group, their decision to leave one country for another while the two are at war is a serious act that could not be without consequences. The termination of the Ethiopian nationality of these persons was not arbitrary and not in violation of international law.

There was no evidence that members of the third group threatened Ethiopian security, and there was no process for identifying individuals warranting special consideration, and no possibility of review or appeal. Such a wide-scale deprivation of Ethiopian nationality of persons remaining in Ethiopia (D) is arbitrary and contrary to international law.

The same is true for members of the fourth group: There is no evidence that they, by their "mere presence" in third countries could be presumed to be security threats, or that Ethiopia (D) employed an individualized assessment process to determine their potential threat. They were allowed to contest their treatment only through Ethiopian diplomatic or consular establishments abroad. Members of this group were arbitrarily deprived of their Ethiopian citizenship in violation of international law.

Ethiopia's (D) denationalization of members of the fifth group was not arbitrary or otherwise unlawful, even though their mere presence in Eritrea (P) was not proof of security risk, because there are evident risks and wartime impediments to communication to provide notice of denationalization.

Finally, the termination of the Ethiopian nationality of all persons in the sixth group was arbitrary and unlawful,

Continued on next page.

since in many cases, most or all dual nationals were sometimes rounded up by local authorities and forced into Eritrea (P) for reasons that cannot be established.

▶ *ANALYSIS*

As the commission stated, the consequences of denationalization are high to the persons affected, and yet the standard applied to determine its legality under international law seems low: The Universal Declaration of Human Rights only requires that denationalization not be "arbitrary." The commission's focus was therefore on the procedures followed by Ethiopia (D) in the denationalization process, the circumstances in which it occurred, and the actions of, and consequences to, the persons affected. Its decision may have been different had the process not taken place during and in the aftermath of war.

■══■

Quicknotes

INTERNATIONAL LAW The body of law applicable to dealings between nations.

NATIONALITY The country in which a person is born or naturalized.

REFERENDUM Right constitutionally reserved to people of state, or local subdivision thereof, to have submitted for their approval or rejection, under prescribed conditions, any law or part of law passed by a lawmaking body.

■══■

Barcelona Traction, Light and Power Company, Ltd.
(Belgium v. Spain)

State of shareholders (P) v. Expropriating state (D)

I.C.J. 1970 I.C.J. 3.

NATURE OF CASE: Action for damages for the expropriation of a corporation.

FACT SUMMARY: Belgium (P) brought an action for damages against Spain (D) on the ground that its nationals as shareholders of the Barcelona Traction Co., incorporated and registered in Canada, had been seriously harmed by actions of Spain (D) resulting in expropriation.

🏛 RULE OF LAW
The state of the shareholders of a corporation has a right of diplomatic protection only when the state whose responsibility is invoked is the national state of the company.

FACTS: The Barcelona Traction, Light, and Power Co. was incorporated and registered in Canada for the purpose of developing and operating electrical power in Spain (D). After the Spanish Civil War, the company was declared bankrupt by a Spanish court and its assets were seized. After the Canadian interposition ceased, Belgium (P) brought an action for damages against Spain (D) for what it termed expropriation of the assets of the Traction Co. on the ground that a large majority of the stock of the company was owned by Belgian (P) nationals. Spain (D) raised the preliminary objection that Belgium (P) lacked standing to bring suit for damages to a Canadian company.

ISSUE: Does the state of the shareholders of a company have a right of diplomatic protection if the state whose responsibility is invoked is not the national state of the company?

HOLDING AND DECISION: [Judge not stated in casebook excerpt.] No. In order for a state to bring a claim in respect of the breach of an obligation owed to it, it must first establish its right to do so. This right is predicated on a showing that the defendant state has broken an obligation toward the national state in respect of its nationals. In the present case it is therefore essential to establish whether the losses allegedly suffered by Belgian (P) shareholders in Barcelona Traction were the consequence of the violation of obligations of which they are beneficiaries. In the present state of the law, the protection of shareholders requires that recourse be had to treaty stipulations or special agreements directly concluded between the private investor and the state in which the investment is placed. Barring such agreements, the obligation owed is to the corporation, and only the state of incorporation has standing to bring an action for violations of such an obligation. Nonetheless, for reasons of equity a theory has been developed to the effect that the state of the shareholders has a right of diplomatic protection when the state whose responsibility is invoked is the national state of the company. This theory, however, is not applicable to the present case, since Spain (D) is not the national state of Barcelona Traction. Barcelona Traction could have approached its national state, Canada, to ask for its diplomatic protection. For the above reasons, the Court is of the opinion that Belgium (P) lacks standing to bring this action.

▶ ANALYSIS

The Restatement of the Foreign Relations Law of the United States, § 185, states that failure of a state to pay just compensation for the taking of the property of an alien is wrongful under international law, regardless of whether the taking itself is conceived as wrongful. Such a wrongful taking is characterized either as tortious conduct or as unjust enrichment.

■=■

Quicknotes

DIPLOMATIC PROTECTION The act by which a state, on behalf of one of its citizens who is an injured party, intervenes when a rule of international law has been violated.

EQUITY Fairness; justice; the determination of a matter consistent with principles of fairness and not in strict compliance with rules of law.

EXPROPRIATION The government's taking of property pursuant to its eminent domain powers.

NATIONALITY The country in which a person is born or naturalized.

SHAREHOLDER An individual who owns shares of stock in a corporation.

STATE OF INCORPORATION Where a corporation's articles of incorporation are filed.

■=■

CHAPTER 8

Rules on State Responsibility

Quick Reference Rules of Law

Application of the Convention on the Prevention and Punishment of the Crime of Genocide
(Bosnia and Herzegovina v. Serbia and Montenegro)

State (P) v. State (D)

2007 I.C.J. 191.

NATURE OF CASE: Action brought in the International Court of Justice to determine whether a state committed a criminal violation of international law.

FACT SUMMARY: In 1993, Bosnia and Herzegovina (P) brought suit against the Federal Republic of Yugoslavia (Serbia and Montenegro) (D) in the International Court of Justice, claiming violations of the Convention on the Prevention and Punishment of the Crime of Genocide.

RULE OF LAW
The conduct of any state organ is to be considered an act of the state under international law, therefore giving rise to the responsibility of the state if the conduct constitutes a breach of an international obligation of the state.

FACTS: The Socialist Federal Republic of Yugoslavia began to break up in the early 1990s, and the republics of Bosnia and Herzegovina (P), Croatia, Macedonia, and Slovenia declared independence. Serbia and Montenegro (D) eventually declared themselves the Federal Republic of Yugoslavia (FRY) (D). During armed conflicts that arose in 1992-1995 within Bosnia and Herzegovina (P), a massacre was perpetrated by Serbian forces on 8000 Bosnian Muslim men of fighting age in a small village called Srebrenica in July 1995. In 1993, Bosnia and Herzegovina (P) brought suit against the FRY (Serbia and Montenegro) (D) in the International Court of Justice, claiming violations of the Convention on the Prevention and Punishment of the Crime of Genocide, on the theory that FRY (D) was responsible for the actions of the Serbian forces.

ISSUE: Is the conduct of any state organ to be considered an act of the state under international law, therefore giving rise to the responsibility of the state if the conduct constitutes a breach of an international obligation of the state?

HOLDING AND DECISION: [Judge not identified in casebook excerpt.] Yes. The conduct of any state organ is to be considered an act of the state under international law, therefore giving rise to the responsibility of the state if the conduct constitutes a breach of an international obligation of the state. This is a rule of customary international law that was codified in Article 4 of the ILC Articles on State Responsibility.

There is no evidence that the Serbian forces were de jure organs of FRY (D). It has not been shown in this case that the army of the FRY (D) took part in the massacres, or that the political leaders of the state had any part in it. There is no doubt that the FRY (D) was providing substantial financial support, in addition to other support, to the Serbian forces that carried out the genocide, but that does not automatically make them organs of the FRY (D).

It is possible to attribute to a state the conduct of persons or groups who, while they do not have the legal status of state organs, are de facto organs of the state, on the theory that they act under strict control by the state. This is so in cases where the persons or groups act in "complete dependence" on the state. In this case, in July 1995, however, the Serbians could not be regarded as mere instruments through which the FRY (D) was acting, or as lacking any real autonomy. The acts of genocide at Srebrenica cannot therefore be attributed to FRY (D) under the "complete dependence" theory.

The conduct of a person or group of persons can also be considered a de facto act of state under international law if in carrying out the offending conduct, the person or group is in fact acting on the instructions of, or under the direction or control of, the state. To determine whether a person or entity may be equated with a state organ even if not having that status under law, it is not necessary to show that the persons who performed the acts were in a relationship of "complete dependence" on the state, but it has to be proved either that they acted in accordance with that state's instructions, or under its "effective control," or that they were under the "overall control" of the state. The "effective control" test is drawn from *Nicaragua v. United States of America,* and requires a showing that the state controlled all aspects of the operation in question. The "overall control" test, unlike the "effective control" test, does not require a showing that every operation by the group was under supervision of the state, but that the state was in general control. The appeals chamber used this test to determine that the acts committed by Serbs rose to international responsibility of the FRY (D).

But the "overall control" test has the major drawback of broadening the scope of state responsibility beyond the fundamental international law principle that a state is responsible only for its own conduct, and for this reason, the test is unsuitable. And there is no evidence that the Serbs were under the effective control of FRY (D) while conducting the massacre at Srebrenica. Thus, the persons or entities that conducted the massacres at Srebrenica were not organs of the FRY (D), and FRY (D) is not responsible under international law for the massacres.

Continued on next page.

▶ *ANALYSIS*

See also the brief for the first part of this case, interpreting the requirements of the Genocide Convention, which is excerpted on page 166 of the casebook. In deciding whether to hold FRY (D) liable for the alleged genocide at Srebrenica by certain Bosnian Serbs, the I.C.J. referred to a standard set by *Nicaragua v. United States,* in which the United States was found not to be legally responsible for the actions of the Contra guerrillas, despite their common goal and public support.

■≡■

Quicknotes

BREACH The violation of an obligation imposed pursuant to contract or law, by acting or failing to act.

GENOCIDE The systematic killing of a particular group.

INTERNATIONAL LAW The body of law applicable to dealings between nations.

■≡■

Barcelona Traction, Light and Power Company, Ltd. (Belgium v. Spain)

Shareholders (P) v. Corporation (D)

I.C.J., 1970 I.C.J. 3.

NATURE OF CASE: Proceeding before the International Court of Justice.

FACT SUMMARY: Belgium (P) claimed that Spain (D) should be held responsible for injury to a Canadian corporation operating in Spain.

🏛 RULE OF LAW
When a state admits into its territory foreign investments or foreign nationals, it assumes an obligation concerning their treatment based on general international law.

FACTS: Belgium (P) sued Spain (D) on behalf of Belgian nationals (P) who had invested in a Canadian corporation. Belgium (P) alleged that Spain (D) was responsible for acts in violation of international law that had caused injury to the Canadian corporation and its Belgian shareholders (P).

ISSUE: When a state admits into its territory foreign investments or foreign nationals, does it assume an obligation concerning their treatment based on general international law?

HOLDING AND DECISION: [Judge not stated in casebook excerpt.] Yes. When a state admits into its territory foreign investments or foreign nationals, it assumes an obligation concerning their treatment based on general international law. An essential distinction should be drawn between those obligations of a state toward the international community as a whole and those arising from the field of diplomatic protection. If a breach of an obligation that is the subject of diplomatic protection occurs, only the party to whom an international obligation is due can bring a claim.

▶ ANALYSIS

The Court mentioned the basic rights of all human persons to be protected against slavery and racial discrimination as deriving from basic general international law. Such rights may derive from international instruments of a universal or quasi-universal character. Such obligations are obligations *erga omnes,* that is, all states have a legal interest in their protection.

■■■

Quicknotes

DIPLOMATIC PROTECTION The act by which a State, on behalf of one of its citizens who is an injured party, intervenes when a rule of international law has been violated.

■■■

Rainbow Warrior
(New Zealand v. France)

[Parties not identified.]

France-New Zealand Arbitration Tribunal, 82 I.L.R. 500 (1990).

NATURE OF CASE: Arbitration regarding removal of prisoners.

FACT SUMMARY: France removed two agents convicted of destroying a ship docked in New Zealand on the basis that they required emergency medical treatment.

 RULE OF LAW
The wrongfulness of an act of a state not in conformity with an international obligation is precluded by the "distress" of the author state if there exists a situation of extreme peril in which the organ of the state has, at that particular moment, no means of saving himself or persons entrusted to his care other than to act in a manner inconsistent with the requirements of the obligation at issue.

FACTS: A team of French agents destroyed a civilian vessel docked in New Zealand. Agents Mafart and Prieur were extradited and New Zealand sought reparations from the incident. Following the transfer of the two agents to a French military facility, they were later transported to Paris on the basis that they each needed medical treatment. The dispute was submitted to an arbitral tribunal. New Zealand demanded a declaration that France had breached its obligations and ordered that it return the agents to the facility for the remainder of their sentences.

ISSUE: Is the wrongfulness of an act of a state not in conformity with an international obligation precluded by the "distress" of the author state if there exists a situation of extreme peril in which the organ of the state has, at that particular moment, no means of saving himself or persons entrusted to his care other than to act in a manner inconsistent with the requirements of the obligation at issue?

HOLDING AND DECISION: [Judge not stated in casebook excerpt.] Yes. The wrongfulness of an act of a state not in conformity with an international obligation is precluded by the "distress" of the author state if there exists a situation of extreme peril in which the organ of the state has, at that particular moment, no means of saving himself or persons entrusted to his care other than to act in a manner inconsistent with the requirements of the obligation at issue. Three conditions here would be required to justify France's conduct: (1) very exceptional circumstances of extreme urgency involving medical or other considerations, provided prompt recognition of such circumstances is provided by New Zealand; (2) the reestablishment of the original situation of compliance;

and (3) a good faith effort to try to obtain the consent of New Zealand. The unilateral removal of Mafart without obtaining New Zealand's consent was justified; however, the removal of Prieur was a material breach of France's obligations.

ANALYSIS

The court rejects France's contention that the circumstances here constituted a force majeure. "Force majeure" is usually invoked to justify unintentional acts, and refers to "unforeseen external events" that render it "materially impossible" to act in conformity with the obligation.

■==■

Quicknotes

FORCE MAJEURE CLAUSE Included in contracts to protect against nonperformance due to causes outside control of the parties; unforeseen external event that results in impossibility.

MATERIAL BREACH Breach of a contract's terms by one party that is so substantial as to relieve the other party from its obligations pursuant thereto.

UNILATERAL One-sided; involving only one person.

■==■

Gabčíkovo-Nagymaros Project
(Hungary/Slovakia)

[Parties not identified.]

I.C.J., 1997 I.C.J. 7.

NATURE OF CASE: Review of countries' obligations pursuant to a treaty.

FACT SUMMARY: Hungary claimed it was no longer bound to a treaty entered into with Czechoslovakia on the basis that it was justified in abandoning and suspending works due to a "state of necessity."

🏛 RULE OF LAW
A state of necessity can only be invoked if it is occasioned by an essential interest of the state authoring the act conflicting with its international obligations, that interest was threatened by a grave and imminent peril, the act being challenged is the only means of safeguarding that interest, the act challenged must not have seriously impaired an essential interest of the state toward which the obligation existed, and the state that authored the act must not have contributed to the state of necessity.

FACTS: Hungary and Czechoslovakia entered into a treaty for the construction and operation of a system of locks on the Danube River, which was started but not completed. The two countries underwent major transformations in government, with Czechoslovakia dividing into two separate states. Hungary gave notice of the termination of the treaty. Hungary and Slovakia later petitioned to the I.C.J. to decide whether Hungary was entitled to suspend and abandon its operations on the basis of changed circumstances and impossibility. Slovakia contended that it was entitled to implement a significant variation from the original plan in response to Hungary's repudiation of the treaty.

ISSUE: Can a state of necessity only be invoked if it is occasioned by an essential interest of the state authoring the act conflicting with its international obligations, that interest was threatened by a grave and imminent peril, the act being challenged is the only means of safeguarding that interest, the act challenged must not have seriously impaired an essential interest of the state toward which the obligation existed, and the state that authored the act must not have contributed to the state of necessity?

HOLDING AND DECISION: [Judge not stated in casebook excerpt.] Yes. A state of necessity can only be invoked if it is occasioned by an essential interest of the state authoring the act conflicting with its international obligations, that interest was threatened by a grave and imminent peril, the act being challenged is the only means of safeguarding that interest, the act challenged

must not have seriously impaired an essential interest of the state toward which the obligation existed, and the state that authored the act must not have contributed to the state of necessity. The perils invoked by Hungary were neither sufficiently established nor imminent; Hungary had available alternative means of responding to the perceived dangers other than suspension and abandonment of the works.

▶ ANALYSIS

Hungary failed in its argument here on the imminency of the perceived peril. While guarding the "ecological balance" had been interpreted to constitute an "essential interest," "imminency" of the peril was interpreted as necessarily being "a threat to the interest at the actual time," even if the peril were to take place at some time in the future. The dangers here remained "at some far-off time" and were too "uncertain" to invoke the justification.

■=■

Quicknotes

REPUDIATION The actions or statements of a party to a contract that evidence his intent not to perform, or to continue performance, of his duties or obligations thereunder.

TREATY An agreement between two or more nations for the benefit of the general public.

■=■

Gabčíkovo-Nagymaros Project
(Hungary/Slovakia)

Treaty partner (P) v. New nation (D)

1997 I.C.J. 7, reprinted in 37 I.L.M. 162 (1998).

NATURE OF CASE: Proceeding before the International Court of Justice.

FACT SUMMARY: Hungary (P) claimed that when Czechoslovakia (D) appropriated waters of the Danube River to construct a dam, it violated provisions of a treaty.

🏛 RULE OF LAW
Watercourse states shall participate in the use, development, and protection of an international watercourse in an equitable and reasonable manner.

FACTS: Hungary (P) and Czechoslovakia (D) had signed a treaty in 1977 for the construction of dams and other projects along the Danube River that bordered both nations. After Hungary (P) stopped working on the project and negotiations failed to resolve the matter, Czechoslovakia (D) began work on damming the river in its territory and Hungary (P) terminated the treaty. Hungary (P) claimed the damming of the river had been agreed to only in the context of a joint operation and sharing of its benefits, and that Czechoslovakia (D) had unlawfully unilaterally assumed control of a shared resource.

ISSUE: Shall watercourse states participate in the use, development, and protection of an international watercourse in an equitable and reasonable manner?

HOLDING AND DECISION: [Judge not stated in casebook excerpt.] Yes. Watercourse states shall participate in the use, development, and protection of an international watercourse in an equitable and reasonable manner. Czechoslovakia (D) deprived Hungary (P) of its right to an equitable and reasonable share of the natural resources of the Danube and failed to respect the proportionality that is required by international law. The parties must reestablish cooperative administration of what remains of the project.

▶ ANALYSIS

The Court held that the joint regime must be restored. Common utilization of shared water resources was necessary for the achievement of several of the Treaty's objectives. Czechoslovakia (D) was not authorized to proceed without Hungary's (P) consent.

■■■

Quicknotes

TREATY An agreement between two or more nations for the benefit of the general public.

UNILATERAL One-sided; involving only one person.

■■■

Dispute Settlement

Quick Reference Rules of Law

Armed Activities on the Territory of the Congo (Democratic Republic of the Congo v. Rwanda)

State (P) v. State (D)

I.C.J., 2006 I.C.J. 126.

NATURE OF CASE: Proceeding in the International Court of Justice.

FACT SUMMARY: The Democratic Republic of the Congo (P) brought an application against Rwanda (D), and Rwanda (D) challenged the jurisdiction of the International Court of Justice.

🏛 RULE OF LAW
Where one party to a treaty excludes dispute settlement obligations under the treaty before becoming a party, and fails to take formal acts to bring about withdrawal of the reservation, the International Court of Justice lacks jurisdiction based on that treaty.

FACTS: The Democratic Republic of the Congo (DRC) (P) brought an application against Rwanda (D). DRC (P) tried to base the jurisdiction of the International Court of Justice on nine treaties with dispute settlement clauses that provided for such jurisdiction. Rwanda (D) was not party to two of the treaties, and with respect to the other seven, Rwanda (D) excluded dispute settlement obligations. Rwanda (D) challenged the jurisdiction of the International Court of Justice on the nature of its obligations. The excerpt omits discussion of some of the treaties. The treaties involved were Genocide Convention, Article IX; Convention on Racial Discrimination, Article 22; Convention on Discrimination against Women, Article 29; World Health Organization Constitution, Article 75; Unesco Convention, Article XIV; Montreal Convention, Article 14; Vienna Convention, Article 66; Convention Against Torture; and Convention on Privileges and Immunities of the Specialized Agencies. Rwanda (D) was not party to the last two.

ISSUE: Where one party to a treaty excludes dispute settlement obligations under the treaty before becoming a party, and fails to take formal acts to bring about withdrawal of the reservation, does the International Court of Justice lack jurisdiction based on that treaty?

HOLDING AND DECISION: [Judge not stated in casebook excerpt.] Yes. Where one party to a treaty excludes dispute settlement obligations under the treaty before becoming a party, and fails to take formal acts to bring about withdrawal of the reservation, the International Court of Justice lacks jurisdiction based on that treaty. First, Rwanda (D) may have committed itself at the time of a 1993 peace agreement to withdrawing all reservations to human rights treaties, and the Rwanda (D) minister of justice effectuated the withdrawal, but Rwanda (D) never took formal acts to bring about withdrawal of the reservation. A decision to withdraw a reservation within a state's domestic legal order is not the same as implementation of that decision by the national authorities within the international legal order, which can only occur by notification to the other state parties to the treaty in question through the Secretary-General of the United Nations.

Second, the existence of a dispute that implicates peremptory norms of general international law is not an exception to the principle that jurisdiction always depends on the consent of parties. The DRC (P) may have made numerous protests against Rwanda's (D) actions at the bilateral and multilateral levels, and therefore satisfied preconditions to the seisin of the I.C.J. in the compromissory clauses within some of the treaties, including the Convention on Discrimination against Women, but whatever the dispute, there was no evidence that the DRC (P) sought negotiations with respect to interpretation or application of the Convention. The DRC (P) also failed to show that it initiated arbitration proceedings with Rwanda (D) under the Convention on Discrimination against Women. The treaty cannot therefore form the basis of jurisdiction.

▸ ANALYSIS

The Court's analysis of all treaties involved was similar to that included in the casebook excerpt. The main principle here is that where a state has apparently not granted consent to the jurisdiction of the I.C.J., the I.C.J. will not advance the case past the preliminary matter of jurisdiction, whatever atrocities have in fact been committed by the non-consenting state. Additionally, where, as here, there is evidence of non-consent, reversal of the position requires an overt act by the state, in order to convince the Court that, after all, consent to the I.C.J.'s jurisdiction was granted.

■══■

Quicknotes

JURISDICTION The authority of a court to hear and declare judgment in respect to a particular matter.

TREATY An agreement between two or more nations for the benefit of the general public.

■══■

Military and Paramilitary Activities in and Against Nicaragua (Nicaragua v. United States)

State (P) v. State (D)

I.C.J., 1984 I.C.J. 392.

NATURE OF CASE: Proceeding in the International Court of Justice.

FACT SUMMARY: Nicaragua (P) filed suit in 1984 against the United States (D) claiming it was responsible for illegal military and paramilitary activities in and against Nicaragua. The United States (D) challenged the jurisdiction of the International Court of Justice to hear the case, as well as the admissibility of Nicaragua's (P) application to the I.C.J.

🏛 RULE OF LAW
(1) The International Court of Justice has jurisdiction to hear a dispute between two states if each accepted the Court's jurisdiction.
(2) The application by a state to the International Court of Justice is admissible where no grounds exist to exclude it.

FACTS: Nicaragua (P) filed suit in 1984 against the United States (D), claiming it was responsible for illegal military and paramilitary activities in and against Nicaragua (P). The United States (D) challenged the jurisdiction of the International Court of Justice to hear the case. Though the United States (D) deposited a declaration accepting the compulsory jurisdiction of the Court in 1946, it attempted to qualify that declaration in a 1984 notification referring to the declaration of 1946 and stating in part that the declaration "shall not apply to disputes with any Central American State. . . ." The United States (D) also argued that Nicaragua (P) had failed to deposit a similar declaration to the I.C.J., and that the I.C.J. lacked jurisdiction on that ground as well. Nicaragua (P) argued that it could rely on the 1946 declaration made by the United States (D) because it was a "state accepting the same obligation" as the United States (D) when it filed charges in the I.C.J. against the United States (D). Nicaragua (P) also pointed to its intent to submit to the compulsory jurisdiction of the I.C.J. through a valid declaration it made in 1929 with I.C.J.'s predecessor, the Permanent Court of International Justice, even though Nicaragua (D) failed to formally deposit it with that court. Finally, the United States (D) also challenged the admissibility of Nicaragua's (P) application to the I.C.J.

ISSUE:
(1) Does the International Court of Justice have jurisdiction to hear a dispute between two states if each accepted the Court's jurisdiction?

(2) Is the application by a state to the International Court of Justice admissible where no grounds exist to exclude it?

HOLDING AND DECISION: [Judge not stated in casebook excerpt.]

(1) Yes. The International Court of Justice has jurisdiction to hear a dispute between two states if each accepted the Court's jurisdiction. Nicaragua's (P) declaration of 1929 is valid even though it was not deposited with the Permanent Court, because it had potential effect that would last for many years. Because it was made unconditionally and was valid for an unlimited period, it retained its potential effect when Nicaragua (P) became a party to the Statute of the I.C.J. The drafters of the current Statute wanted to maintain the greatest possible continuity between it and the Permanent Court. Nicaragua (P) may be deemed to have given its consent to the transfer of its declaration to the I.C.J. when it accepted the Statute.

In addition, the conduct of Nicaragua (P) and the United States (D) suggest that both intended to be bound by the compulsory jurisdiction of the I.C.J., and the conduct of the United States (D) constitutes recognition of the validity of the declaration of Nicaragua (P) of 1929. Because the Nicaraguan declaration of 1929 is valid, Nicaragua (P) was a "state accepting the same obligation" as the United States (D) at the date of filing of the charges with the I.C.J., and therefore could rely on the United States' (D) declaration of 1946.

The 1984 notification by the Untied States (D) does not prohibit jurisdiction in this case, because the United States (D) appended by its own choice a six months' notice clause to its declaration, and it was not free to disregard it with respect to Nicaragua (P). The obligation of the United States (D) to submit to the jurisdiction of the I.C.J. in this case cannot be overridden by the 1984 notification.

The "multilateral treaty reservation" that was appended to the United States' (D) declaration of 1946, which limited the I.C.J.'s compulsory jurisdiction, also does not prohibit jurisdiction in this case. Through the declaration, the United States (D) accepted jurisdiction except with respect to "disputes arising under a multilateral treaty, unless (1) all parties to the treaty affected by the decision are also parties to the case before the

Continued on next page.

Court, or (2) the United States of America specially agrees to jurisdiction." Nicaragua's (P) application in this case relies on four multilateral treaties, and the United States (D) argued that the I.C.J. could exercise jurisdiction only if all treaty parties affected by a decision were also parties to the case. But the effect on other states is not a jurisdictional problem, and the United States' (D) objection to jurisdiction on the basis of the multilateral treaty reservation is unfounded.

(2) Yes. The application by a state to the International Court of Justice is admissible where no grounds exist to exclude it. The United States (D) challenged the admissibility of Nicaragua's (P) application on five separate grounds. The first—that Nicaragua (P) failed to bring forth necessary parties—fails because there is no "indispensable parties" rule. The second and third—that Nicaragua (P) is asking the Court to consider the existence of a threat to peace, which is the exclusive province of the Security Council—fails because the I.C.J. can exercise jurisdiction concurrent with that of the Security Council. Both proceedings can be pursued *pari passu*. The fourth—that the I.C.J. is unable to deal with situations involving ongoing armed conflict—is not a show-stopper because any judgment on the merits is limited to the evidence submitted and proven by the litigants. The fifth—that the case is incompatible with the Contadora process, to which Nicaragua (P) is a party—fails because there is nothing compelling the I.C.J. to decline to consider one aspect of a dispute just because the dispute has other aspects. The fact that negotiations are being conducted subject to the Contadora process does not pose any legal obstacle to the exercise by the Court of its judicial function.

▶ ANALYSIS

The questions of jurisdiction and admissibility are very complicated, but are based primarily on the principle that the I.C.J. has only as much power as that agreed to by the parties. A primary focus of the case was on the declarations—the 1946 declaration of the United States, and the 1929 declaration of Nicaragua—and what each declaration indicated about the respective parties' intent as it relates to the I.C.J.'s jurisdiction.

■══■

Quicknotes

JURISDICTION The authority of a court to hear and declare judgment in respect to a particular matter.

STATUTE A law enacted pursuant to the legislature's power and consistent with specified procedure so that it regulates a particular activity.

■══■

Application of the International Convention on the Elimination of All Forms of Racial Discrimination (Georgia v. Russian Federation)

State (P) v. State (D)

I.C.J., 2008 I.C.J. 140.

NATURE OF CASE: Order on request for the indication of provisional measures.

FACT SUMMARY: Georgia (P) filed proceedings against the Russian Federation (D), claiming that Russia (D) engaged in ethnic cleansing in Georgia (P), in violation of the Convention on Elimination of Racial Discrimination (CERD).

🏛 RULE OF LAW

Under certain circumstances, the International Court of Justice may assess facts and order provisional measures to protect rights under international treaties without deciding the merits of a dispute.

FACTS: Georgia (P) filed proceedings against the Russian Federation (D), claiming violation of the Convention on Elimination of Racial Discrimination (CERD). Georgia (P) alleged that Russia (D) was engaging in ethnic cleansing in the South Ossetia and Abkhazia regions of Georgia (P). Georgia (P) asked the International Court of Justice to decide whether the circumstances required provision measures to protect rights under CERD, not to decide the merits of Georgia's (P) argument that Russia (D) breached CERD.

ISSUE: Under certain circumstances, may the International Court of Justice assess facts and order provisional measures to protect rights under international treaties without deciding the merits of a dispute?

HOLDING AND DECISION: [Judge not stated in casebook excerpt.] Yes. Under certain circumstances, the International Court of Justice may assess facts and order provisional measures to protect rights under international treaties without deciding the merits of a dispute. The evidence shows that the Georgian population in the affected areas remains vulnerable, and there is an imminent risk that the rights of the population and of Georgia (P) under CERD may suffer irreparable prejudice without intervention. In addition, the I.C.J. has the power, under its Statute, to indicate measures to protect those rights, even if they are not exactly as requested, without prejudging the question of the jurisdiction of the I.C.J. to deal with the merits of the case. Therefore, both parties shall refrain from any act of racial discrimination against persons, groups of persons, or institutions, abstain from supporting racial discrimination, and do all in their power to prevent such discrimination.

▶ ANALYSIS

The ruling of the I.C.J. went beyond what Georgia (P) asked for, which was to stop Russia (D) from engaging in racial discrimination and ethnic cleansing, by applying it to both parties. That is the way in which the I.C.J. used its statutory authority to indicate measures that were not exactly as requested. The protective measures are similar to the common law preliminary injunction.

■══■

Quicknotes

BREACH The violation of an obligation imposed pursuant to contract or law, by acting or failing to act.

INJUNCTION A court order requiring a person to do, or prohibiting that person from doing, a specific act.

■══■

Legality of the Threat or Use of Nuclear Weapons

[Parties not identified.]

I.C.J., Advisory Opinion, 1996 I.C.J. 226.

NATURE OF CASE: Advisory opinion.

FACT SUMMARY: The General Assembly and World Health Organization requested advisory opinions from the International Court of Justice regarding the legality of nuclear weapons.

🏛 RULE OF LAW

The International Court of Justice may give an advisory opinion on any legal question at the request of whatever body may be authorized by or in accordance with the Charter of the United Nations to make such a request.

FACTS: [Facts not stated in casebook excerpt.]

ISSUE: May the International Court of Justice give an advisory opinion on any legal question at the request of whatever body may be authorized by or in accordance with the Charter of the United Nations to make such a request?

HOLDING AND DECISION: [Judge not stated in casebook excerpt.] Yes. The International Court of Justice may give an advisory opinion on any legal question at the request of whatever body may be authorized by or in accordance with the Charter of the United Nations to make such a request. Only compelling reasons are justified for a refusal to grant such an advisory opinion. The Charter of the United Nations authorizes the General Assembly to make such a request; however, the Court lacks the jurisdiction to grant such an opinion to the World Health Organization.

▶ ANALYSIS

The Court also rejected arguments that it should refrain from rendering an advisory opinion on the basis that such a reply might negatively affect disarmament negotiations, and that the Court would be exceeding its authority and acting in a law-making capacity. The Court rejected the latter argument on the basis that it simply states the existing law and does not legislate, even if it sometimes must specify the scope and application of such law.

■■■

Quicknotes

ADVISORY OPINION A decision rendered at the request of an interested party as to how the court would rule should the particular issue arise.

■■■

Legal Consequences of the Construction of a Wall in the Occupied Palestinian Territory

United Nations (P) v. Israel (D)

I.C.J., Advisory Opinion, 2004 I.C.J. 136.

NATURE OF CASE: Advisory opinion by International Court Justice.

FACT SUMMARY: Israel (D) constructed a wall in occupied Palestinian territory and the United Nations (P) objected.

🏛 RULE OF LAW
The construction of a wall by Israel, the occupying power, in the occupied Palestinian territory, violates international law, including the Fourth Geneva Convention of 1949, the Hague Convention, and relevant Security Council and General Assembly resolutions.

FACTS: Israel (D) constructed a wall in occupied Palestinian territory. The wall and its route impaired the freedom of the Palestinian population. The U.N. General Assembly (P) demanded that it stop and reverse the construction of the wall. The I.C.J. was asked to provide an advisory opinion on the matter.

ISSUE: Does the construction of a wall by Israel (D), the occupying power, in the occupied Palestinian territory, violate international law, including the Fourth Geneva Convention of 1949, the Hague Convention, and relevant Security Council and General Assembly resolutions?

HOLDING AND DECISION: [Judge not stated in casebook excerpt.] Yes. The construction of a wall by Israel (D), the occupying power, in the occupied Palestinian territory, violates international law, including the Fourth Geneva Convention of 1949, the Hague Convention, and relevant Security Council and General Assembly resolutions. The wall and the Israeli occupation impede the liberty of movement of the inhabitants of the occupied territory, with the exception of Israeli citizens, as guaranteed under Article 12 of the International Covenant on Civil and Political Rights. It also impedes access to work, health facilities, education, and an adequate standard of living under the International Covenant on Economic, Social, and Cultural Rights and the United Nations Convention on the Rights of the Child. Finally, the wall changed the demography of the territory, because of the departure of some Palestinians, which violates Article 49 of the Fourth Geneva Convention. Construction of the wall also breaches Israel's (D) obligations under the Fourth Geneva Convention and the Hague Convention because the route chosen for the wall infringes the rights of Palestinians in the occupied territory, which cannot be justified by military exigencies or the requirement of national security. The legal consequence of Israel's (D) actions in the matter is that all states are under an obligation not to recognize the illegal situation resulting from the construction of the wall, and all the states party to the Fourth Geneva Convention are under an obligation to ensure compliance by Israel (D) with international humanitarian law. Finally, both Israel (D) and Palestine are under an obligation to observe the rules of international humanitarian law. Illegal action and unilateral decisions have been taken on all sides, and implementation of the relevant Security Council resolutions is the only way to end the hostile situation.

SEPARATE OPINION: (Higgins, J.) The International Court of Justice looked at only a part of a much larger conflict between the two states, and should have considered the bigger picture and spelled out what is required of both parties. Of paramount importance is the protection of civilians. In addition, the real impediment to Palestine's ability to exercise its rights as a self-determined people is not the wall, but Israel's (D) refusal to withdraw from Arab occupied territory and for Palestine to provide conditions to allow Israel (D) to feel secure in doing so. Further, while the wall seems to have resulted in a lessening of attacks on Israeli civilians, the necessity and proportionality for the route selected, balanced against the hardships for Palestinians, have not been explained.

DISSENT: (Buergenthal, J.) The construction of the wall raises important issues of humanitarian law, but the Court should have declined to issue an advisory opinion because the Court failed to address Israel's (D) arguments that it was willing to provide compensation and services for Palestinian residents, and that the wall was intended to be a temporary structure. The Court's conclusions are not convincing, because it failed to demonstrate adequately why it was not convinced that military exigencies and concern for security required Israel (D) to erect the wall along the chosen route.

▶ ANALYSIS

Judge Buergenthal, the only dissenter in the matter, is a U.S. citizen. In addition, the United States was one of eight votes against asking the I.C.J. for an advisory opinion. Ninety members voted in favor of the opinion, and 74 members abstained.

■■■■

Continued on next page.

Quicknotes

GENEVA CONVENTION International agreement that governs the conduct of warring nations.

HAGUE SERVICE CONVENTION Multilateral treaty governing service of process in foreign jurisdictions.

■▬■

United States—Final Anti-Dumping Measures on Stainless Steel from Mexico

State (D) v. State (P)

World Trade Organization, Appellate Body, 47 I.L.M. 475 (2008).

NATURE OF CASE: Appeal to Appellate Body of the World Trade Organization (WTO).

FACT SUMMARY: Mexico (P) complained that the United States (D) violated Article VI of GATT 1994 and the Anti-Dumping Agreement by using incorrect methodology for calculation of margins of dumping. The panel that convened for the complaint did not follow the Appellate Body's prior holdings, and instead relied on panel reports that the Appellate Body had reversed.

🏛 RULE OF LAW
In ruling on a dispute brought before a WTO panel, the panel must follow previously adopted Appellate Body reports addressing the same issues.

FACTS: Mexico (P) complained that the United States (D) violated Article VI of GATT 1994 and the Anti-Dumping Agreement by using incorrect methodology for calculation of margins of dumping. The Appellate Body of the WTO had addressed similar complaints filed against the United States (D) by the European Community and Japan, but the panel that convened for Mexico's (P) complaint did not follow the Appellate Body's prior holdings, and instead relied on panel reports that the Appellate Body had reversed.

ISSUE: In ruling on a dispute brought before a WTO panel, must the panel follow previously adopted Appellate Body reports addressing the same issues?

HOLDING AND DECISION: [Judge not identified.] Yes. In ruling on a dispute brought before a WTO panel, the panel must follow previously adopted Appellate Body reports addressing the same issues. While Appellate Body reports are not binding, except with respect to resolving the particular dispute between the parties, subsequent panels are not free to disregard the legal interpretations and reasoning contained in previous Appellate Body reports that have been adopted. The Appellate Body functions to provide consistency and stability in interpretation of rights and obligations under covered agreements, and the panel's failure to follow previously adopted Appellate Body reports undermines the development of a coherent and predictable body of jurisprudence. The panel's erroneous legal interpretation is corrected, and its findings and conclusions that have been appealed are reversed. Whether the panel failed to discharge its duties under Article 11 of the Dispute Settlement Understanding is not ruled upon.

▶ ANALYSIS

"Dumping" is the act of a manufacturer in one country exporting a product to another country at a price that is either below the price it charges in its home market or is below its cost of production. "Free market" advocates view "dumping" as beneficial for consumers and believe that actions to prevent it would have negative consequences. The use of "zeroing" in the context of calculating anti-dumping duties in domestic trade remedy proceedings has been one of the most contentious issues in World Trade Organization dispute settlement, and that in part explains the panel's deviation from prior rulings by the Appellate Body in this case.

■══■

Quicknotes

INTERPRETATION The determination of the meaning of a statute.

REMEDY Compensation for violation of a right or for injuries sustained.

■══■

International Law in National Law

Quick Reference Rules of Law

The Paquete Habana

Country at war (P) v. Fishermen (D)

175 U.S. 677 (1900).

NATURE OF CASE: Appeal from judgment condemning two fishing vessels and their cargoes as prizes of war.

FACT SUMMARY: The owners (D) of fishing vessels seized by officials of the United States (P) argued that international law exempted coastal fishermen from capture as prizes of war.

 RULE OF LAW
Coastal fishing vessels, with their cargoes and crews, are exempt from capture as prizes of war.

FACTS: The owners (D) of two separate fishing vessels brought this appeal of a district court decree condemning two fishing vessels and their cargoes as prizes of war. Each vessel was a fishing smack, running in and out of Havana, sailing under the Spanish flag, and regularly engaged in fishing on the coast of Cuba. The cargoes of both vessels consisted of fresh fish, which had been caught by their respective crews. Until stopped by the blockading United States (P) squadron, the owners (D) had no knowledge of the existence of a war or of any blockage. The owners (D) had no arms or ammunition on board the vessels and had made no attempt to run the blockade after learning of its existence. The owners (D) did not offer any resistance at the time of capture. On appeal, the owners (D) argued that both customary international law and the writings of leading international scholars recognized an exemption from seizure at wartime of coastal fishing vessels.

ISSUE: Are coastal fishing vessels, with their cargoes and crews, exempt from capture as prizes of war?

HOLDING AND DECISION: (Gray, J.) Yes. Coastal fishing vessels, pursuing their vocation of catching and bringing in fresh fish, have been recognized as exempt, with their cargoes and crews, from capture as prizes of war. The doctrine that exempts coastal fishermen, with their vessels and cargoes, from capture as prizes of war, has been familiar to the United States (P) from the time of the War of Independence, and has been recognized explicitly by the French and British governments. Where there are no treaties and no controlling executive or legislative acts or judicial decisions, as is the case here, resort must be had to the customs and usages of civilized nations, and, as evidence of these, to the works of jurists and commentators, who are well acquainted with the field. Such works are resorted to by judicial tribunals, not for the speculations of their authors concerning what the law ought to be, but for trustworthy evidence of what the law really is. At the present time, by the general consent of the civilized nations of the world, and independently of any express treaty or other public act, it is an established rule of international law that coastal fishing vessels, with their implements and supplies, cargoes, and crews, unarmed and honestly pursuing their peaceful calling of catching and bringing in fresh fish, are exempt from capture as prizes of war. Reversed.

▶ ANALYSIS

In a dissenting opinion that was not published in the main body of this casebook, Chief Justice Fuller argued that the captured vessels were of such a size and range as to not fall within the exemption. The Chief Justice also contended that the exemption in any case had not become a customary rule of international law, but was only an act of grace that had not been authorized by the President.

■■■■

Quicknotes

BLOCKADE When one country prevents materials or persons from entering or leaving another.

CUSTOM Generally any habitual practice or course of action that is repeated under like circumstances.

INTERNATIONAL LAW The body of law applicable to dealings between nations.

■■■■

Sosa v. Alvarez-Machain

[Parties not identified.]

542 U.S. 692 (2004).

NATURE OF CASE: Appeal of judgment awarding damages to foreign national.

FACT SUMMARY: [Alvarez-Machain (P) claimed he was involuntarily detained by bounty hunters and brought to the United States.]

 RULE OF LAW
International law is part of U.S. law.

FACTS: [Alvarez-Machain (P) claimed he was involuntarily detained by bounty hunters and brought to the United States.]

ISSUE: Is international law part of U.S. law?

HOLDING AND DECISION: (Souter, J.) Yes. International law is part of U.S. law. The law of nations comprises two principal elements. The fist covers the general norms regarding the relationship of nation states, which is the purview of the Executive and Legislative Branches of government. The second aspect, which falls within the judicial sphere, is a body of judge-made law regulating the conduct of individuals situated outside domestic boundaries. Finally, there is a sphere in which the rules binding individuals for the benefit of other individuals overlaps with the norms of state relationships, including violation of safe conducts, infringement of the rights of ambassadors, and piracy. Thus, federal courts may consider international norms intended to protect individuals.

▶ *ANALYSIS*

This short case excerpt illustrates a seminal case for the concept that international law is part of U.S. domestic law, and that international norms may be considered in determining individual rights in federal cases.

■▬■

Quicknotes

DAMAGES Monetary compensation that may be awarded by the court to a party who has sustained injury or loss to his person, property, or rights due to another party's unlawful act, omission or negligence.

INTERNATIONAL LAW The body of law applicable to dealings between nations.

■▬■

Banco Nacional de Cuba v. Sabbatino

National financial institution (P) v. Court-appointed receiver (D)

376 U.S. 398 (1964).

NATURE OF CASE: Appeal from an action for conversion.

FACT SUMMARY: Banco Nacional de Cuba (P) assigned the bills of lading for a shipment of sugar contracted between Farr, Whitlock & Co., an American commodities broker and another Cuban bank, instituted this action, alleging conversion of the bills of lading and seeking to recover the proceeds thereof from Farr, and to enjoin Sabbatino (D), a court-appointed receiver, from exercising control over such proceeds.

RULE OF LAW

Pursuant to the Act of State Doctrine, the judiciary will not examine the validity of a taking of property within its own territory by a foreign sovereign government, recognized by this country, in the absence of international agreements to the contrary, even if the taking violates customary international law.

FACTS: Farr, Whitlock & Co. (Farr), an American commodities broker, contracted to purchase Cuban sugar from a wholly owned subsidiary of Compania Azucarera Vertientes–Camaquey de Cuba (CAV), a corporation organized under Cuban law whose stock was owned principally by United States residents. Farr agreed to pay for the sugar in New York upon presentation of the shipping documents. Shortly thereafter, a law was enacted in Cuba giving the government power to nationalize by forced expropriation of property or enterprises in which American nationals had an interest. The sugar contracted for by Farr was expropriated from Compania Azucarera. In order to obtain consent from the Cuban government before a ship carrying sugar could leave Cuba, Farr entered into contracts, identical to those it had made with CAV, with the Banco Para el Comercio de Cuba, an instrumentality of the Cuban government. This bank assigned the bills of lading to the Banco Nacional de Cuba (P), also an instrumentality of the Cuban government, who presented the bills and a sight draft as required under the contract to Farr in New York in return for payment. Farr refused the documents after being notified by CAV of its claim to the proceeds as rightful owner of the sugar. Farr was served with a court order that had appointed Sabbatino (D) as receiver of CAV's New York assets and enjoined it from removing the payments from the state. The Banco Nacional (P) then instituted this action, alleging conversion of the bills of lading seeking to recover the proceeds thereof from Farr, and to enjoin Sabbatino (D), the receiver, from exercising dominion over such proceeds. The district court granted summary judgment against Banco Nacional (P), holding

that the Act of State Doctrine does not apply when the questioned foreign act is in violation of international law. The court of appeals affirmed the judgment.

ISSUE: Does the judiciary have the authority to examine the validity of a taking of property within its own territory by a foreign sovereign even if the taking violated international law?

HOLDING AND DECISION: (Harlan, J.) No. The Judicial Branch will not examine the validity of a taking of property within its own territory by a foreign sovereign government, extant and recognized by this country at the time of suit, in the absence of a treaty or other agreement, even if the complaint alleges that the taking violates customary international law. The plain implication of past cases is that the Act of State Doctrine is applicable even if international law has been violated. The Act of State Doctrine does not deprive the courts of jurisdiction once acquired over a case. It requires only that when it is made to appear that the foreign government has acted in a given way on the subject matter of the litigation, the details of such action or the merit of the result cannot be questioned but must be accepted by our courts as a rule for their decision. It results that title to the property in this case must be determined by the result of the expropriation action taken by the authorities of the Cuban government. The damages of adjudicating the propriety of such expropriation acts, regardless of whether the State Department has, as it did in this case, asserted that the act violated international law, are too far-reaching for the judicial branch to attempt. The judgment of the court of appeals is reversed and the case remanded to the district court.

DISSENT: (White, J.) According to the majority opinion, not only are the courts powerless to question acts of state proscribed by international law, but they are likewise powerless to refuse to adjudicate the claim founded upon a foreign law; they must render judgment and thereby validate the lawless act. The Act of State Doctrine does not require American courts to decide cases in disregard of international law and of the rights of litigants to a full determination on the merits.

ANALYSIS

In the instant case the Court also concluded that the Act of State Doctrine, even in diversity of citizenship cases, must be determined according to federal rather than state law. The Court stated that it is constrained to make it clear that

Continued on next page.

an issue concerned with a basic choice regarding the competence and function of the judiciary and national executive in ordering our relationships with other members of the international community must be treated exclusively as an aspect of federal law.

■■■■

Quicknotes

ACT OF STATE DOCTRINE Prohibits United States courts from investigating acts of other countries committed within their borders.

ENJOIN The ordering of a party to cease the conduct of a specific activity.

■■■■

Missouri v. Holland

State (P) v. Game warden (D)

252 U.S. 416 (1920).

NATURE OF CASE: Action seeking a declaratory judgment.

FACT SUMMARY: Missouri (P) brought this suit to prevent Holland (D), a game warden of the United States, from attempting to enforce the Migratory Bird Treaty Act on the ground that the statute was an unconstitutional interference with the rights reserved to the states by the Tenth Amendment.

🏛 RULE OF LAW

Acts of Congress are the supreme law of the land only when made in pursuance of the Constitution, while treaties are declared to be so when made under the authority of the United States.

FACTS: This is a bill in equity brought by the state of Missouri (P) to prevent Holland (D), a game warden of the United States, from attempting to enforce the Migratory Bird Treaty Act, the enactment statute of a treaty between the United States and Great Britain proclaimed by the President. The ground of the bill is that the statute is an unconstitutional interference with the rights reserved to the states by the Tenth Amendment, and that the acts of Holland (D) done and threatened under that authority invade the sovereign right of the state of Missouri (P) and contravene its will manifested in statutes. A motion to dismiss was sustained by the district court on the ground that the act of Congress is constitutional.

ISSUE: Are treaties the supreme law of the land when made under the authority of the United States?

HOLDING AND DECISION: (Holmes, J.) Yes. It is contended that a treaty cannot be valid if it infringes the Constitution, that there are limits, therefore, to the treaty-making power, and that one such limit is that what an act of Congress could not do unaided, in derogation of the powers reserved to the states, a treaty cannot do. Although it is true that acts of Congress are the supreme law of the land only when made in pursuance of the Constitution, treaties are declared to be so when made under the authority of the United States. Furthermore, valid treaties are as binding within the territorial limits of the states as they are elsewhere throughout the dominion of the United States. Since the Migratory Bird Treaty Act was made pursuant to a treaty between the United States and Canada, its provisions are the supreme law of the land and binding on the state of Missouri (P). The treaty and the statute must be upheld. The decree of the lower court is affirmed.

▶ ANALYSIS

Justice Sutherland, in discussing the foreign affairs power in *United States v. Curtiss-Wright Export Corp.,* 299 U. S. 304 (1936), stated that as a result of the separation from Great Britain by the colonies acting as a unit, the powers of external sovereignty passed from the Crown not to the colonies severally but to the colonies in their collective and corporate capacity as the United States. Even before the Declaration, the colonies were a unit in foreign affairs, and the powers to make treaties and maintain diplomatic relations, if they had never been mentioned in the Constitution, would have vested in the federal government as necessary concomitants of nationality.

■▬■

Quicknotes

DECLARATORY JUDGMENT An adjudication by the courts that grants not relief but is binding over the legal status of the parties involved in the dispute.

EQUITY Fairness; justice; the determination of a matter consistent with principles of fairness and not in strict compliance with rules of law.

JURISDICTION The authority of a court to hear and declare judgment in respect to a particular matter.

TENTH AMENDMENT The Tenth Amendment to the United States Constitution reserving those powers therein, not expressly delegated to the federal government or prohibited to the states, to the states or to the people.

TREATY An agreement between two or more nations for the benefit of the general public.

■▬■

Whitney v. Robertson

Importer (P) v. Customs (D)

124 U.S. 190 (1888).

NATURE OF CASE: Appeal from judgment for defendant in customs dispute.

FACT SUMMARY: Whitney (P) claimed that a treaty between the U.S. and the Dominican Republic guaranteed that no higher duty would be assessed on goods from the Dominican Republic than was assessed on goods from any other country and that duties had been wrongfully assessed on his sugar imports.

🏛 RULE OF LAW
Where a treaty and an act of legislation conflict, the one last in date will control.

FACTS: Whitney (P) sought to recover the duties he had paid for importing sugar from the Dominican Republic. Whitney (P) alleged that sugar from Hawaii was admitted free of duty and that under the terms of a treaty, the United States could not assess a higher duty on imports from the Dominican Republic.

ISSUE: Where a treaty and an act of legislation conflict, will the one last in date control?

HOLDING AND DECISION: (Field, J.) Yes. Where a treaty and an act of legislation conflict, the one last in date will control. The act of Congress under which the duties were collected was passed after the treaty and therefore is controlling. Affirmed.

▶ ANALYSIS

A treaty is not abrogated or repealed by a later inconsistent statute. The treaty still exists as an international obligation. The terms of the treaty may not be enforceable, however.

■═■

Quicknotes

TREATY An agreement between two or more nations for the benefit of the general public.

■═■

Breard v. Greene

Convicted murderer (D) v. State (P)

523 U.S. 371 (1998).

NATURE OF CASE: Appeal from denial of habeas corpus.

FACT SUMMARY: Breard (D) claimed that his conviction should be overturned because of alleged violations of the Vienna Convention on Consular Relations.

🏛 RULE OF LAW

When a statute that is subsequent in time is inconsistent with a treaty, the statute to the extent of conflict renders the treaty null.

FACTS: Breard (D) was scheduled to be executed following his conviction for murder. Breard (D) filed for habeas relief in federal court, arguing that the arresting authorities had wrongfully failed to inform him that, as a foreign national, he had the right to contact the Paraguayan consulate (P).

ISSUE: When a statute that is subsequent in time is inconsistent with a treaty, does the statute render the treaty null?

HOLDING AND DECISION: (Per curiam) Yes. When a statute that is subsequent in time is inconsistent with a treaty, the statute to the extent of conflict renders the treaty null. Breard's (D) argument that the Vienna Convention was violated must fail because Congress enacted the Antiterrorism and Effective Death Penalty Act after the Vienna Convention. The Executive Branch has authority over foreign relations and may utilize diplomatic channels to request a stay of execution. Petition denied.

▌ ANALYSIS

The Court also held that the Eleventh Amendment barred suits against states. The Consul General of Paraguay (P) tried to raise a § 1983 suit. The Court found that Paraguay (P) was not authorized to do so.

Quicknotes

42 U.S.C. § 1983 Provides that every person, who under color of state law subjects or causes to be subjected any citizen of the United States or person within its jurisdiction to be deprived of rights, privileges, and immunities guaranteed by the federal constitution and laws, is liable to the injured party at law or in equity.

ELEVENTH AMENDMENT The Eleventh Amendment to the United States Constitution prohibiting the extension of the judicial powers of the federal courts to suits brought against a state by citizens of another state, or of a foreign state, without the state's consent.

HABEAS CORPUS A proceeding in which a defendant brings a writ to compel a judicial determination of whether he is lawfully being held in custody.

Foster v. Neilson

Grantees (P) v. Land owner (D)

27 U.S. (2 Pet.) 253 (1829).

NATURE OF CASE: Appeal from decision for defendant in dispute over land.

FACT SUMMARY: Foster (P) and Elam claimed that a tract of land in Louisiana had been granted to them by the Spanish governor.

🏛 RULE OF LAW
When the terms of a treaty require a legislative act, the treaty cannot be considered law until such time as the legislature ratifies and confirms the terms.

FACTS: Foster (P) and Elam sued to recover a tract of land in Louisiana that the Spanish governor had granted them. Neilson (D) successfully argued that the grant was void because it was made subsequent to the transfer to France and the United States of the territory on which the land was situated. Foster (P) and Elam relied on a treaty between the United States and Spain that provided that all grants of land made by Spain would be ratified by the United States. The case was taken to the U.S. Supreme Court on a writ of error.

ISSUE: When the terms of a treaty require a legislative act, can the treaty be considered law before such time as the legislature ratifies and confirms the terms?

HOLDING AND DECISION: (Marshall, C.J.) No. When the terms of a treaty require a legislative act, the treaty cannot be considered law until such time as the legislature ratifies and confirms the terms. The treaty does not operate in itself to ratify or confirm title in land. The legislature must act before the terms of the contract are binding. Affirmed.

▶ ANALYSIS

Some international agreements are self-executing. Others are non-self-executing. The court must decide whether an agreement is to be given effect without further legislation.

Quicknotes

LAND GRANT Donation of public lands for use by another entity.

TITLE The right of possession over property.

TREATY An agreement between two or more nations for the benefit of the general public.

WRIT OF ERROR A writ issued by an appellate court, ordering a lower court to deliver the record of the case so that it may be reviewed for alleged errors.

Medellín v. Texas

Mexican national (D) v. State (P)

128 S. Ct. 1346 (2008).

NATURE OF CASE: Appeal of death sentence.

FACT SUMMARY: After Texas (P) convicted José Medellín (D) of rape and murder, he appealed on the grounds that Texas (P) failed to inform him of his right to have consular personnel notified of his detention by the state, as required under the Vienna Convention. On appeal to the U.S. Supreme Court, Medellín (D) argued that a case decided by the International Court of Justice suggested that his conviction must be reconsidered to comply with the Vienna Convention.

🏛 RULE OF LAW
(1) The U.S. Constitution does not require state courts to honor a treaty obligation of the United States by enforcing a decision of the International Court of Justice.
(2) The U.S. Constitution does not require state courts to provide review and reconsideration of a conviction without regard to state procedural default rules as required by a Memorandum by the President.

FACTS: José Medellín (D), a Mexican national, was convicted and sentenced to death for participating in the gang rape and murder of two teenage girls in Houston. In his appeal, Medellín (D) argued that the state had violated his rights under the Vienna Convention, to which the United States is a party. Article 36 of the Vienna Convention gives any foreign national detained for a crime the right to contact his consulate. The U.S. Supreme Court dismissed the petition and Medellín's (D) case was remanded to the Texas Court of Criminal Appeals, which also denied him relief. The U.S. Supreme Court took up his case again, and Medellín's (D) argument rested in part on a holding by the International Court of Justice in *Case Concerning Avena and Other Mexican Nationals (Mex. v. U.S.),* 2004 I.C.J. 12, that the United States had violated the Vienna Convention rights of 51 Mexican nationals (including Medellín (D)) and that their state-court convictions must be reconsidered, regardless of any forfeiture of the right to raise the Vienna Convention claims because of a failure to follow state rules governing criminal convictions. Medellín (D) argued that the Vienna Convention granted him an individual right that state courts must respect. Medellín (D) also cited a memorandum from the U.S. President that instructed state courts to comply with the I.C.J.'s rulings by rehearing the cases. Medellín (D) argued that the Constitution gives the President broad power to ensure that treaties are enforced, and that this power extends to the treatment of treaties in state court proceedings.

ISSUE:

(1) Does the U.S. Constitution require state courts to honor a treaty obligation of the United States by enforcing a decision of the International Court of Justice?
(2) Does the U.S. Constitution require state courts to provide review and reconsideration of a conviction without regard to state procedural default rules as required by a Memorandum by the President?

HOLDING AND DECISION: (Roberts, C.J.)

(1) No. The U.S. Constitution does not require state courts to honor a treaty obligation of the United States by enforcing a decision of the International Court of Justice. The Vienna Convention provides that if a person detained by a foreign country asks, the authorities of the detaining national must, without delay, inform the consular post of the detainee of the detention. The Optional Protocol of the Convention provides that the International Court of Justice is the venue for resolution of issues of interpretation of the Vienna Convention. By ratifying the Optional Protocol to the Vienna Convention, the United States consented to the jurisdiction of the I.C.J. with respect to claims arising out of the Vienna Convention. In 2005, however, after *Avena* was decided, the United States gave notice of withdrawal from the Optional Protocol. While *Avena* constitutes an international law obligation on the part of the United States, it does not help Medellín (D) because not all international law obligations automatically constitute binding federal law. *Avena* does not have automatic domestic legal effect such that the judgment if its own force applies in state and federal courts, because it is not a self-executing treaty, and Congress did not enact legislation implementing binding effect. Thus, the I.C.J. judgment is not automatically enforceable domestic law, immediately and directly binging on state and federal courts under the Supremacy Clause.
(2) The U.S. Constitution does not require state courts to provide review and reconsideration of a conviction without regard to state procedural default rules as required by a Memorandum by the President. The presidential memorandum was an attempt by the Executive Branch to enforce a non-self-executing treaty without the necessary congressional action, giving it no binding authority on state courts.

Continued on next page.

CONCURRENCE: (Stevens, J.) Although the judgment is correct, Texas (P) ought to comply with *Avena*. *Avena* may not be the supreme law of the land, but it constitutes an international law obligation on the part of the United States. Since Texas (P) failed to provide consular notice in accordance with the Vienna Convention, thereby getting the United States into this mess, and since that violation probably didn't prejudice Medellín (D), Texas (P) ought to comply with *Avena*.

DISSENT: (Breyer, J.) the Supremacy Clause requires Texas (P) to enforce the I.C.J.'s judgment in *Avena*. The majority does not point to a single ratified U.S. treaty that contains the self-executing language it says is required in this case. The absence or presence of language in a treaty about a provision's self-execution proves nothing. The relevant treaty provisions should be found to be self-executing, because (1) the language supports direct judicial enforceability, (2) the Optional Protocol applies to disputes about the meaning of a provision that is itself self-executing and judicially enforceable, (3) logic requires a conclusion that the provision is self-executing since it is "final" and "binding," (4) the majority's decision has negative practical implications, (5) the I.C.J. judgment is well suited to direct judicial enforcement, (6) such a holding would not threaten constitutional conflict with other branches, and (7) neither the President nor Congress has expressed concern about direct judicial enforcement of the I.C.J. decision.

▶ *ANALYSIS*

Medellín (D) was executed on August 5, 2008, after last-minute appeals to the U.S. Supreme Court were rejected. Governor Rick Perry rejected calls from Mexico and Secretary of State Condoleezza Rice and Attorney General Michael Mukasey to delay the execution, citing the torture, rape, and strangulation of two teenage girls in Houston as just cause for the death penalty. Though a bill was introduced in the House of Representatives to respond to the Court's ruling, Congress took no action.

■═■

Quicknotes

INTERNATIONAL LAW The body of law applicable to dealings between nations.

TREATY An agreement between two or more nations for the benefit of the general public.

■═■

Hamdan v. Rumsfeld

Detained terrorist (P) v. United States (D)

548 U.S. 557 (2006).

NATURE OF CASE: Appeal from circuit court holding that a military commission violated a detainee's rights under the Geneva Convention.

FACT SUMMARY: A U.S. military commission began proceedings against Hamdan (P), who was captured in Afghanistan. Hamdan (P) challenged the authority of the commission.

🏛 RULE OF LAW
(1) The military commission established to try those deemed "enemy combatants" for alleged war crimes in the War on Terror was not authorized by the Congress or the inherent powers of the President.
(2) The rights protected by the Geneva Convention may be enforced in federal court through habeas corpus petitions.

FACTS: Salim Ahmed Hamdan (P) was captured by Afghani forces and imprisoned by the U.S. military in Guantanamo Bay. He filed a petition for a writ of habeas corpus in federal district court to challenge his detention. Before the district court ruled on the petition, a U.S. military commission began proceedings against Hamdan (P), which designated him an enemy combatant. Hamdan (P) challenged the authority of the commission, arguing that the commission trial would violate his rights under Article 102 of the Geneva Convention, which provides that a "prisoner of war can be validly sentenced only if the sentence has been pronounced by the same courts according to the same procedure as in the case of members of the armed forces of the Detaining Power." The district court granted Hamdan's (P) habeas petition, ruling that a hearing to determine whether he was a prisoner of war under the Geneva Convention must have taken place before he could be tried by a military commission. The D.C. Circuit Court of Appeals reversed the decision, finding that the Geneva Convention could not be enforced in federal court and that the establishment of military tribunals had been authorized by Congress and was therefore not unconstitutional.

ISSUE:
(1) Was the military commission established to try those deemed "enemy combatants" for alleged war crimes in the War on Terror authorized by the Congress or the inherent powers of the President?
(2) May the rights protected by the Geneva Convention be enforced in federal court through habeas corpus petitions?

HOLDING AND DECISION: [Judge not stated in casebook excerpt.]

(1) No. The military commission established to try those deemed "enemy combatants" for alleged war crimes in the War on Terror was not authorized by the Congress or the inherent powers of the President. Neither an act of Congress nor the inherent powers of the Executive Branch laid out in the Constitution expressly authorized the sort of military commission at issue in this case. Absent that express authorization, the commission had to comply with the ordinary laws of the United States (D) and the laws of war.
(2) Yes. The rights protected by the Geneva Convention may be enforced in federal court through habeas corpus petitions. The Geneva Convention, as a part of the ordinary laws of war, could be enforced by the U.S. Supreme Court, along with the statutory Uniform Code of Military Justice (UCMJ), since the military commission was not authorized. Hamdan's (P) exclusion from certain parts of his trial deemed classified by the military commission violated both of these, and the trial was therefore illegal. Article 3, or "Common Article 3" as it is sometimes known, does apply to Hamdan (P), despite a holding to the contrary by the court of appeals, and arguments to the contrary by the government. Common Article 3 provides minimal protection to individuals associated with neither a signatory nor a non-signatory "Power" who are involved in a conflict in the territory of a signatory. Common Article 3 is applicable here and requires that Hamdan (P) be tried by a "regularly constituted court affording all the judicial guarantees which are recognized as indispensable by civilized peoples."

▶ ANALYSIS

Many U.S. and international human rights organizations have determined that violations might occur through the non-application of the Geneva Convention to detainees in the U.S. war on terrorism.

■■■

Quicknotes

GENEVA CONVENTION International agreement that governs the conduct of warring nations.

HABEAS CORPUS A proceeding in which a defendant brings a writ to compel a judicial determination of whether he is lawfully being held in custody.

■■■

United States v. Belmont

Government (P) v. Banker (D)

301 U.S. 324 (1937).

NATURE OF CASE: Appeal from denial of claim for payment of money deposited by Russian corporation.

FACT SUMMARY: The United States (P) claimed that it was due funds deposited in a U.S. bank by a Russian corporation that had been nationalized by the Soviet government.

🏛 RULE OF LAW
The national government has complete power in the conduct of international affairs and states cannot curtail or interfere in that power.

FACTS: A Russian corporation had deposited money in Belmont (D), a private bank in New York City, prior to the 1918 nationalization and liquidation by the Soviet government of the corporation. In 1933, the Soviet Union and the United States (P) agreed to a final settlement of claims and counterclaims. The Soviet Union agreed to take no steps to enforce claims against American nationals and assigned and released all such claims to the United States (P). When the U.S. (P) sought to recover the money, the court held that the *situs* of the bank deposit was within the state of New York and was not an intangible property right within Soviet territory and that it would be contrary to the public policy of the State of New York to recognize or enforce the nationalization decree. The United States (P) appealed and the U.S. Supreme Court granted certiorari.

ISSUE: Does the national government have complete power in the conduct of international affairs?

HOLDING AND DECISION: (Sutherland, J.) Yes. The national government has complete power in the conduct of international affairs and states cannot curtail or interfere in that power. The United States (P) recognized the Soviet government coincidentally with the assignment of all claims. The President has the power to conduct foreign relations, without the consent of the Senate. In respect of foreign relations generally, state lines disappear. Reversed and remanded.

▶ ANALYSIS

The Court noted that recognition of the Soviet Union and the release of all claims were interdependent. Thus it was purely in the realm of foreign policy to make this agreement. States cannot interfere in the conduct of foreign relations.

■=■

Quicknotes

CERTIORARI A discretionary writ issued by a superior court to an inferior court in order to review the lower court's decisions; the Supreme Court's writ ordering such review.

TREATY An agreement between two or more nations for the benefit of the general public.

■=■

Roper v. Simmons

Convicted murderer (D) v. State (P)

543 U.S. 551 (2005).

NATURE OF CASE: U.S. Supreme Court review of a state court determination involving a death sentence for a juvenile offender.

FACT SUMMARY: After Christopher Simmons (D) was convicted of a murder he committed when he was 17 years old, the Missouri Supreme Court ruled that the death penalty was unconstitutional as applied to persons under the age of 18. The U.S. Supreme Court reviewed the decision.

🏛 RULE OF LAW
The opinion of the world community is relevant, though not controlling, to consideration of the juvenile death penalty in the United States.

FACTS: The state of Missouri (P) convicted Christopher Simmons (D) of a murder he committed when he was 17 years old. The Missouri Supreme Court ruled that the death penalty was unconstitutional as applied to persons under the age of 18, and set aside the sentence of death imposed on Simmons (D). The U.S. Supreme Court reviewed the decision, and in the process of reaching its conclusion, considered the opinion on the matter of the international community.

ISSUE: Is the opinion of the world community relevant, though not controlling, to consideration of the juvenile death penalty in the United States?

HOLDING AND DECISION: (Kennedy, J.) Yes. The opinion of the world community is relevant, though not controlling, to consideration of the juvenile death penalty in the United States. Precedent suggests that reference to the laws of other countries and to international authorities for interpretation of the prohibition of "cruel and unusual punishments" is proper. Every country in the world has ratified the U.N. Convention on the Rights of the Child, which contains an express prohibition on capital punishment for crimes committed by juveniles under 18, except Somalia and the United States. Since 1990, only seven countries other than the United States have executed juvenile offenders, and since then each country, except the United States, has either abolished capital punishment for juveniles or made public disavowal of the practice. The United Kingdom's abolition of the death penalty for juveniles, which is particularly relevant given the ties between the United Kingdom and the United States, occurred before the international conventions on the subject were created. International opinion against the death penalty for minors is based in large part on the understanding that the instability and emotional imbalance of young people may often be a factor in the crime, and that opinion, while not controlling, is relevant. The Eighth and Fourteenth Amendments forbid imposition of the death penalty on offenders under the age of 18 when the crime was committed. Affirmed.

▶ ANALYSIS

Not stated in the casebook excerpt is that the Court applied the "evolving standards of decency" test. Justice Kennedy cited a body of sociological and scientific research that found that juveniles have a lack of maturity and sense of responsibility compared to adults. The Court reasoned that in recognition of the comparative immaturity and irresponsibility of juveniles, almost every state prohibited those under age 18 from voting, serving on juries, or marrying without parental consent. Kennedy reasoned that the trend internationally against the death penalty for minors was relevant because of its basis in this evolving notion that the death penalty is inappropriate for juvenile offenders because of their instability and emotional imbalance.

■=■

Quicknotes

EIGHTH AMENDMENT The Eighth Amendment to the federal Constitution prohibits the imposition of excessive bail, fines, and cruel and unusual punishment.

FOURTEENTH AMENDMENT Declares that no state shall make or enforce any law that shall abridge the privileges and immunities of citizens of the United States. No state shall deny to any person within its jurisdiction the equal protection of the laws.

■=■

Kadi v. Council and Commission

Terrorists (D) v. European Union (P)

European Court of Justice, 2008 E.C.R. ___ (2008).

NATURE OF CASE: Appeal of judgment by a European Community Court of First Instance.

FACT SUMMARY: A regulation of the Council of the European Union (P) froze the funds of Yassin Abdullah Kadi (D) and Al Barakaat International Foundation (D), following a resolution by the U.N. Security Council. The EU Court of First Instance ruled that it did not have jurisdiction to review measures adopted by the European Community (EC) giving effect to resolutions of the Security Council adopted against the Al Qaeda and Taliban terrorist networks. Kadi (D) and Al Barakaat (D) appealed.

RULE OF LAW

The courts of the member states of the European Union (P) have jurisdiction to review measures adopted by the European Community that give effect to resolutions of the U.N. Security Council.

FACTS: In its effort to fight terrorism, the U.N. Security Council imposed sanctions under Chapter VII of the U.N. Charter against individuals and entities allegedly associated with Osama bin Laden, the Al-Qaeda network, and the Taliban. The U.N. Sanctions Committee made a list of alleged offenders, and sanctions included freezing such persons' and entities' assets. To give effect to the Security Council resolutions, the Council of the European Union (P) adopted a regulation ordering the freezing of the assets of those on the list, which included Yassin Abdullah Kadi (D), a resident of Saudi Arabia, and Al Barakaat International Foundation (D). Kadi (D) and Al Barakaat (D) began proceedings in the Court of First Instance (CFI) and requested annulment of the Council regulation, arguing that the Council lacked jurisdiction to adopt the regulation and that the regulation infringed several of their fundamental rights, including the right to respect for property, the right to be heard before a court of law, and the right to effective judicial review. The CFI rejected all claims and confirmed the validity of the regulation, ruling specifically that it had no jurisdiction to review the validity of the contested regulation and, indirectly, the validity of the relevant Security Council resolution, except in respect of *jus cogens* norms. Kadi (D) and Al Barakaat (D) appealed.

ISSUE: Do the courts of the member states of the European Union (P) have jurisdiction to review measures adopted by the European Community that give effect to resolutions of the U.N. Security Council?

HOLDING AND DECISION: [Judge not stated in casebook excerpt.] Yes. The courts of the member states of the European Union (P) have jurisdiction to review measures adopted by the European Community that give effect to resolutions of the U.N. Security Council. EC courts have the power to review the legality of all Community acts, including the contested regulation, that aim to give effect to resolutions adopted by the Security Council under the U.N. Charter. The review of lawfulness applies only to the EC act purporting to give effect to the international agreement, not to the international agreement itself. Thus, EC courts do not have competence to review the legality of a resolution adopted by an international body, even if the courts limited their review to examination of the compatibility of that resolution with *jus cogens* norms. A judgment by an EU court that an EC measure is contrary to a higher rule of law in the EC legal order would not implicate a challenge to the legitimacy of that resolution in international law.

ANALYSIS

This case marks the first time that the ECJ confirmed its jurisdiction to review the lawfulness of a measure giving effect to Security Council resolutions. It also constitutes the first time the ECJ quashed an EC measure giving effect to a UNSC resolution for being unlawful.

Quicknotes

JUDICIAL REVIEW The authority of the courts to review decisions, actions, or omissions committed by another agency or branch of government.

JURISDICTION The authority of a court to hear and declare judgment in respect to a particular matter.

JUS COGENS NORM Universally understood principles of international law that cannot be set aside because they are based on fundamental human values.

CHAPTER 11

Bases of Jurisdiction

Quick Reference Rules of Law

Al-Skeini v. Secretary of State for Defence

Families of deceased (P) v. United Kingdom (D)

U.K. House of Lords, [2007] UKHL 26.

NATURE OF CASE: Wrongful death proceedings under international convention.

FACT SUMMARY: The families (P) of six Iraqi civilians who were killed in Basra in 2003 where the United Kingdom (D) was an occupying power appealed a decision by U.K. authorities not to conduct an independent investigation into the circumstances of the deaths, arguing that the Human Rights Act 1998 has extraterritorial application where the United Kingdom (D) is an occupying power.

🏛 RULE OF LAW

The Human Rights Act 1998 applied to acts of a U.K. public authority performed outside its territory only where the victim was within the jurisdiction of the United Kingdom (D) for purposes of the European Convention on Human Rights.

FACTS: Six Iraqi civilians were killed in Basra in 2003 where the United Kingdom (D) was an occupying power. Five of them were shot dead by members of U.K. armed forces in the course of patrol operations, and the sixth was arrested and died in a military base. U.K. authorities refused to conduct an independent investigation into the circumstances of the deaths. The U.K. government argued that the deaths occurred outside the territory of the United Kingdom (D), and consequently the European Convention for Human Rights, which imposes an obligation for independent and thorough investigation, does not apply. The families (P) of the deceased sued.

ISSUE: Did the Human Rights Act 1998 apply to acts of a U.K. public authority performed outside its territory only where the victim was within the jurisdiction of the United Kingdom (D) for purposes of the European Convention on Human Rights?

HOLDING AND DECISION: (Rodger of Earlsferry, L. [for the majority]) Yes. The Human Rights Act 1998 applied to acts of a U.K. public authority performed outside its territory only where the victim was within the jurisdiction of the United Kingdom (D) for purposes of the European Convention on Human Rights. The rule of statutory construction adopted by Lord Bingham must be taken against the background of international law, and jurisdiction under the HRA should be co-extensive with the interpretation given by the European Court to jurisdiction under the Convention. The Convention applies outside the territory of the United Kingdom (D) where the deceased were linked to the United Kingdom (D) when they were killed. The HRA does not have a more restrictive jurisdictional scope than the Convention rights it was meant to implement. With the exception of the

claimant who had been mistreated inside a British military detention unit, the claimants were not within U.K. jurisdiction within the meaning of the Convention.

DISSENT: (Bingham of Cornhill, L.) No. The Human Rights Act 1998 has no extraterritorial application. To succeed in this case, the claimants have to show that a public authority acted in contravention of the European Convention on Human Rights and the Human Rights Act 1998. Typically, claims relate to conduct within the borders of contracting states, such as the United Kingdom (D), and the only question is whether a claimant's Convention right has been violated, and if so, by whom. Here, however, the alleged violations took place in Iraq, which is not a contracting state. The rule of statutory construction urged by the U.K. government is that unless contrary intention appears, Parliament should be taken to intend an act to extend to each territory of the United Kingdom (D) but not to any territory outside the United Kingdom (D). In passing the HRA, Parliament could not have intended to legislate for foreign lands, because between 1953 and 1997, British forces were almost always involved in hostilities or peacekeeping activities in some part of the world, and such situations must have been on the minds of members of Parliament when they passed the HRA. Had they intended to legislate for activity by British soldiers in foreign lands, they would have expressly stated as much.

▶ ANALYSIS

There were actually four Lords forming the majority (Lord Rodger included), and Lord Bingham was the sole dissenter. Lord Rodger's basic rule is that the presumption against extraterritoriality must be seen against the background of international law, that Parliament had a legitimate interest in regulating the conduct of its citizens, and therefore could intend its legislation to affect their position in other states.

■=■

Quicknotes

INTERNATIONAL LAW The body of law applicable to dealings between nations.

JURISDICTION The authority of a court to hear and declare judgment in respect to a particular matter.

STATUTORY CONSTRUCTION The examination and interpretation of statutes.

■=■

United States v. Aluminum Co. of America

Federal government (P) v. Corporation (D)

148 F.2d 416 (2d Cir. 1945).

NATURE OF CASE: Appeal from a prosecution for violation of the Sherman Act.

FACT SUMMARY: The United States (P) brought this action against the Aluminum Co. of America (D) and Aluminum Limited (D), a Canadian corporation formed to take over the properties of Aluminum Co. of America (D) outside the United States, for violation of the Sherman Act by the participation of each company in a foreign cartel called the Alliance.

RULE OF LAW

Any state may impose liabilities, even upon persons not within its allegiance, for conduct outside its borders that has consequences within its borders that the state reprehends.

FACTS: A foreign cartel called Alliance, a Swiss corporation, was created by an agreement entered into in 1931 among a French corporation, two German corporations, one Swiss corporation, one British corporation, and Aluminum Limited (D). Aluminum Limited (D) was a Canadian corporation formed to take over properties of the Aluminum Co. of America (D) outside the United States. The original 1931 agreement provided for the issuance of shares to the signatories and a quota of production for each share, the shareholders to be limited to the quantity measured by the number of shares held by each. Alliance was free to sell at any price it chose. No shareholder was to obtain or sell aluminum produced by anyone not a shareholder. Another agreement in 1936 abandoned the system of unconditional quotas and substituted a system of royalties. The shareholders agreed that imports into the United States should be included in the quotas. Thereafter, the United States (P) brought this action against the Aluminum Co. of America (D) and Aluminum Limited (D) for violation of the Sherman Act that prohibits every contract, combination, or other conspiracy in restraint of trade among the several states or with foreign nations. The district court found that the 1931 and 1936 agreements did not suppress or restrain the exportation of aluminum to the United States (P) and that America (D) was not a party to the Alliance. The United States (P) appealed.

ISSUE: May a state impose liabilities, even upon persons not within its allegiance, for conduct outside its borders that has consequences within its borders?

HOLDING AND DECISION: (L. Hand, Swan, and A. Hand, J.) Yes. It is settled law that any state may impose liabilities, even upon persons not within its allegiance, for conduct outside its borders that has consequences within its borders that the state reprehends. Under the Sherman Antitrust Act, both the 1931 and the 1936 agreements of the Alliance would clearly have been unlawful had they been made within the United States (P); and, though made abroad, both are unlawful if they were intended to affect imports and did affect them. The evidence shows that the shareholders of Alliance intended to restrict imports, thus shifting the burden of proof of whether they in fact restricted imports into the United States to Limited (D). In the first place, a depressant on production, as was encompassed within the 1936 agreement, which applies generally, may be assumed to distribute its effect evenly upon all markets. Again, when the parties in the instant case specifically made the depressant apply to a given market, there is reason to suppose that they expected the effect to be a lessening of what would otherwise have been imported. Since the underlying doctrine of the Sherman Act was that all factors that contribute to determining prices must be kept free to operate unhampered by agreements, this court must conclude that the 1936 agreement violated the Act.

▌ *ANALYSIS*

The general words of the Sherman Antitrust Act should not be read without regard to the limitations customarily observed by nations upon the exercise of their powers. Thus, one should not impute to Congress an intent to punish all whom its courts can catch, for conduct that has no consequences within the United States. There may be agreements made beyond the borders of the United States not intended to affect imports or exports that do affect them. Almost any limitation of the supply of goods in Europe, for example, or in South America, may have repercussions in the United States if there is trade between the two. Yet, when one considers the international complications likely to arise from an effort in the United States to treat such agreements as unlawful, it is safe to assume that Congress certainly did not intend the Sherman Antitrust Act to cover them.

■━■

Quicknotes

ANTITRUST ACTS Federal and state statutes to protect trade and commerce from unlawful restraints, price discrimination, price fixing, and monopolies.

CARTEL An agreement between manufacturers or producers of the same product so as to form a monopoly.

■━■

Hartford Fire Insurance Co. v. California

Foreign-based reinsurer (D) v. State (P)

509 U.S. 764 (1993).

NATURE OF CASE: Appeal from a judgment as to jurisdiction and application of domestic law to a foreign company in a federal antitrust action.

FACT SUMMARY: Claiming that Hartford Fire Insurance Co. (D) and other London-based reinsurers (D) had allegedly engaged in unlawful conspiracies to affect the market for insurance in the United States, California (P) instituted an action against Hartford (D), under the Sherman Act, which the reinsurers (D) sought to dismiss under the principle of international comity.

> ## 🏛 RULE OF LAW
> Where a person subject to regulation by two states can comply with the laws of both, jurisdiction may be exercised over foreign conduct since no conflict exists.

FACTS: California (P) brought an action against Hartford Fire Insurance Co. (D) and other London-based reinsurers (D) alleging that they had engaged in unlawful conspiracies to affect the market for insurance in the United States and that their conduct in fact produced substantial effect, thus violating the Sherman Act. Hartford (D) argued that the district court should have declined to exercise jurisdiction under the principle of international comity. The court of appeals agreed that courts should look to that principle in deciding whether to exercise jurisdiction under the Sherman Act but that other factors, including Hartford's (D) express purpose to affect U.S. commerce and the substantial nature of the effect produced, outweighed the supposed conflict, requiring the exercise of jurisdiction in this case. Hartford (D) appealed.

ISSUE: Where a person subject to regulation by two states can comply with the laws of both, may jurisdiction be exercised over foreign conduct since no conflict exists?

HOLDING AND DECISION: (Souter, J.) Yes. Where a person subject to regulation by two states can comply with the laws of both, jurisdiction may be exercised over foreign conduct since no conflict exists. The Sherman Act applies to foreign conduct that was meant to produce and does in fact produce some substantial effect in the United States. Even assuming that a court may decline to exercise Sherman Act jurisdiction over foreign conduct, international comity would not prevent a U.S. court from exercising jurisdiction in the circumstances alleged here. Since Hartford (D) does not argue that British law requires it to act in some fashion prohibited by the law of the United States or claim that its compliance with the laws of both countries is otherwise impossible, there is no conflict with British law. Since there is no irreconcilable

conflict between domestic and British law, the reinsurers (D) may not invoke comity. Affirmed.

DISSENT: (Scalia, J.) The district court had subject-matter jurisdiction over the Sherman Act claims, and it is now well established that the Sherman Act applies extraterritorially, despite the presumption against extraterritoriality. But, even where the presumption against extraterritoriality does not apply, statutes should not be interpreted to regulate foreign persons or conduct if that regulation would conflict with principles of international law. The activity at issue here took place primarily in the United Kingdom, and Hartford (D) and the other reinsurers (D) are British subjects having their principal place of business or residence outside the United States. Great Britain has established a comprehensive regulatory scheme governing the London reinsurance markets and clearly has a heavy interest in regulating the activity. Finally, § 2(b) of the McCarran-Ferguson Act allows state regulatory statutes to override the Sherman Act in the insurance field, subject only to a narrow exception, suggesting that the importance of regulation to the United States is slight.

▶ ANALYSIS

Black's Law Dictionary, p. 242 (5th ed. 1979), defines "comity of nations" as "[t]he recognition which one nation allows within its territory to the legislative, executive, or judicial acts of another nation, having due regard both to international duty and convenience and to the rights of its own citizens or of other persons who are under the protection of its laws." When it enacted the Foreign Trade Antitrust Improvements Act of 1982 (FTAIA), Congress expressed no view on the question of whether a court with Sherman Act jurisdiction should ever decline to exercise such jurisdiction on grounds of international comity, an issue that the Court declined to address in this case. Justice Scalia endorsed the approach of the Restatement (Third) of Foreign Relations Law, advocating that a nation having some basis for jurisdiction should nonetheless refrain from exercising that jurisdiction when the exercise of such jurisdiction is unreasonable.

■═■

Quicknotes

ANTITRUST LAW Body of federal law prohibiting business conduct that constitutes a restraint on trade.

COMITY A rule pursuant to which courts in one state give deference to the statutes and judicial decisions of another.

■═■

Blackmer v. United States

Citizen (D) v. Government (P)

284 U.S. 421 (1932).

NATURE OF CASE: Appeal from contempt conviction.

FACT SUMMARY: Blackmer (D) was found to be in contempt of court for failing to respond to subpoenas served upon him in France requiring his appearance in the United States.

▥ RULE OF LAW
For the exercise of judicial jurisdiction in personam, there must be due process.

FACTS: Blackmer (D) was a U.S. (P) citizen who resided in France. He was served subpoenas to appear in court as a witness in a criminal trial in the United States. When he failed to respond to the subpoenas, contempt proceedings were initiated and Blackmer (D) was found guilty and fined. Blackmer (D) appealed, claiming the federal statute was unconstitutional.

ISSUE: For the exercise of judicial jurisdiction in personam, must there be due process?

HOLDING AND DECISION: (Hughes, C.J.) Yes. For the exercise of judicial jurisdiction in personam, there must be due process. Due process requires appropriate notice of the judicial action and an opportunity to be heard. The statute provides that when the presence of a citizen of the United States who resides abroad is required in court, a subpoena be issued addressed to a consul of the United States. The consul must serve the subpoena on the witness personally with a tender of traveling expenses. Upon proof of such service and of the failure of the witness to appear, a court order may be issued. If the witness fails to comply with the court order, the court may adjudge the witness guilty of contempt. Congress acted pursuant to its authority in enacting the statute and it could prescribe a penalty to enforce it. Affirmed.

▌ *ANALYSIS*

The Court did not find the statute to be unconstitutional. Blackmer (D) alleged that there was inadequate notice. Since Blackmer (D) retained his U.S. citizenship, he was still subject to U.S. authorities.

Quicknotes

CONTEMPT An act of omission that interferes with a court's proper administration of justice.

DUE PROCESS RIGHTS The constitutional mandate requiring the courts to protect and enforce individuals' rights and liberties consistent with prevailing principles of fairness and justice and prohibiting the federal and state governments from such activities that deprive its citizens of a life, liberty, or property interest.

IN PERSONAM JURISDICTION The jurisdiction of a court over a person as opposed to his interest in property.

SERVICE OF PROCESS The communication of reasonable notice of a court proceeding to a defendant in order to provide him with an opportunity to be heard.

United States v. Yousef

Federal government (P) v. Convicted terrorist (D)

327 F.3d 56 (2d Cir. 2003).

NATURE OF CASE: Appeal of criminal conviction.

FACT SUMMARY: Ramzi Yousef (D), Wali Khan Amin Shah (D), and Abdul Hakim Murad (D) appealed from judgments of conviction entered in the United States District Court for the Southern District of New York on charges relating to a conspiracy to bomb twelve U.S. commercial airliners in Southeast Asia.

🏛 RULE OF LAW

The U.S. government (P) did not exceed its authority by trying an alleged terrorist in the United States, when the criminal conduct occurred outside the United States, but involved its airliners.

FACTS: Ramzi Yousef (D) entered Manila under an assumed name in order to execute a plan to attack U.S. airliners. Under the plan, bombs would be placed aboard twelve U.S. aircraft with routes in Southeast Asia by five individuals. The conspirators would board the plane, assemble the bomb while in flight, and then exit the plane during its first layover. The plot was discovered two weeks before the intended execution, when Yousef (D) and Murad (D) accidentally started a fire while burning chemicals in their Manila apartment. The fire department involved the police department, which found the bomb components, a laptop with notes on the plan, and other evidence. Philippine authorities arrested Murad (D) and Shah (D), but Shah (D) escaped and evaded capture until a year later. Yousef (D) fled to Pakistan, but was captured the following month. Through a multi-count indictment, Yousef (D), Murad (D), and Shah (D) were charged with various crimes related to their conspiracy to bomb the planes. A jury found all three guilty on all counts.

ISSUE: Did the U.S. government (P) exceed its authority by trying an alleged terrorist in the United States, when the criminal conduct occurred outside the United States, but involved its airliners?

HOLDING AND DECISION: [Judge not stated in casebook excerpt.] No. The U.S. government (P) did not exceed its authority by trying an alleged terrorist in the United States, when the criminal conduct occurred outside the United States but involved its airliners. Jurisdiction is supported by both domestic and international law. Because the federal court had jurisdiction over the substantive crimes charged, including attempted destruction of aircraft in the special aircraft jurisdiction of the United States, it also had derivative jurisdiction over the conspiracy charges. Congress is presumed to intend extraterritorial application of criminal statutes where the nature of the crime does not depend on the locality of the criminal acts and where restricting the statute to U.S. territory would severely diminish the statute's effectiveness. With respect to whether customary international law provides a basis for jurisdiction over the case, United States law is not subordinate to customary international law or necessarily subordinate to treaty-based international law. Moreover, customary international law does provide a substantial basis for jurisdiction by the United States through the "passive personality principle," because the case involved a plot to bomb U.S. aircraft that would have been carrying U.S. citizens and crews destined for cities in the United States. Jurisdiction is also appropriate under the "objective territorial principle" because the purpose of the attack was to influence U.S. foreign policy. Finally, Yousef's (D) conduct constitutes conduct proscribed by the Montreal Convention, and his prosecution and conviction is both consistent with and required by the United States' treaty obligations and domestic law.

▶ ANALYSIS

The Tokyo Convention on Offences and Certain Other Acts Committed on Board Aircraft generally regulates jurisdiction over crimes committed on aircraft. International law generally requires that there be a genuine link between the state and the aircraft in order for the state to lawfully assert jurisdiction over crimes committed on board.

■■■

Quicknotes

INDICTMENT A formal written accusation made by a prosecutor and issued by a grand jury, charging an individual with a criminal offense.

INTERNATIONAL LAW The body of law applicable to dealings between nations.

JURISDICTION The authority of a court to hear and declare judgment in respect to a particular matter.

TREATY An agreement between two or more nations for the benefit of the general public.

■■■

United States v. Vasquez-Velasco

United States (P) v. Foreign drug trafficker (D)

15 F.3d 833 (1994).

NATURE OF CASE: Appeal of criminal conviction.

FACT SUMMARY: Javier Vasquez-Velasco (D), a member of a drug cartel in Guadalajara, and several other members, beat and killed [John] Walker [an American citizen writing a novel in Mexico] and [Alberto] Radelat [a photographer and U.S. legal resident]. He was convicted under U.S. law. On appeal, Vasquez-Velasco (D) argued that U.S. penal laws do not apply extraterritorially.

 RULE OF LAW
Extraterritorial application of a penal statute to the murder of a U.S. citizen mistaken for a federal agent is consistent with principles of international law.

FACTS: *United States v. Felix-Gutierrez,* 940 F.2d 1200 (9th Cir. 1991), cert. denied, 508 U.S. 906 (1993), a case in which a defendant was convicted of kidnapping and murdering Enrique Camarena, an American Drug Enforcement Agency (DEA) agent, and Alfredo Zavala, a DEA informant, was the basis for the appeal by the defendant in this case, Javier Vasquez-Velasco (D). Vasquez-Velasco (D), a member of a drug cartel in Guadalajara, and several other members, beat and killed [John] Walker [an American citizen writing a novel in Mexico] and [Alberto] Radelat [a photographer and U.S. legal resident]. At trial, the U.S. government (P) argued that Vasquez-Velasco (D) and his three co-defendants committed the crimes to further their positions in a Guadalajara drug cartel. The murders Velasco (D) was charged with were allegedly retaliatory actions against a DEA crackdown. He was convicted in a jury trial of committing violent crimes in aid of a racketeering enterprise in violation of 18 U.S.C. § 1959. On appeal, Vasquez-Velasco (D) argued that U.S. penal laws do not apply extraterritorially.

ISSUE: Is the extraterritorial application of a penal statute to the murder of a U.S. citizen mistaken for a federal agent consistent with principles of international law?

HOLDING AND DECISION: (Fletcher, J.) Yes. Extraterritorial application of a penal statute to the murder of a U.S. citizen mistaken for a federal agent is consistent with principles of international law. International law generally permits the exercise of extraterritorial jurisdiction under the objective territorial principle, under which jurisdiction is asserted over acts performed outside the United States (P) that produce detrimental effects within the United States (P), and the protective principle, under which jurisdiction is asserted over foreigners for an act committed outside the United States (P) that may impinge on the territorial integrity, security, or political independence

of the United States (P). Extraterritorial application of 18 U.S.C. § 1959 to violent crimes associated with drug trafficking is reasonable under international law principles, since it is a serious and universally condemned offense. Despite the fact that the crimes in this case did not involve the murder of a DEA agent, extraterritorial jurisdiction is still appropriate because, according to the government's theory, the cartel members mistook Walker and Radelat for DEA agents. As in *Felix-Gutierrez,* the crime was directed against the United States (P).

▶ ANALYSIS

The objective territorial and protective principles apply because the defendant in this case murdered the two U.S. citizens on the mistaken belief they were DEA agents, and their murders might intimidate the DEA and local police and drug agencies, who might otherwise cooperate with the DEA. The case therefore turns on the defendant's subjective beliefs; if the government had been unsuccessful in its argument that the murders were committed as retaliation against the DEA, extraterritorial jurisdiction would be harder to apply.

Quicknotes

INTERNATIONAL LAW The body of law applicable to dealings between nations.

JURISDICTION The authority of a court to hear and declare judgment in respect to a particular matter.

RACKETEERING A conspiracy organized for the commission or attempted commission of extortion or coercion.

Regina v. Bartle, Bow Street Stipendiary Magistrate and Commissioner of Police, Ex parte Pinochet

Government (P) v. Alleged torturer (D)

U.K. House of Lords, 2 W.L.R. 827, 38 I.L.M. 581 (1999).

NATURE OF CASE: Appeal from arrest and extradition order.

FACT SUMMARY: Pinochet (D) claimed that he could not be extradited because he was not guilty of any crime under English law.

RULE OF LAW
Torture is an international crime.

FACTS: An English magistrate issued an arrest warrant for Pinochet (D), the former head of state of Chile, at the request of a Spanish investigating judge for extradition. The House of Lords found that Pinochet (D) could not claim immunity in regard to torture that had been made a universal crime by the International Convention Against Torture and other Cruel, Inhuman, or Degrading Treatment or Punishment of 1984. Pinochet (D) claimed torture was not strictly an international crime in the highest sense.

ISSUE: Is torture an international crime?

HOLDING AND DECISION: (Lord Browne-Wilkinson) Yes. Torture is an international crime. The Torture Convention was agreed not to create an international crime that had not previously existed but to provide an international system under which the international criminal—the torturer—could find no safe haven. All state parties are required to prohibit torture on their territory and to take jurisdiction over any alleged offender who is found within their territory. Torture is to be treated as an extraditable offense and will be considered to have been committed not only in the place where it occurred but also in the state where either the alleged offender or victim is a national.

▌ANALYSIS

The Torture Convention created an exception to the otherwise applicable immunity of present and former heads of state from criminal process. Pinochet (D) ultimately was found to be too sick to stand trial. He was allowed to return to Chile.

■══■

Quicknotes

EXTRADITION The surrender by one state or nation to another of an individual allegedly guilty of committing a crime in that area.

IMMUNITY Exemption from a legal obligation.

■══■

United States v. Yousef

Federal government (P) v. Convicted terrorist (D)

327 F.3d 56 (2d Cir. 2003).

NATURE OF CASE: Appeal of criminal conviction.

FACT SUMMARY: Ramzi Yousef (D), Wali Khan Amin Shah (D), and Abdul Hakim Murad (D) appealed from judgments of conviction entered in the United States District Court for the Southern District of New York on charges relating to a conspiracy to bomb twelve U.S. commercial airliners in Southeast Asia. The district court held that the principle of universal jurisdiction was applicable, because Yousef's (D) conduct qualified as a "terrorist" act.

🏛 RULE OF LAW

Universal jurisdiction arises under customary international law only where crimes (1) are universally condemned by the community of nations, and (2) by their nature occur either outside of a state or where there is no state capable of punishing, or competent to punish, the crime.

FACTS: Ramzi Yousef (D) entered Manila under an assumed name in order to execute a plan to attack U.S. airliners. Under the plan, bombs would be placed aboard twelve U.S. aircraft with routes in Southeast Asia by five individuals. The conspirators would board the plane, assemble the bomb while in flight, and then exit the plane during its first layover. The plot was discovered two weeks before the intended execution, when Yousef (D) and Murad (D) accidentally started a fire while burning chemicals in their Manila apartment. The fire department involved the police department, which found the bomb components, a laptop with notes on the plan, and other evidence. Philippine authorities arrested Murad (D) and Shah (D), but Shah (D) escaped and evaded capture until a year later. Yousef (D) fled to Pakistan, but was captured the following month. Through a multi-count indictment, Yousef (D), Murad (D), and Shah (D) were charged with various crimes related to their conspiracy to bomb the planes. A jury found all three guilty on all counts. The district court held that the principle of universal jurisdiction was applicable, because Yousef's (D) conduct qualified as a "terrorist" act.

ISSUE: Does universal jurisdiction arise under customary international law only where crimes (1) are universally condemned by the community of nations, and (2) by their nature occur either outside of a state or where there is no state capable of punishing, or competent to punish, the crime?

HOLDING AND DECISION: [Judge not stated in casebook excerpt.] Yes. Universal jurisdiction arises under customary international law only where crimes (1) are universally condemned by the community of nations, and (2) by their nature occur either outside of a state or where there is no state capable of punishing, or competent to punish, the crime. Universal jurisdiction is historically restricted to piracy, war crimes, and crimes against humanity, and unlike those offenses, "terrorism" does not have a precise definition and has not achieved universal condemnation.

▶ ANALYSIS

One of the biggest impediments to defining "terrorism" is state-sponsored terrorism, or acts of state employed to effect coercion. The terrorism that is commonly understood in the United States is not similarly defined in many parts of the world. Whenever the acts of terrorism are a case's focus—whether one involving universal jurisdiction or another issue—courts will be hesitant to impose a definition.

■═■

Quicknotes

INDICTMENT A formal written accusation made by a prosecutor and issued by a grand jury, charging an individual with a criminal offense.

INTERNATIONAL LAW The body of law applicable to dealings between nations.

JURISDICTION The authority of a court to hear and declare judgment in respect to a particular matter.

■═■

United States v. Alvarez-Machain

Federal government (P) v. Foreign national (D)

504 U.S. 655 (1992).

NATURE OF CASE: Review of dismissal of federal indictment.

FACT SUMMARY: Alvarez-Machain (D), abducted from Mexico for trial in the United States (P) by Drug Enforcement Agency (DEA) agents, contended that his abduction was illegal because of an extradition treaty between the United States (P) and Mexico.

RULE OF LAW
The presence of an extradition treaty between the United States and another nation does not necessarily preclude obtaining a citizen of that nation through abduction.

FACTS: Alvarez-Machain (D) was abducted from his office in Mexico by persons working for DEA agents. He was wanted in the United States (P) for alleged complicity in the torture-murder of a DEA agent. Alvarez-Machain (D) moved to dismiss the indictment, contending that his abduction violated a U.S.-Mexico extradition treaty. The district court agreed and dismissed the indictment. The court of appeals affirmed, and the U.S. Supreme Court granted review.

ISSUE: Does the presence of an extradition treaty between the United States and another nation necessarily preclude obtaining a citizen of that nation through abduction?

HOLDING AND DECISION: (Rehnquist, C.J.) No. The presence of an extradition treaty between the United States (P) and another nation does not necessarily preclude obtaining a citizen of that nation through abduction. It has long been the rule that abduction, in and of itself, does not invalidate a prosecution against a foreign national. The only question, therefore, is whether the abduction violates any extradition treaty that may be in effect between the United States (P) and the nation in which the abductee was to be found. Here, the U.S.-Mexican authorities presumably were aware of the United States' (P) long-standing law regarding abductions and did not insist on including a prohibition against abductions. Alvarez-Machain (D) argued that since international law prohibits abductions, the drafters of the treaty had no reason to consider a prohibition thereof necessary. However, this body of law only applies to situations where no extradition treaty exists, so it is irrelevant here. Consequently, since the extradition treaty does not prohibit an abduction such as occurred here, it was not illegal. Reversed.

DISSENT: (Stevens, J.) The majority opinion fails to distinguish between acts of private citizens, which do not violate any treaty obligations, and conduct expressly authorized by the executive branch, which undoubtedly constitutes a fragrant violation of international law and a breach of the U.S. (P) treaty obligations.

▶ ANALYSIS

Alvarez-Machain (D) lost this battle but won the war. He was tried in Los Angeles in 1993. At the close of the prosecution's case, the trial judge, Edward Rafeedie, dismissed the case for lack of evidence. The judge used some harsh language in his order, apparently believing the case should never have been brought.

Quicknotes

EXTRADITION The surrender by one state or nation to another of an individual allegedly guilty of committing a crime in that area.

INDICTMENT A formal written accusation made by a prosecutor and issued by a grand jury, charging an individual with a criminal offense.

TREATY An agreement between two or more nations for the benefit of the general public.

Wilson v. Girard

U.S. Secretary of Defense (P) v. U.S. soldier (D)

354 U.S. 524 (1957).

NATURE OF CASE: Appeal from an injunction against extradition.

FACT SUMMARY: Girard (D), a Specialist Third Class in the United States Army, wounded a Japanese woman during a military exercise in Japan. Japan indicted Girard (D) for causing death by wounding, but Girard (D) was granted an injunction against his delivery to the Japanese authorities.

🏛 RULE OF LAW
A sovereign nation has exclusive jurisdiction to punish offenses against its laws committed within its borders, unless it expressly or impliedly consents to surrender its jurisdiction.

FACTS: Girard (D), a Specialist Third Class in the United States Army, wounded a Japanese woman during a military exercise in Japan. A security treaty between Japan and the United States authorized the making of administrative agreements between the two governments concerning the conditions that would govern the disposition of the United States Armed Forces in Japan. Such an agreement provided that the United States might waive its jurisdiction over offenses committed in Japan by members of its armed forces. Subsequently, another protocol agreement was signed by the two governments, pursuant to the NATO agreement. It authorized that in criminal cases where the right to jurisdiction is concurrent, the military authorities of the United States would have the primary right to exercise jurisdiction over members of the armed forces for offenses arising out of any act or omission done in the performance of official duty. The United States claimed the right to try Girard (D) on the ground that his act was done in the performance of official duty giving the United States primary jurisdiction. Japan insisted that Girard's (D) action was not within the scope of his official duty and therefore it had the primary right of jurisdiction. The United States ultimately waived whatever jurisdiction it might have. Girard (D) sought a writ of habeas corpus that was denied, but he was granted an injunction against delivery to the Japanese authorities. Wilson (P), Secretary of Defense, appealed.

ISSUE: Does a sovereign nation have exclusive jurisdiction to punish offenses against its laws committed within its borders, unless it expressly or impliedly consents to surrender its jurisdiction?

HOLDING AND DECISION: (Per curiam) Yes. A sovereign nation has exclusive jurisdiction to punish offenses against it committed within its borders, unless it expressly or impliedly consents to surrender its jurisdiction. Japan's cession to the United States of jurisdiction to try American military personnel for conduct constituting an offense against the laws of both countries was conditioned by the protocol agreement, which provided that "the authorities of the state having the primary right shall give sympathetic consideration to a request from the authorities of the other state for a waiver of its right in cases where that other state considers such a waiver to be of particular importance." Furthermore, there has been no prohibition against this under the Constitution or legislation subsequent to the security treaty. In the absence of such statutory or constitutional barriers, the wisdom of the arrangement is exclusively for the determination of the executive and legislative branches. These branches have decided to waive jurisdiction and deliver Girard (D) to the Japanese authorities. Therefore, the judgment of the district court is reversed.

▶ ANALYSIS

The trend toward granting limited immunities in cases relating to official acts and archives appears to be on the increase. This is to be distinguished from the normal diplomatic immunities that are part of customary international law. The agreements between the United States and Japan are good examples of the willingness of one nation to grant a special position to foreign government employees.

■▬■

Quicknotes

EXTRADITION The surrender by one state or nation to another of an individual allegedly guilty of committing a crime in that area.

INJUNCTION A court order requiring a person to do or prohibiting that person from doing a specific act.

TREATY An agreement between two or more nations for the benefit of the general public.

WAIVER The intentional or voluntary forfeiture of a recognized right.

WRIT OF HABEAS CORPUS A proceeding in which a defendant brings a writ to compel a judicial determination of whether he is lawfully being held in custody.

■▬■

Immunity from Jurisdiction

Quick Reference Rules of Law

The Schooner Exchange v. McFaddon

Government (D) v. Claimants (P)

11 U.S. (7 Cranch) 116 (1812).

NATURE OF CASE: Appeal from reversal of dismissal of claim of ownership.

FACT SUMMARY: Two Americans (P) claimed that they owned and were entitled to possession of the schooner Exchange.

 RULE OF LAW
National ships of war entering the port of a friendly power are to be considered as exempted by the consent of that power from its jurisdiction.

FACTS: Two Americans (P) claimed they had seized the schooner Exchange on the high seas and that they now owned it and were entitled to possession of the ship. The United States Attorney (D) claimed that the United States and France were at peace and that a public ship of the Emperor of France had been compelled by bad weather to enter the port of Philadelphia and was prevented by leaving by process of the court. The district court granted the United States' (D) request to dismiss the claims of ownership and ordered that the ship be released. The circuit court reversed, and the United States (D) appealed to the U.S. Supreme Court.

ISSUE: Are national ships of war entering the port of a friendly power to be considered as exempted by the consent of that power from its jurisdiction?

HOLDING AND DECISION: (Marshall, C.J.) Yes. National ships of war entering the port of a friendly power are to be considered as exempted by the consent of that power from its jurisdiction. The jurisdiction of the nation within its own territory is exclusive and absolute. The Exchange, a public armed ship, in the service of a foreign sovereign, with whom the United States is at peace, and having entered an American port open for her reception, must be considered to have come into the American territory, under an implied promise, that while necessarily within it, and demeaning herself in a friendly manner, she should be exempt from the jurisdiction of the country. Reversed.

▶ ANALYSIS

This case implicated the absolute form of sovereign immunity from judicial jurisdiction. The Court highlighted three principles: the exemption of the person of the sovereign from arrest or detention within a foreign country; the immunity that all civilized nations allow to foreign ministers; that a sovereign is understood to cede a portion of his territorial jurisdiction when he allows troops of a foreign prince to pass through his dominions.

Quicknotes

JURISDICTION The authority of a court to hear and declare judgment in respect to a particular matter.

SOVEREIGN IMMUNITY Immunity of government from suit without its consent.

Argentine Republic v. Amerada Hess Shipping Corp.

Country at war (D) v. Foreign corporations (P)

488 U.S. 428 (1989).

NATURE OF CASE: Review of reversal of dismissal of action seeking damages for property destruction.

FACT SUMMARY: A pair of Liberian corporations (P) sought to sue the Argentine Republic (D) in U.S. courts under the Alien Tort Statute.

RULE OF LAW
The Alien Tort Statute does not confer jurisdiction over foreign states.

FACTS: United Carriers, Inc. (P), a Liberian corporation, chartered a vessel called the Hercules to Amerada Hess Shipping Corporation (P), another Liberian corporation. The ship was to be used to transport fuel. While off the South American coast during the 1983 Falkland Islands War, it was irreparably damaged and had to be scuttled. United (P) and Amerada (P) sued Argentina (D) in U.S. district court. The court dismissed, holding jurisdiction to be absent. The Second Circuit reversed, holding that jurisdiction existed under the Alien Tort Statute of 1789. The U.S. Supreme Court granted review.

ISSUE: Does the Alien Tort Statute confer jurisdiction over foreign states?

HOLDING AND DECISION: (Rehnquist, C.J.) No. The Alien Tort Statute does not confer jurisdiction over foreign states. The statute confers jurisdiction in district courts over suits brought by aliens in tort for violations of international law or U.S. treaties. The law, as an initial matter, is silent as to whether it applies to suits against foreign states. More importantly, in 1976, Congress enacted the Foreign Sovereign Immunities Act (FSIA), which dealt in a comprehensive manner with the issue of jurisdiction over foreign states. The law provides that, except as provided in the Act, foreign states shall be immune from U.S. courts' jurisdiction. While the FSIA does not explicitly repeal the Alien Tort Statute to the extent that it may confer jurisdiction over a foreign state, it is clear that this was an intent behind the FSIA. This being so, the FSIA can be the only source of jurisdiction over a foreign state. Reversed.

▶ ANALYSIS

The main focus of the FSIA appears to be commercial. There are a variety of commercial activities that occur outside the United States that can lead to a foreign state's being sued in a U.S. court. The same is not true in the tort arena.

Quicknotes

DAMAGES Monetary compensation that may be awarded by the court to a party who has sustained injury or loss to his person, property or rights due to another party's unlawful act, omission, or negligence.

JURISDICTION The authority of a court to hear and declare judgment in respect to a particular matter.

TORT A legal wrong resulting in a breach of duty by the wrongdoer, causing damages as a result of the breach.

Austria v. Altmann

Sovereign (D) v. Art heiress (P)

541 U.S. 677 (2004).

NATURE OF CASE: Appeal from affirmance of denial of motion to dismiss action to determine rightful ownership of art.

FACT SUMMARY: Austria (D) contended that the United States federal courts did not have jurisdiction to hear an action brought by Altmann (P) claiming that valuable art displayed in an Austrian museum was obtained through wrongful conduct by the Nazis during and after World War II and rightfully belonged to her.

🏛 RULE OF LAW

The Foreign Sovereign Immunities Act of 1976 (FSIA) applies to claims that are based on conduct that occurred before the FSIA's enactment and before the United States adopted a "restrictive theory" of sovereign immunity in 1952.

FACTS: Upon learning of evidence that certain of her uncle's valuable art works had either been seized by the Nazis or expropriated by Austria (D) after World War II, Altmann (P) filed an action in federal district court to recover six paintings by Gustav Klimt from Austria (D) and its instrumentality, the Austrian Gallery (Gallery) (D). Altmann (P) claimed that her uncle had bequeathed the paintings to her in his will after he fled Austria (D). Austria (D) and the Gallery (D) moved to dismiss, claiming sovereign immunity. Altmann (P) claimed that the FSIA applied to deny sovereign immunity through an exception for cases in which rights in property have been taken in violation of international law. The district court denied Austria's (D) motion and the court of appeals affirmed. The U.S. Supreme Court granted certiorari.

ISSUE: Does the FSIA apply to claims that are based on conduct that occurred before the FSIA's enactment and before the United States adopted a "restrictive theory" of sovereign immunity in 1952?

HOLDING AND DECISION: (Stevens, J.) Yes. The FSIA applies to claims that are based on conduct that occurred before the FSIA's enactment and before the United States adopted a "restrictive theory" of sovereign immunity in 1952. Foreign sovereign immunity is a matter of grace and comity, rather than a constitutional requirement. Accordingly, the Court has long deferred to Executive Branch sovereign immunity decisions, and until 1952, Executive policy was to request immunity in all actions against friendly sovereigns. In that year, the State Department began to apply the "restrictive theory" of sovereign immunity. Although this change had little impact on federal courts, which continued to abide by the Department's immunity suggestions, the change threw immunity decisions into some disarray.

Foreign nations' diplomatic pressure sometimes prompted the Department to file suggestions of immunity in cases in which immunity would not have been available under the restrictive theory, and when foreign nations failed to ask the Department for immunity, the courts had to determine whether immunity existed, so responsibility for such determinations lay with two different branches. To remedy these problems, Congress enacted the FSIA to codify the restrictive principle and transferred primary responsibility for immunity determinations to the Judicial Branch. The FSIA grants federal courts jurisdiction over civil actions against foreign states and carves out the expropriation and other exceptions to its general grant of immunity. In any such action, the district court's subject matter jurisdiction depends on the applicability of one of those exceptions. Evidence that Congress intended the FSIA to apply to preenactment conduct lies in its preamble's statement that foreign states' immunity "[c]laims . . . should henceforth be decided by [United States] courts . . . in conformity with the principles set forth in this chapter," § 1602. This language is unambiguous and means that immunity "claims"—not actions protected by immunity, but assertions of immunity to suits arising from those actions—are the relevant conduct regulated by the FSIA and are "henceforth" to be decided by the courts. Thus, Congress intended courts to resolve all such claims in conformity with the FSIA's principles regardless of when the underlying conduct occurred. The FSIA's overall structure strongly supports this conclusion, since many of its provisions unquestionably apply to cases arising out of conduct that occurred before 1976, and its procedural provisions undoubtedly apply to all pending cases. In this context, it would be anomalous to presume that an isolated provision (such as the expropriation exception on which respondent relies) is of purely prospective application absent any statutory language to that effect. Finally, applying the FSIA to all pending cases regardless of when the underlying conduct occurred is most consistent with two of the FSIA's principal purposes: clarifying the rules judges should apply in resolving sovereign immunity claims and eliminating political participation in the resolution of such claims. This holding does not prevent the State Department from filing statements of interest suggesting that courts decline to exercise jurisdiction in particular cases implicating foreign sovereign immunity. Nor does the holding express an opinion on whether deference should be granted such filings in cases covered by the FSIA. Instead, the issue resolved by the holding here concerns only the interpretation of the FSIA's reach—a "pure question of statutory construction . . . well within the province of the Judiciary." Affirmed.

Continued on next page.

▶ *ANALYSIS*

Under the "restrictive theory," immunity is recognized with regard to a foreign state's sovereign or public acts (*jure imperii*), but not its private acts (*jure gestionis*). This theory "restricts" the classical or absolute theory of sovereign immunity, under which a sovereign cannot, without his consent, be made a respondent in the courts of another sovereign.

■━━■

Quicknotes

CERTIORARI A discretionary writ issued by a superior court to an inferior court in order to review the lower court's decisions; the Supreme Court's writ ordering such review.

COMITY A rule pursuant to which courts in one state give deference to the statutes and judicial decisions of the court of another state.

INTERNATIONAL LAW The body of law applicable to dealings between nations.

SOVEREIGN IMMUNITY Immunity of government from suit without its consent.

■━━■

Siderman de Blake v. Republic of Argentina

Property owner and torture victim (P) v. Sovereign (D)

965 F.2d 699 (9th Cir. 1992).

NATURE OF CASE: Appeal from a judgment dismissing torture claims lodged against the government of another country.

FACT SUMMARY: After the military regime governing Argentina (D) tortured Jose Siderman (P) and threatened his family with death, the Sidermans (P) fled to the United States, later filing this complaint for damages due to the torture and for the expropriation of their property.

🏛 RULE OF LAW
The right to be free from official torture is fundamental and universal, a right deserving of the highest status under international law.

FACTS: After the Argentine (D) military regime subjected Jose Siderman (P) to seven days of torture, during which they shouted anti-Semitic epithets at him, they left him in an isolated area, threatening his family with death unless they left Argentina (D) immediately. Forced to sell an interest in 127,000 acres of land at a steep discount in order to finance their flight, the Sidermans (P) came to the United States. Argentine (D) military officials diverted to themselves the profits and revenues from the Sidermans' (P) corporation, INOSA. The Sidermans (P) filed this complaint, alleging torture and expropriation of their property. When Argentina (D) did not appear, the court entered a default judgment for the Sidermans (P) on the torture claim but dismissed the expropriation claims. The district court later vacated the default judgment, dismissing the action on the grounds of Argentina's (D) immunity under the Foreign Sovereign Immunity Act (FSIA). The Sidermans (P) appealed.

ISSUE: Is the right to be free from official torture fundamental and universal, a right deserving of the highest status under international law?

HOLDING AND DECISION: [Judge not stated in casebook excerpt.] Yes. The right to be free from official torture is fundamental and universal, a right deserving of the highest status under international law. The record reveals no ground for shielding Argentina (D) from the Sidermans' (P) claims that their family business was stolen from them by the military junta. It further suggests that Argentina (D) has implicitly waived its sovereign immunity with respect to the Sidermans' (P) claims for torture. Thus, the district court erred in dismissing the Sidermans' (P) torture claims. Reversed and remanded.

▌ ANALYSIS

While not all customary international law carries with it the force of a *jus cogens* norm, which is derived from values taken to be fundamental by the international community, the prohibition against official torture has attained that status. Thus, under international law, any state that engages in official torture violates a *jus cogens* norm. The court concluded, however, that if violations of a *jus cogens* norm committed outside the United States were to be exceptions to immunity, Congress must make them so. The fact that there had been a violation of a *jus cogens* norm did not confer jurisdiction under the FSIA.

Quicknotes

JUS COGENS NORM Universally understood principles of international law that cannot be set aside because they are based on fundamental human values.

SOVEREIGN IMMUNITY Immunity of government from suit without its consent.

Republic of Argentina v. Weltover, Inc

Bond issuer (D) v. Bond holders (P)

504 U.S. 607 (1992).

NATURE OF CASE: Review of denial of dismissal of action for breach of contract.

FACT SUMMARY: Argentina (D) contended that it could not be sued in a U.S. court for defaulting on bonds it had issued.

RULE OF LAW
A foreign government may be amenable to suit in a U.S. court for defaulting on its bonds.

FACTS: Due to currency instability, Argentine businesses often had trouble participating in foreign transactions. The Argentine government (D), to ameliorate this problem, instituted a program wherein it agreed to sell to domestic borrowers U.S. dollars in exchange for Argentine currency. The dollars could be used to pay foreign creditors of Argentine businesses. Argentina (D) issued bonds, called "Bonods," to reflect its obligations. In 1986, Argentina (D), facing a shortage of reserves of U.S. dollars, defaulted on bond payments. Several bond holders (P), who collectively owned $1.3 million worth of bonds payable in New York, sued for breach of contract in federal court in New York. Argentina (D) moved to dismiss, asserting sovereign immunity. The district court denied the motion, and the Second Circuit affirmed. The U.S. Supreme Court granted review.

ISSUE: May a foreign government be amenable to suit in a U.S. court for defaulting on its bonds?

HOLDING AND DECISION: (Scalia, J.) Yes. A foreign government may be amenable to suit in a U.S. court for defaulting on its bonds. The Foreign Sovereign Immunities Act of 1976 creates an exception to foreign sovereign immunity "commercial" activities. For purposes of the FSIA, an activity falls within the exception if (1) it occurs outside the United States, (2) is in connection with commerce, and (3) causes a direct effect in the United States. Here, the first element without question has been satisfied. Whether a government's activity is "commercial" must be determined with reference to the nature of the act. The issuing of a bond is a commercial rather than a sovereign act—private concerns can and often do issue bonds; it is not an activity given only to sovereigns. Finally, an effect is "direct" if an effect is the natural and immediate consequence of the activity in question. Here, the effect in the United States was direct because the bonds were payable in New York, so the breach occurred there. In sum, the activities of Argentina (D) with respect to the bonds were commercial in nature, so the commercial activity exception to the FSIA applies. Affirmed.

► ANALYSIS

The key to determining if the commercial activity exception applies in any given case is whether the government has entered the marketplace. If it has, it is to be treated, under the FSIA, as a private player. If it undertakes an activity peculiar to a sovereign, the exception does not apply.

◼━◼

Quicknotes

BOND A debt instrument issued by the issuing entity evidencing a promise to repay the loan with a specified amount of interest on a particular date.

BREACH OF CONTRACT Unlawful failure by a party to perform its obligations pursuant to contract.

SOVEREIGN IMMUNITY Immunity of government from suit without its consent.

◼━◼

Saudi Arabia v. Nelson

Host country (D) v. Foreign citizen (P)

507 U.S. 349 (1993).

NATURE OF CASE: Appeal from a judgment for the plaintiff in a personal injury action against a sovereign government.

FACT SUMMARY: Saudi Arabia (D) claimed foreign sovereign immunity from the subject-matter jurisdiction of the federal courts after Nelson (P) filed suit against it, alleging wrongful arrest, imprisonment, and torture.

🏛 RULE OF LAW
Foreign states are entitled to immunity from the jurisdiction of courts in the United States, unless the action is based upon a commercial activity in the manner of a private player within the market.

FACTS: Nelson (P) was recruited in the United States for employment as a monitoring systems engineer at a hospital in Riyadh, Saudi Arabia (D). When Nelson (P) discovered safety defects in the hospital's oxygen and nitrous oxide lines, he repeatedly advised hospital officials of the defects and reported them to a Saudi government (D) commission as well. Hospital officials instructed Nelson (P) to ignore the problems. Several months later, he was called in to the hospital's security office, arrested, and transported to a jail cell, where he was shackled, tortured, beaten, and kept without food for four days. After thirty-nine days, the Saudi government (D) released Nelson (P), allowing him to leave the country. Nelson (P) and his wife (P) filed this action in the United States, seeking damages for personal injury. They also claimed a basis for recovery in Saudi Arabia's (D) failure to warn Nelson (P) of the hidden dangers associated with his employment. The Saudi government (D) appealed the judgment of the court of appeals.

ISSUE: Are foreign states entitled to immunity from the jurisdiction of courts in the United States, unless the action is based upon a commercial activity in the manner of a private player within the market?

HOLDING AND DECISION: (Souter, J.) Yes. Foreign states are entitled to immunity from the jurisdiction of courts in the United States, unless the action is based upon a commercial activity in the manner of a private player within the market. Saudi Arabia's (D) tortious conduct in this case fails to qualify as "commercial activity" within the meaning of the Foreign Sovereign Immunities Act of 1976. Its conduct boils down to abuse of the power of its police by the Saudi government (D). A foreign state's exercise of the power of its police is peculiarly sovereign in nature and is not the sort of activity engaged in by private parties. Furthermore, Nelson's (P)

failure to warn claim must also fail; sovereign nations have no duty to warn of their propensity for tortious conduct. The Nelsons' (P) action is not based upon a commercial activity within the meaning of the Act and therefore is outside the subject-matter jurisdiction of the federal courts. Motion to dismiss is granted. Reversed.

CONCURRENCE: (White, J.) Neither the hospital's employment practices nor its disciplinary procedures have any apparent connection to this country. Absent a nexus to the United States, the Act does not grant the Nelsons (P) access to our courts.

DISSENT: (Stevens, J.) If the same activities had been performed by a private business, jurisdiction would be upheld.

▶ ANALYSIS

Under the "restrictive," as opposed to the "absolute," theory of foreign sovereign immunity, a state is immune from the jurisdiction of foreign courts as to its sovereign or public acts but not as to those that are private or commercial in character. A state engages in commercial activity under the restrictive theory where it exercises only those powers that can also be exercised by private citizens, as distinct from those powers peculiar to sovereigns. Whether a state acts in the manner of a private party is a question of behavior, not motivation. While it is difficult to distinguish the purpose of conduct from its nature, the Court recognized that the Act unmistakably commands it to observe the distinction.

◼▬◼

Quicknotes

FAILURE TO WARN The failure of an owner or occupier of land to inform persons present on the property of defects or active operations that may cause injury.

JURISDICTION The authority of a court to hear and declare judgment in respect to a particular matter.

SOVEREIGN IMMUNITY Immunity of government from suit without its consent.

◼▬◼

Permanent Mission of India to the United Nations v. City of New York

Sovereign's permanent mission (D) v. Municipality (P)

551 U.S. 193 (2007).

NATURE OF CASE: Appeal from affirmance of decision denying immunity from declaratory judgment action to establish the validity of tax liens.

FACT SUMMARY: India (D) and Mongolia (D) contended that they were immune under the Foreign Sovereign Immunities Act from New York City's (City) (P) action seeking declaratory judgments that tax liens the City (P) had on buildings owned by India (D) and Mongolia (D) were valid to the extent the buildings were used to house diplomatic employees.

🏛️ **RULE OF LAW**

The Foreign Sovereign Immunities Act of 1976 (FSIA) does not immunize a foreign government from a lawsuit to declare the validity of tax liens on property held by the sovereign for the purpose of housing its employees.

FACTS: India (D) and Mongolia (D) owned buildings in New York City (City) (P) that in part were used to house lower-level diplomatic employees. Under New York law, real property owned by a foreign government is exempt from taxation when used exclusively for diplomatic offices or quarters for ambassadors or ministers plenipotentiary to the United Nations. For years, the City (P) levied property taxes against India (D) and Mongolia (D) for that portion of their diplomatic office buildings used to house lower-level employees and their families, but the governments (D) refused to pay the taxes. By operation of state law, the unpaid taxes converted into tax liens held by the City (P) against the properties. The City (P) filed a state-court suit seeking declaratory judgments to establish the liens' validity, but the governments (D) removed the cases to federal court, where they argued that they were immune under the FSIA, which is "the sole basis for obtaining jurisdiction over a foreign state in federal court." The district court disagreed, relying on a FSIA exception withdrawing a foreign state's immunity from jurisdiction where "rights in immovable property situated in the United States are in issue." The court of appeals affirmed, holding that the "immovable property" exception applied, and thus the district court had jurisdiction over the City's (P) suits. The U.S. Supreme Court granted certiorari.

ISSUE: Does the FSIA immunize a foreign government from a lawsuit to declare the validity of tax liens on property held by the sovereign for the purpose of housing its employees?

HOLDING AND DECISION: (Thomas, J.) No. The FSIA does not immunize a foreign government from a lawsuit to declare the validity of tax liens on property held by the sovereign for the purpose of housing its employees. Under the FSIA, a foreign state is presumptively immune from suit unless a specific exception applies. In determining the immovable property exception's scope, the Court begins, as always, with the statute's text. Section 1605(a)(4) of the FSIA does not expressly limit itself to cases in which the specific right at issue is title, ownership, or possession, nor does it specifically exclude cases in which a lien's validity is at issue. Rather, it focuses more broadly on "rights in" property. At the time of the FSIA's adoption, "lien" was defined as a "charge or security or incumbrance upon property," and "incumbrance" was defined as "[a]ny right to, or interest in, land which may subsist in another to the diminution of its value." New York law defines "tax lien" in accordance with these general definitions. A lien's practical effects bear out the definitions of liens as interests in property. Because a lien on real property runs with the land and is enforceable against subsequent purchasers, a tax lien inhibits a quintessential property ownership right—the right to convey. It is thus plain that a suit to establish a tax lien's validity implicates "rights in immovable property." Such an interpretation is supported by two of the FSIA's purposes: adoption of the restrictive view of sovereign immunity and codification of international law at the time of the FSIA's enactment. First, property ownership is not an inherently sovereign function. Moreover, the FSIA was intended to codify the preexisting real property exception to sovereign immunity recognized by international practice. That practice supports the City's (P) view that India (D) and Mongolia (D) are not immune, as does the contemporaneous restatement of foreign relations law. That restatement stated that a foreign sovereign's immunity does not extend to "an action to obtain possession of or establish a property interest in immovable property located in the territory of the state exercising jurisdiction." Restatement (Second) of Foreign Relations Law of the United States § 68(b), p. 205 (1965). Because an action seeking the declaration of the validity of a tax lien on property is a suit to establish an interest in such property, such an action would be allowed under this rule. Affirmed and remanded.

DISSENT: (Stevens, J.) The true dispute in this case is over a foreign sovereign's tax liability—not about the

Continued on next page.

validity of the City's (P) lien. Had Congress intended to waive sovereign immunity in tax litigation, it would have said as much.

▶ *ANALYSIS*

Even if the tax liens in this case are declared valid, India (D) and Mongolia (D) would be immune from foreclosure proceedings. Nevertheless, the benefit to the City (P) of having the liens validated is that once a court has declared property tax liens valid, foreign sovereigns traditionally concede and pay. Even if the foreign sovereign fails to pay in the face of a valid court judgment, that country's foreign aid may be reduced by the United States by 110 percent of the outstanding debt. Finally, the liens would be enforceable against subsequent purchasers.

■■■■

Quicknotes

CERTIORARI A discretionary writ issued by a superior court to an inferior court in order to review the lower court's decisions; the Supreme Court's writ ordering such review.

LIEN A claim against the property of another in order to secure the payment of a debt.

SOVEREIGN IMMUNITY Immunity of government from suit without its consent.

■■■■

Argentine Republic v. Amerada Hess Shipping Corp.

Country at war (D) v. Foreign corporations (P)

488 U.S. 428 (1989).

NATURE OF CASE: Review of reversal of dismissal of action seeking damages for property destruction.

FACT SUMMARY: A pair of Liberian corporations (P) sought to sue the Argentine Republic (D) in U.S. courts under the Alien Tort Statute.

🏛 RULE OF LAW
The Foreign Sovereign Immunities Act's (FSIA) exception for noncommercial torts does not apply to acts occurring on the high seas.

FACTS: United Carriers, Inc. (P), a Liberian corporation, chartered a vessel called the Hercules to Amerada Hess Shipping Corporation (P), another Liberian corporation. The ship was to be used to transport fuel. While off the South American coast during the 1983 Falkland Islands War, it was irreparably damaged and had to be scuttled. United (P) and Amerada (P) sued Argentina (D) in U.S. district court. The court dismissed, holding jurisdiction to be absent. The Second Circuit reversed, holding that jurisdiction existed under the Alien Tort Statute of 1789. The U.S. Supreme Court granted review.

ISSUE: Does the FSIA's exception for noncommercial torts apply to acts occurring on the high seas?

HOLDING AND DECISION: (Rehnquist, C.J.) No. The FSIA's exception for noncommercial torts does not apply to acts occurring on the high seas. The FSIA is the only source of jurisdiction over a foreign state. The only exception to immunity found in the statute that even arguably applies here is that involving noncommercial torts. However, this exception only applies to torts occurring in the United States. As the tort here occurred on the high seas, the exception does not apply. Since no section of the FSIA applies here, jurisdiction over Argentina (D) does not exist. Reversed.

▌ ANALYSIS

The main focus of the FSIA appears to be commercial. There are a variety of commercial activities that occur outside the United States that can lead to a foreign state's being sued in a U.S. court. The same is not true in the tort arena.

Quicknotes

JURISDICTION The authority of a court to hear and declare judgment in respect to a particular matter.

TORT A legal wrong resulting in a breach of duty by the wrongdoer, causing damages as a result of the breach.

Gates v. Syrian Arab Republic

Beheading victim's mother (P) v. Sovereign (D)

580 F. Supp. 2d 53 (D.D.C. 2008).

NATURE OF CASE: Claims brought under state law and the Foreign Sovereign Immunities Act (FSIA) against a sovereign and its principals for money damages for terrorist acts committed by an organization supported by the sovereign.

FACT SUMMARY: Families (P) of U.S. civilian contractors, Armstrong and Hensley, who were beheaded by al-Qaeda in Iraq, claimed that the Syrian Arab Republic (Syria) (D), its president (D), and its intelligence minister (D) were liable under the FSIA for money damages for the beheadings because Syria (D) actively and knowingly supported al-Qaeda in Iraq.

🏛 RULE OF LAW

(1) State-law claims must be dismissed where plaintiffs assert that they are victims of state-sponsored terrorism.

(2) A sovereign may be held liable under the FSIA's state-sponsored terrorism exception where it is shown that terrorist acts against U.S. citizens were committed by terrorists knowingly supported by the sovereign to advance the sovereign's policy objectives.

(3) Money damages for economic damages, solatium, pain and suffering, and punitive damages may be awarded under the FSIA against a state sponsor of terrorism for outrageous acts of terrorism against U.S. citizens committed by terrorists supported by the state sponsor.

FACTS: Al-Tawhid wal-Jihad ("al-Qaeda in Iraq") beheaded U.S. civilian contractors Armstrong and Hensley, and their families (P) brought suit against the Syrian Arab Republic (Syria) (D), its president (D), and its intelligence minister (D), seeking damages under the FSIA and asserting state-law claims for battery, assault, false imprisonment, intentional infliction of emotional distress, wrongful death, survival damages, conspiracy, and aiding and abetting. The plaintiffs alleged that Syria (D), acting through the principals named as defendants, provided material support and resources to al-Qaeda in Iraq and its leader, Zarqawi. Because none of the defendants filed an answer or otherwise appeared, the court proceeded to a default setting, which under the FSIA requires the entry of a default judgment against a non-responding foreign state where the claimant proves its case to the court's satisfaction. The court, after reviewing the evidence presented, concluded that support for Zarqawi and his al-Qaeda network from Syrian territory or Syrian government actors could not have been accomplished without the authorization of the Syrian government

and its military intelligence. The court then addressed the issue of whether Syria (D) could be held liable for money damages under the FSIA for the beheadings of Armstrong and Hensley.

ISSUE:

(1) Must state-law claims be dismissed where plaintiffs assert that they are victims of state-sponsored terrorism?

(2) May a sovereign be held liable under the FSIA's state-sponsored terrorism exception where it is shown that terrorist acts against U.S. citizens were committed by terrorists knowingly supported by the sovereign to advance the sovereign's policy objectives?

(3) May money damages for economic damages, solatium, pain and suffering, and punitive damages be awarded under the FSIA against a state sponsor of terrorism for outrageous acts of terrorism against U.S. citizens committed by terrorists supported by the state sponsor?

HOLDING AND DECISION: [Judge not stated in casebook excerpt.]

(1) Yes. State-law claims must be dismissed where plaintiffs assert that they are victims of state-sponsored terrorism. Under FSIA § 1605A(c), U.S. citizens who are victims of state-sponsored terrorism can sue a responsible foreign state directly. Thus, Congress has provided the "specific source of law" for recovery and has thereby eliminated the inconsistencies arising under state law in such cases. Here, the families (P) effectively brought suit only against Syria (D) because they claimed that all the named defendants should be treated as the foreign state itself. The only cause of action permissible against Syria (D) is a federal cause of action under the FSIA, and the state-law claims must be dismissed.

(2) Yes. A sovereign may be held liable under the FSIA's state-sponsored terrorism exception where it is shown that terrorist acts against U.S. citizens were committed by terrorists knowingly supported by the sovereign to advance the sovereign's policy objectives. Here, it has been shown to the court's satisfaction that it was Syria's (D) foreign policy to support al-Qaeda in Iraq in order to topple the nascent Iraqi democratic government and thwart the U.S. invasion of Iraq. Syria's (D) aid to Zarqawi for at least three years was not unknowing, and, given prior acts of terrorism against civilians by al-Qaeda in Iraq, it was foreseeable that Zarqawi and his terrorist organization would again engage in such acts. Thus, the murders of Armstrong and Hensley were a foreseeable consequence of Syria's (D) aid and support to Zarqawi

Continued on next page.

and al-Qaeda in Iraq, and there is jurisdiction over Syria (D) to support damages under the FSIA.

(3) Yes. Money damages for economic damages, solatium, pain and suffering, and punitive damages may be awarded under the FSIA against a state sponsor of terrorism for outrageous acts of terrorism against U.S. citizens committed by terrorists supported by the state sponsor. Damages for a private action for proven acts of terrorism by foreign states under the FSIA § 1605A(c) may include economic damages, solatium, pain and suffering, and punitive damages. The amount of punitive damages awarded for personal injury or death resulting from an act of state-sponsored terrorism depends on the nature of the injury, the character of the terrorist act, the need for deterrence, and the wealth of the state sponsor. As with other punitive damages, the goal is to punish those who engage in outrageous conduct and to deter others from engaging in similar conduct. Additionally, if several large punitive damages awards issue against a foreign state sponsor of terrorism, the state's financial capacity to provide funding will be curtailed. Therefore, default judgment is entered against Syria (D) in the following amounts: For the Armstrong family: economic damages of $1,051,377; pain and suffering of $50,000,000; punitive damages of $150,000,000; and solatium of $4,500,000. For the Hensley family: economic damages of $1,358,210; pain and suffering of $50,000,000; punitive damages of $150,000,000; and solatium of $6,000,000.

▶ ANALYSIS

The damages provision used by the court to award various money damages in this case, § 1605A(c), was enacted in 2008 in an effort by Congress to assist victims in satisfying their judgments against state sponsors of terrorism as well as to clarify that the cause of action provided in the terrorist-state exception applies not only to agents, employees, or officials of the state sponsor, but also applies to the state itself.

■■■

Quicknotes

PUNITIVE DAMAGES Damages exceeding the actual injury suffered for the purposes of punishment of the defendant, deterrence of the wrongful behavior or comfort to the plaintiff.

SOLATIUM Damages awarded in order to provide solace to the victim or to otherwise compensate for emotional injury.

■■■

Dole Food Company v. Patrickson

Corporation (D) v. Food worker (P)

538 U.S. 468 (2003).

NATURE OF CASE: Appeal from judgment denying removal to federal district court to foreign corporations impleaded in a state-court tort action.

FACT SUMMARY: Dead Sea Bromine Co. and Bromine Compounds, Ltd. (collectively, the Dead Sea Companies (D)), which were impleaded by Dole Food Company and others (Dole petitioners) (D) in a state-court tort action, contended that as subsidiaries of an instrumentality of Israel they were entitled to remove the case to federal district court under the Foreign Sovereign Immunities Act of 1976 (FSIA).

🏛 RULE OF LAW
(1) Under the FSIA, a state must own a majority of the shares of a corporation if the corporation is to be deemed an instrumentality of the state.
(2) Instrumentality status under the FSIA is determined at the time the complaint is filed.

FACTS: Farm workers (P) filed a state-court action against Dole Food Company and others (Dole petitioners) (D), alleging injury from chemical exposure. The Dole petitioners (D) impleaded Dead Sea Bromine Co. and Bromine Compounds, Ltd. (collectively, the Dead Sea Companies (D)). As to the Dead Sea Companies (D), the court of appeals rejected their claim that they were instrumentalities of a foreign state (Israel) as defined by the FSIA, and that they were therefore entitled to removal to federal district court. The court instead ruled that a subsidiary of an instrumentality is not itself entitled to instrumentality status. The U.S. Supreme Court granted certiorari.

ISSUE:
(1) Under the FSIA, must a state own a majority of the shares of a corporation if the corporation is to be deemed an instrumentality of the state?
(2) Is instrumentality status under the FSIA determined at the time the complaint is filed?

HOLDING AND DECISION: (Kennedy, J.)
(1) Yes. Under the FSIA, a state must own a majority of the shares of a corporation if the corporation is to be deemed an instrumentality of the state. Removal of actions against foreign states is governed by 28 U.S.C. § 1441(d). Section 1603(a) of the FSIA defines "foreign state" to include its "instrumentality," which in turn is defined, in part, as any entity "which is a . . . corporat[ion]" whose shares are majority-owned by the foreign state, and that is not a U.S. citizen or created under

the laws of a third country. Thus, the issue is whether the Dead Sea Companies (D) were an instrumentality of Israel. Israel did not have any direct ownership of shares in these companies, which were separated from Israel by one or more intermediate corporate tiers. Therefore, the Dead Sea Companies (D) were only indirect subsidiaries of Israel. They do not satisfy the FSIA requirement that the state own a "majority" of the shares of the corporation to qualify for instrumentality status. Only direct ownership satisfies the statutory requirement. In issues of corporate law structure often matters. The statutory reference to ownership of "shares" shows that Congress intended coverage to turn on formal corporate ownership. As a corporation and its shareholders are distinct entities, a corporate parent that owns a subsidiary's shares does not, for that reason alone, own or have legal title to the subsidiary's assets; and, it follows with even greater force, the parent does not own or have legal title to the subsidiary's subsidiaries. The veil separating corporations and their shareholders may be pierced in certain exceptional circumstances, but the Dead Sea Companies (D) refer to no authority for extending the doctrine so far that, as a categorical matter, all subsidiaries are deemed to be the same as the parent corporation. Affirmed as to this issue.
(2) Yes. Instrumentality status under the FSIA is determined at the time the complaint is filed. The plain language of FSIA § 1603(b)(2), which requires that a corporation show that it is an entity "a majority of whose shares . . . is owned by a foreign state," and is expressed in the present tense, requires that instrumentality status be determined at the time the action is filed. Here, any relationship recognized under the FSIA between the Dead Sea Companies (D) and Israel had been severed before suit was commenced, so the companies would not be entitled to instrumentality status even if their theory that such status could be conferred on a subsidiary were accepted. Affirmed as to this issue. Affirmed.

▶ ANALYSIS

Under corporate law principles, which the Court looked to in this case, the fact that Israel might have exercised considerable control over the Dead Sea Companies (D) would not have changed the outcome of the Court's decision, since control and ownership are distinct concepts, and it is majority ownership by a foreign state, not control, that is the benchmark of instrumentality status.

∎≡∎

Continued on next page.

Quicknotes

CERTIORARI A discretionary writ issued by a superior court to an inferior court in order to review the lower court's decisions; the Supreme Court's writ ordering such review.

IMPLEADER Procedure by which a third party, who may be liable for all or part of liability, is joined to an action so that all issues may be resolved in a single suit.

■━━■

First National City Bank v. Banco Para El Comercio Exterior de Cuba

American bank (D) v. Cuban state bank (P)

462 U.S. 611 (1983).

NATURE OF CASE: Review of suit to collect on a letter of credit and counterclaim for a setoff.

FACT SUMMARY: First National City Bank (now Citibank) (D) claimed that it could set off the value of its seized assets in Cuba against a claim by Banco Para El Comercio Exterior de Cuba (Bancec) (P) for payment on a letter of credit issued before the Cuban government nationalized all assets.

🏛 RULE OF LAW
The Foreign Sovereign Immunities Act of 1976 (FSIA) does not affect the attribution of liability among instrumentalities of a foreign state.

FACTS: The Cuban government established Bancec (P) in 1960 and later sued Citibank (D) on a letter of credit. Cuba then seized all of Citibank's (D) assets in Cuba. The Cuban government was later substituted as plaintiff when Bancec (P) was declared dissolved. Citibank (D) counterclaimed, asserting a right to set off the value of its seized Cuban assets. Bancec (P) claimed it was immune from suit as an instrumentality owned by a foreign government under the FSIA. The U.S. Supreme Court granted certiorari.

ISSUE: Does the FSIA affect the attribution of liability among instrumentalities of a foreign state?

HOLDING AND DECISION: (O'Connor, J.) No. The FSIA does not affect the attribution of liability among instrumentalities of a foreign state. The FSIA is not intended to affect the substantive law of liability. When a foreign sovereign asserts a claim in a United States court the consideration of fair dealing bars the state from asserting a defense of sovereign immunity to defeat a setoff or counterclaim. Citibank (D) may set off the value of its assets seized by the Cuban government against the amount sought by Bancec (P).

▶ ANALYSIS

The court here first dismissed the notion that the Cuban bank could claim sovereign immunity. Then it applied principle of both international and federal common law. Under the Cuban Assets Control Regulations, any judgment entered in favor of an instrumentality of the Cuban government would be frozen pending settlement of claims between the U.S. and Cuba.

■■■

Quicknotes

CERTIORARI A discretionary writ issued by a superior court to an inferior court in order to review the lower court's decisions; the Supreme Court's writ ordering such review.

LETTER OF CREDIT An agreement by a bank or other party that it will honor a customer's demand for payment upon the satisfaction of specified conditions.

NATIONALIZATION Government acquisition of a private enterprise.

SETOFF A claim made pursuant to a counterclaim, arising from a cause of action unrelated to the underlying suit, in which the defendant seeks to have the plaintiff's claim of damages reduced.

■■■

Chuidian v. Philippine National Bank

Client (P) v. Bank (D)

912 F.2d 1095 (9th Cir. 1990).

NATURE OF CASE: Action to determine sovereign immunity.

FACT SUMMARY: Chuidian (P) sued Daza (D), an official of the Philippine government, after Daza (D) instructed a Philippine bank not to honor a letter of credit issued by the Republic of the Philippines to Chuidian (P).

🏛 RULE OF LAW
Foreign officials acting in an official capacity can claim sovereign immunity under the Foreign Sovereign Immunities Act of 1976 (FSIA).

FACTS: Daza (D) was a member of an executive agency created by the Philippine government after the overthrow of former President Marcos. When Daza (D) instructed the Bank not to make payment on a letter of credit issued to Chuidian (P) during Marcos's regime, Chuidian (P) sued. Daza (D) claimed sovereign immunity under the FSIA.

ISSUE: Can foreign officials acting in an official capacity claim sovereign immunity under the Foreign Sovereign Immunities Act of 1976?

HOLDING AND DECISION: [Judge not stated in casebook excerpt.] Yes. Foreign officials acting in an official capacity can claim sovereign immunity under the FSIA. No authority supports the continued validity of the pre-1976 common law in light of the FSIA. It is generally recognized that a suit against an individual acting in his official capacity is the practical equivalent of a suit against the sovereign directly.

▶ ANALYSIS

Most courts have agreed with this decision. Some courts have denied immunity under the Alien Tort Act if human rights abuses are involved. Before the FSIA was enacted, the State Department decided such issues.

■═■

Quicknotes

LETTER OF CREDIT An agreement by a bank or other party that it will honor a customer's demand for payment upon the satisfaction of specified conditions.

SOVEREIGN IMMUNITY Immunity of government from suit without its consent.

■═■

Yousuf v. Samantar

Somali native (P) v. Somali official (D)

552 F.3d 371 (4th Cir. 2009).

NATURE OF CASE:
Appeal from dismissal of action for damages for acts of torture and human rights violations under the Torture Victim Protection Act of 1991.

FACT SUMMARY:
Natives of Somalia (P) brought suit under the Torture Victim Protection Act of 1991 against Samantar (D), claiming that they were victims of acts of torture and human rights violations committed against them by Somali government agents commanded by Samantar (D), who claimed immunity under the Foreign Sovereign Immunities Act (FSIA).

🏛 RULE OF LAW
The FSIA does not apply to individual officials of a foreign state.

FACTS:
Natives of Somalia (P) brought suit under the Torture Victim Protection Act of 1991 against Samantar (D), claiming that they were victims of acts of torture and human rights violations committed against them by Somali government agents commanded by Samantar (D), who claimed immunity under the Foreign Sovereign Immunities Act (FSIA). The district court, following the majority view that individuals acting within the scope of their official duties qualifies them as an "agency or instrumentality of a foreign state" under the FSIA, and finding that Samantar (D) had acted in his official capacity, held that Samantar (D) had immunity from suit, and dismissed the case. The court of appeals granted review.

ISSUE:
Does the FSIA apply to individual officials of a foreign state?

HOLDING AND DECISION:
(Traxler, J.) No. The FSIA does not apply to individual officials of a foreign state. A majority of the courts considering the scope of the meaning of "agency or instrumentality" under the FSIA have concluded that an individual foreign official acting within the scope of his official duties qualifies as an "agency or instrumentality of a foreign state." However, the language and overall structure and purpose of the statute must also be considered. The FSIA defines an "agency or instrumentality" as an "entity" that is a "separate legal person . . . ." The phrase "separate legal person" seems to be drawn from corporate law, which holds that a corporation and its shareholders are distinct entities. If Congress had intended to cover individuals, it could have said so, without using a corporate concept. Thus, the FSIA's use of the phrase suggests that natural persons are not covered thereby. Moreover, in ensuring that an "agency or instrumentality" seeking the benefits of sovereign immunity is

actually connected to a "foreign state," the FSIA requires that the "entity" be "neither a citizen of a State of the United States as defined in § 1332(c) and (e) . . . nor created under the laws of any third country." Sections 1332(c) and (e) govern the citizenship of corporations and legal representatives of estates, and are inapplicable to individuals. Also, it is nonsensical to speak of an individual, rather than a corporate entity, being "created" under the laws of a country. Therefore, these references support the interpretation that natural persons are not covered by the FSIA. Such an interpretation is also consistent with the FSIA's overall statutory scheme. For example, the rules for service of process under the FSIA are strikingly similar to the general procedural rules for service on a corporation or other business entity, and do not contain the rules for service of process on an individual. Finally, the legislative history also supports the interpretation that "an agency or instrumentality of foreign state" cannot be an individual. The House Committee Report on the FSIA explained that "separate legal person" was "intended to include a corporation, association, foundation, or any other entity that, under the law of the foreign state where it was created, can sue or be sued in its own name, contract in its own name or hold property in its own name." Because the FSIA does not apply to individual foreign government agents like Samantar (D), the district court erred that he had immunity. Reversed.

▶ ANALYSIS

One criticism of the approach taken by the court in this case is that since there is little practical difference between a suit against a state and a suit against an individual acting in his official capacity, plaintiffs will be able to circumvent state immunity by suing government officials in their individual capacities, thus undermining one of the FSIA's primary goals.

■≡■

Quicknotes

SOVEREIGN IMMUNITY Immunity of government from suit without its consent.

■≡■

Regina v. Bartle and Commissioner of Police, Ex parte Pinochet

Government (P) v. Former head of state (D)

U.K. House of Lords, 2 W.L.R. 827, 38 I.L.M. 581 (1999).

NATURE OF CASE: Appeal from extradition proceedings.

FACT SUMMARY: Pinochet (D) claimed that he was immune from prosecution as a former head of state.

RULE OF LAW
The notion of continued immunity for former heads of state is inconsistent with the provisions of the Torture Convention.

FACTS: The House of Lords (P) considered charges that Pinochet (D), the former head of state of Chile, had violated the Torture Convention. Chile, Spain, and the United Kingdom were all parties to the Torture Convention, which became law on December 8, 1988. Pinochet (D) claimed he was immune as a former head of state under principle of international law.

ISSUE: Is the notion of continued immunity for former heads of state inconsistent with the provisions of the Torture Convention?

HOLDING AND DECISION: (Lord Browne-Wilkinson) Yes. The notion of continued immunity for former heads of state is inconsistent with the provisions of the Torture Convention. If, as alleged, Pinochet (D) organized and authorized torture after December 8, 1988, he was not acting in any capacity that gives rise to immunity because such conduct was contrary to international law. The torture proceedings should proceed on the allegation that torture in pursuance of a conspiracy to commit torture was being committed by Pinochet (D) after December 1988 when he lost his immunity.

ANALYSIS

The court discussed the common law as well. Under common law, a former head of state enjoys immunity for official acts done while in office. The purpose of the Torture Convention was to provide that there is no safe haven for torturers.

Quicknotes

EXTRADITION The surrender by one state or nation to another of an individual allegedly guilty of committing a crime in that area.

SOVEREIGN IMMUNITY Immunity of government from suit without its consent.

Arrest Warrant of 11 April 2000
(Democratic Republic of the Congo v. Belgium)

Sovereign state (P) v. Sovereign state (D)

I.C.J., 2002 I.C.J. 3.

NATURE OF CASE: Application claiming violations of international law and seeking order of provisional measures of protection relating to an arrest warrant for a sovereign's foreign minister.

FACT SUMMARY: The Democratic Republic of the Congo (D.R.C.) (P) contended that an international arrest warrant for its foreign minister, issued by Belgium (D), violated international law by purporting to exercise jurisdiction over another state's foreign minister, and the D.R.C. (P) sought an order of provisional measures of protection on the ground that the warrant effectively prevented the foreign minister from leaving the D.R.C. (P).

🏛 RULE OF LAW
A state's foreign minister enjoys full immunity from criminal jurisdiction in another state's courts, even where the minister is suspected of humanitarian violations.

FACTS: Under Belgian law, which provided for universal jurisdiction in the case of grave breaches of the Geneva Conventions, crimes against humanity, and other serious offenses, a Belgian judge issued an international arrest warrant for the foreign minister of the D.R.C. (P), seeking his extradition on allegations of grave violations of humanitarian law. Belgian law also provided that any immunity conferred by an individual's official capacity did not prevent application of universal jurisdiction. The Belgian warrant was transmitted to the International Criminal Police Organization (Interpol) and was circulated internationally. The D.R.C. (P) brought an application against Belgium (D) in the International Court of Justice (I.C.J.), asserting that the warrant violated international law by purporting to exercise jurisdiction over another state's foreign minister, and that the minister should enjoy immunity equivalent to that enjoyed by diplomats and heads of state. The D.R.C. (P) also sought an order of provisional measures of protection on the ground that the warrant effectively prevented the foreign minister from leaving the D.R.C. (P). The I.C.J. issued its judgment.

ISSUE: Does a state's foreign minister enjoy full immunity from criminal jurisdiction in another state's courts, even where the minister is suspected of humanitarian violations?

HOLDING AND DECISION: [Judge not identified in casebook excerpt.] Yes. A state's foreign minister enjoys full immunity from criminal jurisdiction in another state's courts, even where the minister is suspected of war

crimes or crimes against humanity. A foreign minister's duties involve overseeing the state's diplomatic activities, acting as the state's representative in international negotiations and meetings, and traveling internationally. The minister may bind the state, and must be able to be in constant communication with the state and its diplomatic missions around the world, as well as with representatives of other states. Such a minister is recognized under international law as a representative of the state solely by virtue of his or her office. Based on these functions, an acting Minister of Foreign Affairs enjoys full immunity from criminal jurisdiction and inviolability so that he or she may not be hindered in the performance of his or her duties. Such immunity inheres regardless of whether the alleged criminal acts were performed in the minister's "official" capacity or "private" capacity, and regardless of when the conduct occurred. Otherwise, even the mere risk that by traveling to or transiting another state the minister might be exposed to legal proceedings could deter the minister from traveling internationally and fulfilling his or her official functions. Belgium's (D) argument that immunities cannot protect foreign ministers when they are accused of having committed war crimes or crimes against humanity is rejected. Belgium (D) points to instruments creating international criminal tribunals and decisions of national courts that state expressly that an individual's official capacity is not a bar to the exercise by such tribunals or courts of their jurisdiction. As support, it points to a judge's statement that "[i]nternational law cannot be supposed to have established a crime having the character of a *jus cogens* and at the same time to have provided an immunity that is coextensive with the obligation it seeks to impose." It also points to another judge's statement that "no established rule of international law requires state immunity *ratione materiae* to be accorded in respect of prosecution for an international crime." The D.C.R. (P), by contrast, points to statements by judges in the cases cited by Belgium (D) that support its assertion that, under international law as it currently stands, there is no exception to absolute immunity from criminal prosecution of an incumbent foreign minister accused of crimes under international law. The D.C.R. (P) also would limit the instruments creating war crimes tribunals to those tribunals and not extend them to other proceedings before national courts. Based on current practice and court decisions of some nations, there is no exception to the rule according immunity from criminal jurisdiction and inviolability to incumbent foreign ministers suspected of having

Continued on next page.

committed war crimes or crimes against humanity. Also, the rules regarding immunity for officials in the instruments creating war crimes tribunals are limited to those tribunals and do not create an exception to customary international law in regard to national courts. Decisions issued by those tribunals have not addressed the issue at bar and therefore do not affect this conclusion. Another consideration is that even if a national court has jurisdiction to prosecute an individual who is acting in an official capacity, such jurisdiction does not negate the individual's immunity under customary international law. Nevertheless, it must be emphasized that immunity from jurisdiction enjoyed by an incumbent foreign minister does not mean that he or she enjoys impunity for crimes he or she may have committed. Jurisdictional immunity is procedural, whereas criminal responsibility is a matter of substantive law, so that jurisdictional immunity does not operate to exonerate the minister, who may, under certain circumstances, be prosecuted for his or her crimes. The minister may be tried in the domestic courts of his or her state, and may cease to enjoy immunity if the state that the minister represents waives it. After the minister ceases to hold office, the minister will no longer enjoy all the immunities he or she previously enjoyed, and may be prosecuted for acts committed prior to or subsequent to the time the minister was in office, as well as in respect of acts committed during that period of office in a private capacity. Finally, the minister may be tried by international criminal courts where they have jurisdiction.

▶ ANALYSIS

This case did not decide the tenability of the claim of universal jurisdiction by domestic courts. However, some of the Court's judges, in a separate opinion, expressed the belief that universal jurisdiction is permitted in the case of those crimes considered the most heinous by the international community, so that the warrant for the arrest of the D.R.C.'s foreign minister did not as such violate international law. It thus appears that the judges of the I.C.J. are split on the issue of universal jurisdiction as exercised by local or domestic courts. In any event, a domestic court's exercise of universal jurisdiction is not without precedent: in 1961, Israel claimed universal jurisdiction when it kidnapped the former Nazi Adolf Eichmann from Argentina, tried him in an Israeli court and executed him.

■■■■

Quicknotes

INTERNATIONAL LAW The body of law applicable to dealings between nations.

JURISDICTION The authority of a court to hear and declare judgment in respect to a particular matter.

JUS COGENS NORM Universally understood principles of international law that cannot be set aside because they are based on fundamental human values.

■■■■

CHAPTER **13**

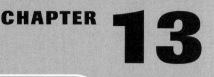

Human Rights

Quick Reference Rules of Law

Şahin v. Turkey

Turkish Muslim (P) v. Sovereign state (D)

Eur. Ct. of Human Rights, App. No. 44774/98, 44 Eur. H.R. Rep. 99 (2005).

NATURE OF CASE: Application alleging violations of rights and freedoms under the Convention for the Protection of Human Rights and Fundamental Freedoms.

FACT SUMMARY: Şahin (P), a Turkish Muslim, claimed the Republic of Turkey (Turkey) (D) violated her rights and freedoms under the Convention for the Protection of Human Rights and Fundamental Freedoms by banning the wearing of the Islamic headscarf in institutions of higher education.

🏛 RULE OF LAW
The ban by a secular country on wearing religious clothing in institutions of higher education does not violate students' rights and freedoms under the Convention for the Protection of Human Rights and Fundamental Freedoms.

FACTS: Şahin (P), a Turkish Muslim, came from a traditional family of practicing Muslims and considered it her religious duty to wear the Islamic headscarf. When she was a fifth-year student at the faculty of medicine of the University of Istanbul, in 1998, the Vice-Chancellor of the University issued a circular directing that students with beards and students wearing the Islamic headscarf would be refused admission to lectures, courses and tutorials. Subsequently, Şahin (P) was denied access to a written examination on one of the subjects she was studying because was wearing the Islamic headscarf, and university authorities refused on the same grounds to enroll her in a course, or to admit her to various lectures and another written examination. She left Istanbul in 1999 to pursue her medical studies at the Faculty of Medicine at Vienna University and has lived in Vienna since then. Before moving, Şahin (P) filed an application against the Republic of Turkey (Turkey) (P) with the European Commission of Human Rights under the Convention for the Protection of Human Rights and Fundamental Freedoms, alleging that her rights and freedoms under the Convention had been violated by the ban on the wearing of the Islamic headscarf in institutions of higher education. The European Court of Human Rights heard the case and rendered a judgment.

ISSUE: Does the ban by a secular country on wearing religious clothing in institutions of higher education violate students' rights and freedoms under the Convention for the Protection of Human Rights and Fundamental Freedoms?

HOLDING AND DECISION: [Judge not stated in casebook excerpt.] No. The ban by a secular country on wearing religious clothing in institutions of higher education does not violate students' rights and freedoms under

the Convention for the Protection of Human Rights and Fundamental Freedoms (Convention). Turkey (D) is constitutionally a secular ("laik" in Turkish) state founded on the principles of equality without regard to distinctions based on sex, religion, or denomination. Historically, Turkey (D) banned wearing religious attire other than in places of worship or at religious ceremonies, and the nation's religious schools were closed and came under public control. The wearing of the Islamic headscarf in educational institutions is a relatively recent development and has engendered much debate in Turkish society, which has taken on strong political overtones. Some see the Islamic headscarf as a symbol of a political Islam, and this has been perceived as a threat to republican values and civil peace. Turkey's (D) Constitutional Court decided in 1989 that granting legal recognition to a religious symbol such as the Islamic headscarf was not compatible with the principle that state education must be neutral and might generate conflicts between students of different religions. In 1990, transitional section 17 of Law no. 2547 entered into force, providing that: "Choice of dress shall be free in higher-education institutions, provided that it does not contravene the laws in force." In 1991, the Constitutional Court ruled that this provision did not permit headscarves to be worn in higher-education institutions on religious grounds and so was consistent with the Constitution. In explaining the ban on the headscarf at the University School of Medicine, the school's Vice Chancellor circulated a memorandum in which he emphasized that the ban was not intended to infringe on students' freedom of conscience or religion, but to comply with the laws and regulations in force, and that such compliance would be sensitive to patients' rights. In arguing that the ban on wearing the Islamic headscarf in higher-education institutions constituted an unjustified interference with her right to freedom of religion, and, in particular, her right to manifest her religion, Şahin (P) relied on Article 9 of the Convention, which provides: "(1) Everyone has the right to freedom of thought, conscience and religion; this right includes freedom to change his religion or belief and freedom, either alone or in community with others and in public or private, to manifest his religion or belief, in worship, teaching, practice and observance. (2) Freedom to manifest one's religion or beliefs shall be subject only to such limitations as are prescribed by law and are necessary in a democratic society in the interests of public safety, for the protection of public order, health or morals, or for the protection of the rights and freedoms of others." Thus, the Court must decide whether the ban interfered with Şahin's

Continued on next page.

(P) rights under Article 9, and, if so, whether the interference was "prescribed by law," pursued a legitimate aim and was "necessary in a democratic society" within the meaning of Article 9 § 2 of the Convention. As to the first issue, because Şahin (P) was wearing the headscarf to obey a religious precept, the ban interfered with her right to manifest her religion. This leads to the second issue—whether such interference was supported under Article 9 § 2. The phrase "prescribed by law" not only requires that the impugned measure should have some basis in domestic law, but also refers to the quality of the law in question, requiring that it should be accessible to the person concerned and foreseeable as to its effects. Here, transitional section 17 of Law no. 2547 provided the legal basis for interference under Turkish law and satisfies the requirements that it be specific and its consequences foreseeable. Additionally, the impugned interference primarily pursued the legitimate aims of protecting the rights and freedoms of others and of protecting public order. The freedom enshrined in Article 9, which is a foundation of democratic society, is the freedom to hold or not to hold religious beliefs, and to practice or not practice a religion. While religious freedom is primarily a private matter, it also implies freedom to manifest one's religion in community with others, in public and within the circle of those whose faith one shares. Nonetheless, Article 9 does not protect every act motivated or inspired by religious belief. In democratic societies, in which several religions coexist within the same population, it may be necessary to place restrictions on freedom to manifest one's religion or belief in order to reconcile the interests of the various groups and ensure that everyone's beliefs are respected. The state has a duty to be neutral in ensuring that there is public order, religious harmony and tolerance in a democratic society, and ensuring that there is mutual tolerance between opposing groups. This does not entail the elimination of pluralism, which along with tolerance and broadmindedness are hallmarks of a democratic society. Instead, this requires a balancing that ensures fair treatment of minorities without abuse of a dominant group, even if individual interests must sometimes be subordinated to those of a group. Where there is great divergence of opinion on certain issues—such as the wearing of an Islamic headscarf—the national decision-making body's role must be given great importance. Rules on such issues may vary greatly from one country to the next according to national traditions and the requirements imposed by the need to protect the rights and freedoms of others and to maintain public order. Each state, therefore, must, to a certain degree, be permitted to decide the extent and form such regulations should take based on the domestic context. This "margin of appreciation" requires the Court to decide whether the measures taken at the national level were justified and proportionate. In determining the boundaries of this margin of appreciation, the Court must keep in mind the state's need to protect the rights and freedoms of others, to preserve public order, and to secure civil peace and true religious pluralism, which is vital to the survival of a democratic society. The Court has previously stressed that the headscarf is a "powerful external symbol" that is hard to reconcile with the principle of gender equality or the message of tolerance, respect for others, and, above all, equality and non-discrimination. Applying these principles here, considering the question of the Islamic headscarf in the Turkish context, it is observed that the wearing of the headscarf may have a great impact on those who choose not to wear it, given that the majority of the population, while professing a strong attachment to the rights of women and a secular way life, are Muslims. The impugned interference therefore serves the key goals of secularism and equality. Additionally, the headscarf has taken on political significance as extremist political movements in Turkey (D) seek to impose on society as a whole their religious symbols and conception of a society founded on religious precepts. It has previously been held that each Contracting State may, in accordance with the Convention provisions, take a stance against such political movements, based on its historical experience. Here, the ban serves to preserve pluralism in the university. Accordingly, the objectives of the ban were legitimate. This leads to the issue of whether there was a reasonable relationship of proportionality between the means employed and the legitimate objectives pursued by the interference. The ban did not prohibit Muslim students from manifesting their religion in accordance with habitual forms of Muslim observance, and it was not directed only at Muslim attire. Thus, the Court should not substitute its view for that of the university authorities, who are better placed to evaluate local needs. Article 9 does not always guarantee the right to behave in a manner governed by a religious belief and does not confer on people who do so the right to disregard rules that have proved to be justified. Giving due regard to Turkey's (D) margin of appreciation, the interference here was justified in principle and proportionate to the aim pursued. Therefore, Article 9 has not been breached.

DISSENT: (Tulkens, J.) Not only is secularism necessary for the protection of a democratic society, so is religious freedom. The Court should have established, therefore, that the ban on wearing the Islamic headscarf was necessary to secure compliance with secularism and met a "pressing social need." However the Court does not adduce concrete examples that support such a position. The religious freedom at issue is the freedom to manifest one's religion, but the Court has not had much opportunity to opine on this freedom. In the instant case, the Court failed to address Şahin's (P) argument that she had no intention of calling into question the principle of secularism—because she believes in it. Second, no evidence was adduced to show that Şahin (P) in fact contravened the principle of secularism by wearing the headscarf. Further, the Court relies on precedent concerning a teacher—not students. Whereas teachers are role-models, students are not. There was also

Continued on next page.

no evidence that the headscarf worn by Şahin (P) was intended to proselytize, spread propaganda, or undermine others' convictions, or that there was any disruption in teaching or in everyday life at the University, or any disorderly conduct, that resulted from her wearing the headscarf. In fact, the Court finds justification for the ban on the need to mitigate the threat posed by "extremist political movements." While everyone agrees on the need to prevent radical Islamism, there has not been a showing that wearing a headscarf is associated with fundamentalism. Not all women who wear the headscarf are extremists. Accordingly, the ban on wearing the headscarf was not based on relevant or sufficient reasons and therefore cannot be deemed interference that is "necessary in a democratic society" within Article 9 § 2's meaning. Şahin's (P) right to freedom of religion under the Convention has therefore been violated.

▶ *ANALYSIS*

Margin of appreciation is the word-for-word English translation of the French phrase "marge d'appreciation," a concept used in a number of courts in Europe, among them the Strasbourg human rights court and the European Union courts in Luxembourg. It means, roughly, the range of discretion. As this case demonstrates, it is a concept the European Court of Human Rights has developed when considering whether a signatory of the European Convention on Human Rights has breached the declaration. The margin of appreciation doctrine allows the Court to account for the fact that the Convention will be interpreted differently in different signatory states, so that judges are obliged to take into account the cultural, historic, and philosophical contexts of the particular nation in question.

■■■

Legal Consequences of the Construction of a Wall in the Occupied Palestinian Territory

[Parties not identified.]

I.C.J., Advisory Opinion, 2004 I.C.J. 136.

NATURE OF CASE: Advisory opinion of the International Court of Justice.

FACT SUMMARY: [Facts not stated in casebook excerpt.]

🏛 RULE OF LAW

The International Covenant on Civil and Political Rights is applicable in respect of acts done by a state in the exercise of its jurisdiction outside its own territory.

FACTS: [Facts not stated in casebook excerpt.]

ISSUE: Is the International Covenant on Civil and Political Rights applicable in respect of acts done by a state in the exercise of its jurisdiction outside its own territory?

HOLDING AND DECISION: [Judge not stated in casebook excerpt.] Yes. The International Covenant on Civil and Political Rights (Covenant) is applicable in respect of acts done by a state in the exercise of its jurisdiction outside its own territory. The scope of the Covenant's application is defined by Article 2, paragraph 1, which provides that "Each State Party to the present Covenant undertakes to respect and to ensure to all individuals within its territory and subject to its jurisdiction the rights recognized in the present Covenant . . . ." This language can be interpreted to mean that only individuals in a state's territory and subject to its jurisdiction are covered by the Covenant. However, it can also be interpreted as covering both individuals present in a state's territory and those outside the territory, but subject to the State's jurisdiction. A state's jurisdiction is primarily territorial, but may in certain cases also be exercised extraterritorially. Given the Covenant's goals and purpose, it seems natural that this latter interpretation should apply. This is in keeping with the practice of the Human Rights Committee, which has found the Covenant applicable where the state exercises jurisdiction on foreign territory. The Covenant's history, found in the travaux préparatoires (preparatory work), confirms such an interpretation by showing that the drafters did not intend to permit states to escape their obligations when they exercise jurisdiction outside their national territory, but only intended to prevent persons residing abroad from asserting, vis-à-vis their state of origin, rights that do not fall within the competence of that state, but that of the state of residence.

▶ ANALYSIS

Contrary to the I.C.J.'s view in this Advisory Opinion, the history of the Covenant seems to support the plain meaning of Article 2, paragraph 1, namely that only individuals in a state's territory and subject to its jurisdiction are covered by the Covenant. As originally drafted, the Covenant would have required each state party to ensure Covenant rights to everyone "within its jurisdiction." The United States, however, amended this to "within its territory." The Covenant was passed with the amendment. Thus, the original intent of the drafters and the practice of the ratifying states is at odds with the I.C.J.'s opinion.

Quicknotes

ADVISORY OPINION A decision rendered at the request of an interested party of how the court would rule should the particular issue arise.

JURISDICTION The authority of a court to hear and declare judgment in respect to a particular matter.

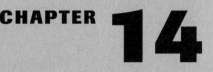
Injury to Aliens and Foreign Investors

Quick Reference Rules of Law

Fireman's Fund Insurance Co. v. Mexico

Debentures owner (P) v. Sovereign state (D)

Int'l Centre for Settlement of Investment Disputes, ICSID Case No. ARB(AF)/02/1,

Award, July 17, 2006.

NATURE OF CASE: Arbitration of claims by a debentures owner alleging violations of the North American Free Trade Agreement (NAFTA) and expropriation of property.

FACT SUMMARY: Fireman's Fund Insurance Company (Fireman's Fund) (P), a U.S. insurance company that owned debentures issued by a Mexican financial services company, pursued an arbitration against Mexico (D) for expropriation of its property.

🏛 RULE OF LAW

An expropriation of property under NAFTA includes the following elements: a taking (which includes destruction) that is permanent and either de jure or de facto, direct or indirect, in the form of a single measure or several measures over time; tangible or intangible property; a substantially complete deprivation of the economic use and enjoyment of the rights to the property; usually a transfer of ownership, but not always; as measured by the effect of the state's measures, not the underlying intent; as possibly determined by the investor's reasonable "investment-backed expectations"; and the compensability of which is determined by whether the measure is within the state's recognized police powers, the public purpose and effect of the measure, the measure's discriminatory nature, the proportionality between the means used and the goals intended to be realized, and the bona fide nature of the measure.

FACTS: Fireman's Fund Insurance Company (Fireman's Fund) (P), a U.S. insurance company that owned debentures issued by a Mexican financial services company, pursued an arbitration against Mexico (D) for expropriation of its property, claiming that Mexico (D) had helped to facilitate the purchase of debentures issued at the same time by the same company that were denominated in Mexican pesos and owned by Mexican investors, but did not facilitate the purchase of the debentures denominated in U.S. dollars owned by Fireman's Fund (P). The tribunal determined that Mexico's (D) acts did not constitute an expropriation. However, in doing so, it delineated the contours of what "expropriation" means.

ISSUE: Does an expropriation of property under NAFTA include the following elements: a taking (which includes destruction) that is permanent and either de jure or de facto, direct or indirect, in the form of a single measure or several measures over time; tangible or intangible property; a substantially complete deprivation of the economic use and

enjoyment of the rights to the property; usually a transfer of ownership, but not always; as measured by the effect of the state's measures, not the underlying intent; as possibly determined by the investor's reasonable "investment-backed expectations;" and the compensability of which is determined by whether the measure is within the state's recognized police powers, the public purpose and effect of the measure, the measure's discriminatory nature, the proportionality between the means used and the goals intended to be realized, and the bona fide nature of the measure?

HOLDING AND DECISION: [Judge not identified in casebook excerpt.] Yes. An expropriation of property under NAFTA includes the following elements: a taking (which includes destruction) that is permanent and either de jure or de facto, direct or indirect, in the form of a single measure or several measures over time; tangible or intangible property; a substantially complete deprivation of the economic use and enjoyment of the rights to the property; usually a transfer of ownership, but not always; as measured by the effect of the state's measures, not the underlying intent; as possibly determined by the investor's reasonable "investment-backed expectations;" and the compensability of which is determined by whether the measure is within the state's recognized police powers, the public purpose and effect of the measure, the measure's discriminatory nature, the proportionality between the means used and the goals intended to be realized, and the bona fide nature of the measure. NAFTA does not define "expropriation." In the ten or so cases in which Article 1110(1) of NAFTA has been considered, the definitions vary. Considering those cases and customary international law, the present Tribunal retains the following elements:

(a) Expropriation requires a taking (which may include destruction) by a government-type authority of an investment by an investor covered by NAFTA.

(b) The covered investment may include intangible as well as tangible property.

(c) The taking must be a substantially complete deprivation of the economic use and enjoyment of the rights to the property, or of identifiable distinct parts thereof (i.e., it approaches total impairment).

(d) The taking must be permanent, and not ephemeral or temporary.

(e) The taking usually involves a transfer of ownership to another person (frequently the government authority

Continued on next page.

concerned), but that need not necessarily be so in certain cases (e.g., total destruction of an investment due to measures by a government authority without transfer of rights).

(f) The effects of the host state's measures are dispositive, not the underlying intent, for determining whether there is expropriation.

(g) The taking may be de jure or de facto.

(h) The taking may be direct or indirect.

(i) The taking may have the form of a single measure or a series of related or unrelated measures over a period of time (the so-called "creeping" expropriation).

(j) To distinguish between a compensable expropriation and a noncompensable regulation by a host state, the following factors (usually in combination) may be taken into account: whether the measure is within the recognized police powers of the host state; the (public) purpose and effect of the measure; whether the measure is discriminatory; the proportionality between the means employed and the aim sought to be realized; and the bona fide nature of the measure.

(k) The investor's reasonable "investment-backed expectations" may be a relevant factor whether (indirect) expropriation has occurred.

▶ ANALYSIS

The Restatement (Third) of Foreign Relations Law of the United States provides that for compensation for a taking by a state of a foreign national's property to be just, it must, in the absence of exceptional circumstances, be in an amount equal to the value of the taken property and be paid at the time of the taking, or within a reasonable time thereafter with interest from the date of taking, and in a form economically usable by the foreign national whose property has been taken.

■■■

Quicknotes

BONA FIDE In good faith.

■■■

Tecnicas Medioambientales Tecmed S.A. ("Tecmed") v. Mexico

Foreign company (P) v. Sovereign state (D)

Int'l Centre for Settlement of Investment Disputes, ICSID Case No. ARB(AF)/00/2,

Award, 43 I.L.M. 133 (2004).

NATURE OF CASE: Arbitration of claims by foreign company against sovereign state for damages from expropriation of investment.

FACT SUMMARY: Tecnicas Medioambientales Tecmed S.A. (Claimant) (P) a Spanish company, claimed that Mexico (D) had expropriated its investment in Tecmed, Tecnicas Medioambientales de Mexico, S.A. de C.V. (Tecmed), a Mexican company, which in turn owned Cytrar, S.A. de C.V. (Cytrar), also a Mexican company, by refusing to renew Cytrar's annual license to run a hazardous industrial waste landfill (the "Landfill").

🏛 RULE OF LAW

(1) The denial by a state of a permit to a nonnational to operate property for its only intended use is an expropriation of the property where the denial is prompted by political considerations that do not constitute a social emergency.

(2) The duty of fair and equitable treatment is violated where a state's conduct frustrates an investor's fair expectations, deprives the investor of clear guidelines as to the investor's required actions, and fails to provide the investor with any alternatives other than a complete loss of its investment.

(3) A state does not violate a guarantee of full protection and security where it neither participates in nor promotes adverse actions against an investor and reacts to such adverse actions reasonably in accord with the parameters inherent in a democratic state.

FACTS: Tecnicas Medioambientales Tecmed S.A. (Claimant) (P) a Spanish company, owned over 99 percent of the shares of Tecmed, Tecnicas Medioambientales de Mexico, S.A. de C.V. (Tecmed), a company incorporated under Mexican law. Tecmed in turn held over 99 percent of the stock of Cytrar, S.A. de C.V. (Cytrar), also a Mexican company, that Tecmed had organized for the purpose of running a hazardous industrial waste landfill (the "Landfill") in the municipality of Hermosillo, located in the State of Sonora, Mexico. In 1996, at Tecmed's request, the Mexican agency for hazardous waste management, INE, issued Cytrar a license to operate the Landfill. This license had to be renewed annually at the applicant's request, and was renewed by the INE at Cytrar's request until 1998, when INE, pursuant to a resolution (the "Resolution") refused to renew the license and instead sought to have Cytrar close the Landfill. The INE's changed position allegedly was the result

primarily of political circumstances associated with a change in government of the Municipality of Hermosillo. Whereas the municipality had previously supported Cytrar's running of the Landfill, in 1998 new authorities encouraged a movement of citizens against the Landfill, which sought the nonrenewal of the Landfill's operating permit and its closure. The community engaged in demonstrations and disruptive conduct, including blocking access to the Landfill. The Claimant (P) claimed that the denial of the license constituted expropriation and sought damages, including compensation for damage to reputation, and interests in connection with damage alleged to have accrued as of the date INE rejected the application for renewal. Claimant (P) also sought the granting of permits that would enable it to operate the Landfill until the end of its useful life. It brought a claim for arbitration before the International Centre for Settlement of Investment Disputes (ICSID) under its Rules and under the Agreement on the Reciprocal Promotion and Protection of Investments (the "Agreement") between Spain and Mexico (D). The Claimant (P) alleged that the Agreement protected foreign investors and their investments from direct and indirect expropriation, such as measures tantamount to direct expropriation. Because the denial of the permit effectively deprived Cytrar of its rights to use and enjoy the real and personal property constituting the Landfill in accordance with its sole intended purpose, Claimant (P) claimed it was denied the benefits and economic use of its investment. Without the permit, the property had no market value and the Landfill's existence as an ongoing business was completely destroyed. Mexico (D) countered that INE had the discretionary powers required to grant and deny permits, and that such issues, except in special cases, are exclusively governed by domestic and not international law. It also asserted that INE's Resolution was neither arbitrary nor discriminatory and constituted a regulatory measure issued in compliance with the state's police power.

ISSUE:

(1) Is the denial by a state of a permit to a non-national to operate property for its only intended use an expropriation of the property where the denial is prompted by political considerations that do not constitute a social emergency?

(2) Is the duty of fair and equitable treatment violated where a state's conduct frustrates an investor's fair expectations, deprives the investor of clear guidelines as to the investor's required actions, and fails to provide the investor with any alternatives other than a complete loss of its investment?

Continued on next page.

(3) Does a state violate a guarantee of full protection and security where it neither participates in nor promotes adverse actions against an investor and reacts to such adverse actions reasonably in accord with the parameters inherent in a democratic state?

HOLDING AND DECISION: [Judge not stated in casebook excerpt.]

(1) Yes. The denial by a state of a permit to a non-national to operate property for its only intended use is an expropriation of the property where the denial is prompted by political considerations that do not constitute a social emergency. The term "expropriation" is not defined in the Agreement. Generally expropriation means a forcible taking by the government of property owned by private persons, although it can also cover a de facto taking, where Government actions or laws transfer assets to third parties, or where such actions or laws deprive persons of their ownership over such assets, without transfer to third parties or the government. It is this last meaning of expropriation that is referred to in the applicable sections of the Agreement, and is sometimes referred to as "indirect" or "creeping" expropriation. Creeping expropriation, however, must be distinguished from de facto expropriation, since the former occurs gradually or stealthily, whereas the latter can occur through a single action or several sequential or simultaneous actions. In any event, to determine whether there has been an indirect expropriation, the actions must be examined on a case-by-case basis. Here, the first step of the analysis is to determine whether the Resolution deprived the Claimant (P) of the economical use and enjoyment of its investments to the point where the rights related thereto ceased to exist. Ordinarily, a regulatory measure that is made pursuant to the state's police power entails only a decrease in assets or rights, whereas a de facto expropriation is a complete deprivation of those assets or rights. Thus, the effect of the Resolution is important in determining whether there was an indirect expropriation by Mexico (D), and the Agreement says as much. In addition to interpreting the Agreement, the tribunal must also apply international law. Under customary international law, it is understood that the measures adopted by a state, whether regulatory or not, are an indirect de facto expropriation if they are irreversible and permanent and destroy the owner's assets or rights. Additionally, under international law, the owner is also deprived of property where the use or enjoyment of benefits related thereto is exacted or interfered with to a similar extent, even where legal ownership over the assets in question is not affected, and so long as the deprivation is not temporary. As under the Agreement, the key is the measure's effect, rather than the intent behind it. Here, the Resolution meets these characteristics of an indirect expropriation: it has provided for the non-renewal of the permit and the closing of the Landfill permanently

and irrevocably and thereafter, based on INE regulations, the Landfill will not be useable for its intended purpose, so that Cytrar's economic and commercial operations in the Landfill after such denial have been fully and irrevocably destroyed. Moreover, the Landfill could not be used for a different purpose, and therefore could not be sold. The Claimant (P) invested in the Landfill only to engage in hazardous waste landfill activities and to profit therefrom; it is now deprived of that investment. Under the Agreement's plain meaning, regulatory administrative actions are not per se excluded from the Agreement's scope, even if they are beneficial to society, if they neutralize an investment's economic value without compensation. This includes environmental measures such as the one at issue. The next step in the analysis is to determine whether the measures are proportional to the public interest and to the protection legally granted to investments. In other words, there must be proportionality between the means employed and the aim sought to be realized. The measure will not be deemed proportional if the investor bears an undue burden under it. Here, the factors motivating INE's Resolution were political, not environmental, and the community's desires were not so great as to lead to social crisis or public unrest, so that the public interest did not outweigh the Claimant's (P) loss of value, and therefore the Resolution was not proportionate to the deprivation of rights sustained by the Claimant (P). Accordingly, the Resolution and its effects amounted to an expropriation in violation of the Agreement and international law.

(2) Yes. The duty of fair and equitable treatment is violated where a state's conduct frustrates an investor's fair expectations, deprives the investor of clear guidelines as to the investor's required actions, and fails to provide the investor with any alternatives other than a complete loss of its investment. The requirement of fair and equitable treatment in the Agreement is an expression of the bona fide principle of international law, under which states must provide to international investments treatment that does not affect the foreign investor's basic expectations used in making the investment. The foreign investor expects the host state to act in a consistent manner, free from ambiguity and totally transparently in its relations with the foreign investor, so that it may know beforehand any and all rules and regulations that will govern its investments, as well as the goals of the relevant policies and administrative practices or directives, to be able to plan its investment and comply with such regulations. The expectation of consistency applies to the revocation of preexisting decisions or permits that were relied on by the investor, and the state must not use the legal instruments that govern the investor's actions or the investment in a

Continued on next page.

manner that does not conform to their usual function, or to deprive the investor of its investment without compensation. Compliance with these principles is necessary for the state to be in compliance with the bona fide principle and with the fair and equitable treatment principle. So as not to be deemed arbitrary, the state's actions must not shock, or at least not surprise, a sense of juridical propriety. Applying these principles here, INE's behavior frustrated Cytrar's fair expectations and negatively affected the generation of clear guidelines that would allow the Claimant (P) or Cytrar to direct its actions or behavior to prevent the non-renewal of the permit, or weakened its position to enforce rights or explore ways to maintain the permit by relocating. Despite Cytrar's good faith expectation that the permit would be renewed at least until Cytrar's relocation of the Landfill to a new site had been completed, INE did not consider Cytrar's proposals in that regard, and not only did it deny the renewal of the permit, even though the relocation had not yet taken place, but it also did so in the understanding that this would lead Cytrar to relocate. This behavior, attributable to Mexico (D), resulted in losses and damages to the Claimant (P) and constituted a violation of the duty to accord fair and equitable treatment to the Claimant (P) and its investment.

(3) No. A state does not violate a guarantee of full protection and security where it neither participates in nor promotes adverse actions against an investor and reacts to such adverse actions reasonably in accord with the parameters inherent in a democratic state. Claimant (P) asserts that Mexican government officials at all levels of government failed to act as quickly, efficiently, and thoroughly as they should have to prevent or eliminate the community's adverse conduct toward the Landfill and Cytrar's staff, and therefore, Mexico (D) breached the guarantee of full protection and security provided in the Agreement. First, there is insufficient evidence that Mexican government officials encouraged, fostered, or contributed support to those who conducted the demonstrations and other adverse activities against the Landfill, or that they participated in such activities. Thus, there is insufficient evidence to attribute the activities to Mexico (D) under international law. In any event, the guarantee of full protection and security is not absolute and does not impose strict liability on a state that grants it. Furthermore, there was insufficient evidence that the Mexican officials or judiciary reacted unreasonably to the adverse activities in a manner that was not in accordance with the parameters inherent in a democratic state.

been consulted on its adoption. Thus, according to the European Court of Human Rights, although a taking of property must always be effected in the public interest, different considerations may apply to nationals and non-nationals and there may well be legitimate reason for requiring nationals to bear a greater burden in the public interest than non-nationals. Thus, as demonstrated by this case, interference with a non-national's property rights that is an indirect expropriation rather than an outright taking will require compensation. In this case, the tribunal awarded the Claimant (P) such compensation (over $5.5 million plus interest).

■■■

Quicknotes

ARBITRATION An alternative resolution process where a dispute is heard and decided by a neutral third party, rather than through legal proceedings.

BONA FIDE In good faith.

DAMAGES Monetary compensation that may be awarded by the court to a party who has sustained injury or loss to his person, property, or rights due to another party's unlawful act, omission or negligence.

SOVEREIGN A state or entity with independent authority to govern its affairs.

■■■

▶ ANALYSIS

Non-nationals are more vulnerable to domestic legislation, since unlike nationals, they will generally have played no part in the election or designation of its authors nor have

Texaco Overseas Petroleum Co. v. Libya

Oil company (P) v. Country (D)

Int'l Arbitral Award, 104 J. Droit Int'l 350 (1977), *translated in* 17 I.L.M. 1 (1978).

NATURE OF CASE: Arbitration decree.

FACT SUMMARY: Libya (D) promulgated a decree attempting to nationalize all of Texaco's (P) rights, interest, and property in Libya.

⚖ RULE OF LAW
The reference to general principles of law in the international arbitration context is always regarded to be a sufficient criterion for the internationalization of a contract.

FACTS: Libya (D) promulgated a decree attempting to nationalize all of Texaco's (P) rights, interest, and property in Libya (D). Texaco (P) requested arbitration and Libya (D) refused to arbitrate. The International Court of Justice appointed a sole arbitrator pursuant to Texaco's (P) request, who found Libya (D) in breach of its obligations under the Deeds of Concessions and legally bound to perform in accordance with their terms.

ISSUE: Is the reference to general principles of law in the international arbitration context always regarded to be a sufficient criterion for the internationalization of a contract?

HOLDING AND DECISION: [Judge not stated in casebook excerpt.] Yes. The reference to general principles of law in the international arbitration context is always regarded to be a sufficient criterion for the internationalization of a contract. The recourse to general principles is justified by the lack of adequate law in the state considered and the need to protect the private contracting party against unilateral and abrupt modifications of law in the contracting state. Legal international capacity is not solely attributable to a state; international law encompasses subjects of a diversified nature. Unlike a state, however, a private contracting party has only a limited capacity and he is entitled to invoke only those rights that he derives from his contract.

▌ *ANALYSIS*

One conflict here was whether to apply Libyan law or international law in the arbitration proceedings. While the contract itself deferred to Libyan law, the court notes that Libyan law does not preclude the application of international law, but that the two must be combined in order to verify that Libyan law complies with international law. Furthermore, even though international law recognizes the right of a state to nationalize, that right in itself is not a sufficient justification to disregard its contractual obligations.

Quicknotes

ARBITRATION Attempted resolution of a dispute by a neutral third party rather than through legal proceedings.

CONTRACTUAL OBLIGATION A duty agreed to be performed pursuant to a contract.

NATIONALIZATION Government acquisition of a private enterprise.

Ahmadou Sadio Diallo
(Guinea v. Democratic Republic of the Congo)

Sovereign state (P) v. Sovereign state (D)

I.C.J., 2007 I.C.J. ___.

NATURE OF CASE: A state responsibility, diplomatic protection case before the International Court of Justice.

FACT SUMMARY: The Republic of Guinea (Guinea) (P) filed a state responsibility, diplomatic protection case on behalf of its national, Diallo, against the Democratic Republic of Congo (D.R.C.) (D) for its alleged violations of Diallo's rights; the D.R.C. (D) contended that the claims were inadmissible because local remedies had not been exhausted.

🏛 RULE OF LAW
The possibility of reconsideration by an administrative authority of an administrative decision as a matter of grace does not constitute a local remedy that must be exhausted before the decision can be challenged in an international proceeding.

FACTS: Guinea (P) filed a state responsibility, diplomatic protection case on behalf of its national, Diallo, against the D.R.C. (D) in the International Court of Justice. Guinea (P) claimed that Diallo, who had resided in the D.R.C. (D) for 32 years, had been unlawfully arrested and imprisoned without trial by D.R.C.'s (D) authorities, detained in violation of his human rights, and his investments, property, and businesses unlawfully expropriated. After Diallo, in local proceedings, unsuccessfully attempted to recover sums owed to him by D.R.C.'s (D) companies, the D.R.C. (D) effectively expelled him by refusing him entry into the country. Such "refusal of entry" is not appealable under D.R.C.'s (D) law. Guinea (P) claimed that Diallo's arrest, detention, and expulsion violated international law, for which violation the D.R.C. (D) was responsible. The D.R.C. (D) contended that the claims were inadmissible because local remedies had not been exhausted, including reconsideration by its Prime Minister, so that Diallo did not meet the requirement for the exercise of diplomatic protection, which includes exhaustion of local remedies.

ISSUE: Does the possibility of reconsideration by an administrative authority of an administrative decision as a matter of grace constitute a local remedy that must be exhausted before the decision can be challenged in an international proceeding?

HOLDING AND DECISION: [Judge not stated in casebook excerpt.] No. The possibility of reconsideration by an administrative authority of an administrative decision as a matter of grace does not constitute a local

remedy that must be exhausted before the decision can be challenged in an international proceeding. The rule that local remedies must be exhausted before international proceedings may be instituted is a well-established rule of customary international law that provides the state against whom the claim is made the opportunity to redress any wrongs by its own means and within the framework of its own legal system. The issue posed by this case is whether the D.R.C.'s (D) legal system actually provided local remedies that Diallo could have exhausted. Guinea (P) must prove either that local remedies were exhausted or that there were exceptional circumstances that excused such exhaustion. The D.R.C. (D), however, must prove that its legal system offered effective remedies that were not exhausted. Guinea (P) did not present evidence as to remedies for the arrest and detention, and the D.R.C. (D) did not address exhaustion of remedies in regard to these alleged illegal acts. The D.R.C. (D) only addressed the issue of expulsion, saying that remedies for expulsion were institutionally provided by its legal system. The Court, therefore, will only address the issue of local remedies in respect of expulsion. The expulsion, which was characterized as a "refusal of entry" is not appealable under the D.R.C.'s (D) law, so that the D.R.C. (D) cannot now rely on an error allegedly made by its administrative agencies at the time Diallo was "refused entry" to claim that he should have treated the measure as an expulsion. Instead, Diallo was justified in relying on the D.R.C.'s (D) authorities when they informed him that he could not appeal the refusal of entry, including for purposes of the local remedy rule. Even if the D.R.C.'s (D) action in fact constituted an expulsion, the D.R.C. (D) has failed to show that there is any means of legal redress against expulsion decisions under its law. Although Diallo could request reconsideration by the appropriate administrative authority of its decision, such reconsideration does not qualify as a local remedy. Remedies that must be exhausted include legal and administrative remedies, but administrative remedies can only be considered for purposes of the local remedies rule if they are aimed at vindicating a right and not at obtaining a favor, unless they constitute an essential prerequisite for the admissibility of subsequent contentious proceedings. Here, the possibility of having the administrative authority—the D.R.C. (D) Prime Minister—retract his decision as a matter of grace does not constitute a local remedy to be exhausted. Because the D.R.C. (D) has failed to show, at least in regard to expulsion, that it provides

Continued on next page.

effective remedies to be exhausted, the D.R.C.'s (D) objection to the expulsion claim must be dismissed.

▶ *ANALYSIS*

The "rule of local remedies" at issue in this case originally developed in the area of diplomatic protection, but has been extended to the area of human rights as well, and is primarily designed to ensure respect for the sovereignty of the host state, which is permitted to resolve the dispute by its own means before international mechanisms are invoked.

■═■

Quicknotes

REMEDY Compensation for violation of a right or for injuries sustained.

■═■

Ahmadou Sadio Diallo
(Guinea v. Democratic Republic of the Congo)

Sovereign state (P) v. Sovereign state (D)

I.C.J., 2007 I.C.J. ___.

NATURE OF CASE: A state responsibility, diplomatic protection case before the International Court of Justice.

FACT SUMMARY: The Republic of Guinea (Guinea) (P) filed a state responsibility, diplomatic protection case on behalf of its national, Diallo, against the Democratic Republic of Congo (D.R.C.) (D) for its alleged violations of Diallo's rights, including his rights as a shareholder (associé) of limited companies (SPRLs) incorporated in the D.R.C. (D). The D.R.C. (D) contended that Guinea (P) did not have standing to protect Diallo.

🏛 **RULE OF LAW**

(1) A state has standing to bring a diplomatic protection claim on behalf of its national who is a shareholder in a company organized under the laws of a host state where it alleges that internationally wrongful acts by the host state have caused injury to the national's rights as a shareholder.

(2) There is no exception in the customary international law of diplomatic protection that permits "substitution" of a shareholder for a company in exceptional circumstances.

FACTS: Guinea (P) filed a state responsibility, diplomatic protection case on behalf of its national, Diallo, against the D.R.C. (D) for its alleged violations of Diallo's rights, including his rights as a shareholder (associé) of two limited companies (SPRLs) incorporated in the D.R.C. (D)—Africom-Zaire and Africontainers-Zaire. Diallo was also a manager (gérant) of these companies. Guinea (P) claimed that its diplomatic protection claim was viable because it was claiming that D.R.C.'s (D) acts infringed on Diallo's rights as a shareholder, rather than just on the companies' rights. Guinea (P) also contended it could bring a claim on a "theory of substitution" based on the companies' rights. The D.R.C. (D) objected to the admissibility of these claims, arguing that Guinea (P) lacked standing to bring them.

ISSUE:

(1) Does a state have standing to bring a diplomatic protection claim on behalf of its national who is a shareholder in a company organized under the laws of a host State where it alleges that internationally wrongful acts by the host state have caused injury to the national's rights as a shareholder?

(2) Is there an exception in the customary international law of diplomatic protection that permits "substitution" of a shareholder for a company in exceptional circumstances?

HOLDING AND DECISION: [Judge not stated in casebook excerpt.]

(1) Yes. A state has standing to bring a diplomatic protection claim on behalf of its national who is a shareholder in a company organized under the laws of a host state where it alleges that internationally wrongful acts by the host state have caused injury to the national's rights as a shareholder. In support of its diplomatic protection claim on behalf of Diallo as associé, Guinea (P) refers to the judgment in the Court's *Barcelona Traction* case, where the Court ruled that "an act directed against and infringing only the company's rights does not involve responsibility toward the shareholders, even if their interests are affected" but added that "[t]he situation is different if the act complained of is aimed at the direct rights of the shareholder as such." Guinea (P) also asserts that a similar position was taken up in Article 12 of the International Law Commission's (ILC) draft Articles on Diplomatic Protection, which provides that: "To the extent that an internationally wrongful act of a state causes direct injury to the rights of shareholders as such, as distinct from those of the corporation itself, the state of nationality of any such shareholders is entitled to exercise diplomatic protection in respect of its nationals." Guinea (P) asserts that under the Decree of 27 February 1887 on commercial corporations, Diallo is entitled to property rights, including dividends, from the companies, as well as "functional rights," encompassing the right to control and manage the companies. It further claims that the D.R.C.'s (D) investment code also entitles Diallo additional shareholder rights, including the right to share in the companies' profits and the right of ownership of the companies. Guinea (P) has standing to assert these rights because it is essentially asserting a diplomatic protection claim on behalf of a natural or legal person. An internationally wrongful act against a shareholder is the violation by the host state of the shareholder's direct rights in relation to a legal person that are defined by the domestic law of the host state. Thus, diplomatic protection of the direct rights of shareholders of a public limited company is not an exception to the general

Continued on next page.

legal régime of diplomatic protection for natural or legal persons, as derived from customary international law. At this point in the proceedings, the Court need not determine which of Diallo's rights appertain to his status as a shareholder versus his status as a manager, as the Court will define the precise nature of those rights at the merits stage. Accordingly, the D.R.C.'s (D) objections to standing are rejected and dismissed as to Diallo's direct rights as a shareholder.

(2) No. There is no exception in the customary international law of diplomatic protection that permits "substitution" of a shareholder for a company in exceptional circumstances. The Court considers whether Guinea (P) may advance a claim encompassing harm to the companies themselves based on a "theory of substitution." Such a theory deviates from the normal rules of state responsibility. The Court, in dictum, has hinted that such a theory might be available in exceptional circumstances. However, state practice and decisions of international courts and tribunals in this area of diplomatic protection do not support such a theory. The role of diplomatic protection has been minimized in the area of the protection of rights of shareholders and of companies because disputes in this area are largely governed by agreement and recourse is made to diplomatic protection for shareholders only rarely where such an agreement does not govern or has proved inoperative. It is in this relatively limited context that protection by substitution might be raised, but it would appear to constitute the very last resort for the protection of foreign investments. At present, such an exception does not exist in customary international law, and Guinea (P) may not assert a claim based on such an exception.

▶ ANALYSIS

In contemporary international law, the protection of the rights of companies and the rights of their shareholders, and the settlement of the associated disputes, are essentially governed by bilateral or multilateral agreements for the protection of foreign investments. Examples of such agreements are the treaties for the promotion and protection of foreign investments, and the Washington Convention of 18 March 1965 on the Settlement of Investment Disputes between States and Nationals of Other States, which created an International Centre for Settlement of Investment Disputes (ICSID), and also by contracts between states and foreign investors.

■═■

Tecnicas Medioambientales Tecmed S.A. ("Tecmed") v. Mexico

Foreign company (P) v. Sovereign state (D)

Int'l Centre for Settlement of Investment Disputes, ICSID Case No. ARB(AF)/00/2,

Award, 43 I.L.M. 133 (2004).

NATURE OF CASE: Award of damages in arbitration for expropriation of investment.

FACT SUMMARY: After determining that Mexico (D) had expropriated Tecnicas Medioambientales Tecmed S.A.'s (Claimant's) (P) property by refusing to issue a permit for the operation of a landfill (the "Landfill") owned by the Claimant's (P) subsidiary [for the facts of the case and the tribunal's findings and ruling, see the brief at page 130, supra], the arbitral tribunal awarded the Claimant (P) money damages and interest, but not moral damages or litigation expenses and attorneys' fees.

⚖ RULE OF LAW
(1) An award for compensatory money damages for expropriated property may include amounts proven to constitute the market value of the property, including amounts for projections of increased revenue and goodwill.
(2) An award for compensatory money damages for expropriated property may include compound interest.
(3) Moral damages will not be awarded where there is no evidence of injury to reputation.
(4) Arbitration expenses and counsel fees will not be awarded to a claimant who has been only partially successful.

FACTS: An arbitral tribunal determined that Mexico (D) had expropriated Tecnicas Medioambientales Tecmed S.A.'s (Claimant's) (P) property by refusing to issue a permit for the operation of a landfill (the "Landfill") owned by the Claimant's (P) subsidiary [for the facts of the case and the tribunal's findings and ruling, see the brief at page 130, supra]. The tribunal then had to determine the appropriate damages. The Claimant (P) primarily requested money damages and secondarily restitution in kind. It also requested interest, moral damages, litigation expenses, and attorneys' fees. The tribunal explained its decision in regard to each of these items.

ISSUE:
(1) May an award for compensatory money damages for expropriated property include amounts proven to constitute the market value of the property, including amounts for projections of increased revenue and goodwill?
(2) May an award for compensatory money damages for expropriated property include compound interest?

(3) Will moral damages be awarded where there is no evidence of injury to reputation?
(4) Will arbitration expenses and counsel fees be awarded to a claimant who has been only partially successful?

HOLDING AND DECISION: [Judge not stated in casebook excerpt.]

(1) Yes. An award for compensatory money damages for expropriated property may include amounts proven to constitute the market value of the property, including amounts for projections of increased revenue and goodwill. Based on the Landfill's acquisition value of $4,028,788, capital investments and profits for the two years in which the Landfill was operational, the market value of the Landfill is $5,553,017.12. The Claimant's (P) expert witness assessed the value of additional investments at $1,951,473,237, but there is no evidence supporting that value, whereas Mexico (D) claims that amount is $439,000, based on accounting data. The tribunal accepts Mexico's (D) value of this item. The tribunal also finds, based on the Landfill's growing revenues and profits and increasing goodwill, that profits were $1,085,229.12. Moreover, to provide an integral compensation for the damage inflicted, the amount of closing the Landfill will not be deducted from such amount, since the decision forcing such closure was in violation of the Agreement between Spain and Mexico (D).

(2) Yes. An award for compensatory money damages for expropriated property may include compound interest. Compound—versus simple—interest has been awarded in other expropriation cases and is at present deemed the appropriate standard of interest in international law for expropriation cases. Here, compound interest at a rate of 6 percent is justified.

(3) No. Moral damages will not be awarded where there is no evidence of injury to reputation. There is no evidence that the actions attributable to Mexico (D) cause injury to the Claimant's (P) reputation and therefore caused it to lose business opportunities. Any adverse press coverage of the Claimant's (P) companies cannot be attributed to Mexico (D).

(4) No. Arbitration expenses and counsel fees will not be awarded to a claimant who has been only partially successful. Here, the Claimant (P) has been successful only with respect to some of its claims, and some of Mexico's (D) defenses and challenges were admitted. Therefore,

Continued on next page.

each party will bear its own costs, expenses, and legal counsel fees. The costs incurred by the tribunal and the ICSID will be shared equally between the parties. After Mexico (D) pays the amounts required by this award, the Claimant (P) will take all necessary steps to transfer the Landfill to Mexico (D).

▶ ANALYSIS

This damages award illustrates that in respect of expropriated or nationalized property, tribunals tend to value the expropriated business on a going concern basis, rather than on a liquidation basis, and that, therefore, they will include measures of goodwill and profitability in the value determination. As with other measures of value, those indicia must be based on reliable data and projections.

■▬■

Quicknotes

ARBITRATION An alternative resolution process where a dispute is heard and decided by a neutral third party, rather than through legal proceedings.

■▬■

Use of Force

Quick Reference Rules of Law

Judgment of the International Military Tribunal

[Parties not identified.]

Nuremberg, Sept. 30, 1946, reprinted in 41 A.J.I.L. 186-218 (1946).

NATURE OF CASE: Indictment for war crimes.

FACT SUMMARY: Officials of Hitler's Third Reich were indicted for instigating wars of aggression against neighboring countries.

🏛 RULE OF LAW

The planning or waging of war that is a war of aggression or a war in violation of international treaties is a crime.

FACTS: Officials of Hitler's Third Reich were indicted for instigating wars of aggression against neighboring countries.

ISSUE: Is the planning or waging of war that is a war of aggression or a war in violation of international treaties a crime?

HOLDING AND DECISION: [Judge not stated in casebook excerpt.] Yes. The planning or waging of war that is a war of aggression or a war in violation of international treaties is a crime. The legal effect of the Kellogg-Briand Pact is that the nations who signed it or adhered to it unconditionally condemned recourse to war as an instrument of policy and expressly renounced it. War for the solution of international controversies undertaken as an instrument of national policy includes a war of aggression, and such war is therefore outlawed by the Pact.

▶ ANALYSIS

This trial involved the indictment of German officials for the seizure of Austria and Czechoslovakia and the war against Poland, as part of Germany's foreign policy. The Tribunal concluded that Germany planned wars against 12 separate nations and therefore was guilty of violating the Charter's prohibition against wars of aggression and wars in violation of international treaties (namely, the Treaty of Versailles).

Quicknotes

KELLOGG-BRIAND PACT A treaty between the United States and other powers, ratified in 1929, which provided for the renunciation of war as an instrument of national policy.

TREATY OF VERSAILLES An agreement produced in 1919 by the League of Nations (or "the Allies," headed up by Britain, France, Italy and the United States), which, following World War I, levied restrictive military sanctions against Germany, divested Germany of its colonies and gave over German land to other countries. Poland, Lithuania, Latvia, Estonia, and Finland were formed by the treaty from land lost by Russia, and a multi-party system was imposed on German politics to inhibit any one group from taking power.

Military and Paramilitary Activities in and Against Nicaragua (Nicaragua v. United States of America)

Country aiding subversives (P) v. Military intervenor (D)

I.C.J., 1986 I.C.J. 14, 103–123.

NATURE OF CASE: Proceeding before the International Court of Justice.

FACT SUMMARY: The United States (D) claimed collective self-defense as a justification for various hostile acts toward Nicaragua (P).

🏛 **RULE OF LAW**
Collective self-defense cannot justify hostile behavior unless the aggrieved state requests aid.

FACTS: The Sandinistas took control of Nicaragua in 1979. Not long after, they began supplying aid to subversive elements in neighboring Honduras and El Salvador. In response to this, the United States (D) commenced a series of military and paramilitary activities against Nicaragua (P), such as support of counterrevolutionaries, airspace overflights, and harbor mining. Neither El Salvador nor Honduras requested U.S. (D) intervention. Nicaragua (P) brought an action against the United States (D) in the International Court of Justice. The United States (D) claimed collective self-defense as a justification.

ISSUE: May collective self-defense justify hostile behavior if the aggrieved state does not request aid?

HOLDING AND DECISION: (Per curiam) No. Collective self-defense cannot justify hostile behavior unless the aggrieved state requests aid. Particularly where, as here, the acts of the allegedly offending state do not constitute an armed attack, a state may not come to the defense of another state, under the doctrine of collective self-defense, unless requested to do so. This is true under both the U.N. Charter and customary international law. In this instance, neither Honduras nor El Salvador was under armed attack and neither requested aid. This being so, the United States (D) could not properly invoke collective self-defense as a basis for justifying its hostile activities toward Nicaragua (P). [The Court went on to order the United States (D) to cease its activities and make reparations.]

▶ **ANALYSIS**

Nicaragua (P) claimed breaches of certain international agreements, such as the U.N. Charter, the Charter of the OAS, and a 1956 treaty. The United States (D) claimed the agreements to be inapplicable. The Court was of the opinion that applicability was irrelevant, as customary international law coincided with law as provided in the agreements.

Quicknotes

BREACH The violation of an obligation imposed pursuant to contract or law, by acting or failing to act.

INTERNATIONAL LAW The body of law applicable to dealings between nations.

International Criminal Law

Quick Reference Rules of Law

"The Justice Case" (Case 3), United States v. Josef Altstoetter et al.

Allied country (P) v. Nazi judges (D)

Trials of Individuals Before the Nuremberg Military Tribunals Under Control Council

Law No. 10, 1946-1949, Vol. III (1951). Opinion and Judgment, at 954-84.

NATURE OF CASE: Post-World War II trial of Nazi judges by a U.S. military tribunal in Germany.

FACT SUMMARY: Judges (D) who were part of the Nazi regime were charged with various crimes, including crimes against humanity, conspiracy to commit war crimes, and "judicial murder," on the grounds that they had destroyed law and justice in Germany and then utilized the emptied forms of legal process for persecution, enslavement, and extermination on a large scale.

🏛 **RULE OF LAW**
(1) The military tribunal draws its power and jurisdiction to punish violations of international law from the Control Council, as an international body temporarily governing Germany.
(2) International law recognizes more than violations of laws and customs of war as offenses.
(3) The *ex post facto* rule does not apply to international law, so that the principle *nullum crimen sine lege* cannot be used as a defense to international crimes.

FACTS: After World War II, a series of trials took place at Nuremberg and other locations in Germany under Control Council Law No. 10 (C.C. Law 10). The Control Council governed occupied Germany, and was made up of representatives from the U.S. (P), U.S.S.R (P), France (P), and England (P). In U.S. occupied zones, trials were held before U.S. judges. In 1947, the U.S. Military Government for Germany created Military Tribunal III to try what was called the "Justice Case", where the Defendants (D) were judges in the Nazi regime. They were charged with "judicial murder and other atrocities, which they committed by destroying law and justice in Germany, and then utilizing the emptied forms of legal process for the persecution, enslavement, and extermination on a large scale," and were accused of conspiracy to commit war crimes against civilians in German-occupied territories (including German civilians and nationals) and against soldiers of countries at war with Germany. They were also accused of crimes against humanity. In addition, some were charged with being members of the SS, SD, and Nazi Party leadership corps, all of which had been declared criminal organizations. All the Defendants (D) pled not guilty. Military Tribunal III rendered its judgment.

ISSUE:
(1) Does the military tribunal draw its power and jurisdiction to punish violations of international law from the

Control Council, as an international body temporarily governing Germany?
(2) Does international law recognize more than violations of laws and customs of war as offenses?
(3) Does the *ex post facto* rule apply to international law, so that the principle *nullum crimen sine lege* can be used as a defense to international crimes?

HOLDING AND DECISION: [Judge not stated in casebook excerpt.]

(1) Yes. The military tribunal draws its power and jurisdiction to punish violations of international law from the Control Council, as an international body temporarily governing Germany. It has always been recognized that a state with a functioning government may punish war crimes of perpetrators that come within the state's jurisdiction, but at the state's discretion. The situation here is different, since there is no functioning German government. Thus, the power to punish violations of international law in Germany is not solely dependent on the enactment of rules of substantive criminal law that are applicable only in Germany. Instead, the military tribunal may punish violations of the common international law because Germany is under the temporary control of the Control Council, an international body that has assumed and exercised the power to establish judicial machinery for the punishment of such violations. Such an international body could not, without consent, assume or exercise such power in a state that had a functioning national government that could exercise its sovereignty.

(2) Yes. International law recognizes more than violations of laws and customs of war as offenses. Violations of laws and customs of war are no longer the only offenses recognized by common international law. Given the "force of circumstance, the grim fact of worldwide interdependence, and the moral pressure of public opinion," crimes against humanity committed by the Nazis have also been recognized as violations of international law. One such crime is genocide, which has been confirmed as a crime under international law by the U.N. General Assembly. The commission of genocide is punishable regardless of whether those who committed it were private individuals, public officials, or statesmen, and regardless of whether it was committed on religious, racial, political, or any other grounds. Whether the crime against humanity is the product of statute,

Continued on next page.

international law, or both, it is not unjust to try the perpetrators, who are chargeable with the knowledge that their acts were wrong and punishable when committed. The Defendants' (D) contention that they should not be found guilty because they acted within the authority and by the command of German laws must be rejected, since C.C. Law 10 provides for punishment regardless of whether the acts were in accord with or in violation of domestic laws at the time. The Nuremberg Tribunals are not German courts and are not enforcing German law, nor are the charges based on violations of German law. Instead, they are international tribunals enforcing international law as superior to any German statute or decree. Although German courts during the Nazi regime were required to follow German law (i.e., Hitler's will) even though it was contrary to international law, no such limitation may be applied to the tribunal here. In fact, the very essence of the case here is that German law—the Hitlerian decrees and corrupt and perverted Nazi judicial system—itself constituted the substance of war crimes and crimes against humanity. Thus, the participation in the enactment and enforcement of that law amounts to complicity in crime. Moreover, governmental participation is a material element of the crime against humanity, since only when public officials participate in atrocities and persecutions do those crimes assume international proportions. Because governmental participation is an element of the crime, it cannot also be a defense thereto.

(3) No. *The ex post facto* rule does not apply to international law, so that the principle *nullum crimen sine lege* cannot be used as a defense to international crimes. The *ex post facto* rule, which under written constitutions condemns statutes that define as criminal those acts committed before the law was enacted, cannot apply to international law, which is not the product of statute, but of multipartite treaties, conventions, judicial decisions, and customs. It is "sheer absurdity" to suggest that the rule can be applied to a treaty, custom, or decision of an international tribunal. If the rule were applied to these, there would be no common international law—it would have been strangled at birth. Thus, the principle of *nullum crimen sine lege* does not limit the tribunal's power to punish violations of international law when committed. Not only is this principle not a limitation of sovereignty, it is a principle of justice, so that to assert that it is unjust to punish those who defy treaties and international assurances is untrue, since the perpetrators must know that what they have done is wrong and it would be unjust to allow the perpetrators to go unpunished.

ANALYSIS

A basic precept of criminal law prohibits *ex post facto* prosecutions (*nullum crimen sine lege; nulla poena sine*

lege). Arguably, since many of the crimes against humanity, such as genocide and mass killing, were already crimes under every legal system, it would not be unjust under *ex post facto* principles to prosecute and punish perpetrators of such crimes, since arguably the crimes were merely "internationalized" by the IMT Charter.

Quicknotes

EX POST FACTO After the fact; a law that makes subsequent activity criminal or increases the punishment for a crime that occurred, or eliminates a defense that was available to the defendant prior to its passage.

INTERNATIONAL LAW The body of law applicable to dealings between nations.

JURISDICTION The authority of a court to hear and declare judgment in respect to a particular matter.

Prosecutor v. Milutinović et al.

International prosecutor (P) v. Government official accused of international crimes (D)

Int'l Crim. Trib. for the former Yugoslavia, I.C.T.Y. Case No. IT-05-87-T, Summary of

Trial Chamber Judgment (Feb. 26, 2009).

NATURE OF CASE: Trial before the International Criminal Tribunal for the former Yugoslavia of Serbian and Yugoslavian government officials accused of instigating and aiding and abetting war crimes and crimes against humanity in Kosovo.

FACT SUMMARY: Milutinović (D), Šainović (D), Ojdanić (D), Pavković (D), Lazarević (D), and Lukić (D), who were either Serbian or Yugoslavian government officials, were each accused of participating in a joint criminal enterprise to modify the ethnic balance in Kosovo and instigating and aiding and abetting various war crimes and crimes against humanity, as set out in Articles 7(1) and 7(3) of the Statute of the Tribunal of the International Criminal Tribunal for the former Yugoslavia, to further the goals of that criminal enterprise.

🏛 RULE OF LAW

Government officials accused of engaging in a joint criminal enterprise and instigating and aiding and abetting war crimes and crimes against humanity will be convicted only where there is sufficient compelling evidence of their participation in such an enterprise and crimes.

FACTS: Milutinović (D), Šainović (D), Ojdanić (D), Pavković (D), Lazarević (D), and Lukić (D), who were either Serbian or Yugoslavian government officials, were each accused of participating in a joint criminal enterprise to modify the ethnic balance in Kosovo and instigating and aiding and abetting various war crimes and crimes against humanity, as set out in Articles 7(1) and 7(3) of the Statute of the Tribunal of the International Criminal Tribunal for the former Yugoslavia, to further the goals of that criminal enterprise. Specifically, the crimes the accused were alleged to be responsible for were: deportation, a crime against humanity (count 1); forcible transfer as "other inhumane acts," a crime against humanity (count 2); murder, a crime against humanity and a violation of the laws or customs of war (counts 3 and 4); and persecution, a crime against humanity (count 5). The accused allegedly participated, along with others, in a joint criminal enterprise to modify the ethnic balance in Kosovo to ensure continued control by the Federal Republic of Yugoslavia (FRY) and Serbian authorities over the province. The purpose of the joint criminal enterprise was to be achieved through a widespread or systematic campaign of terror or violence against the Kosovo Albanian population, including various crimes specified in each of the counts of the indictment. The Kosovo Albanians were forced out of Kosovo through

a campaign of violence and terror, which included killings, property destruction, destruction or damage of religious sites, theft, sexual assaults, beatings, and other crimes that were carried out by the FRY and Serbian forces. At the time of these alleged crimes, approximately from the end of March 1999 to the beginning of June 1999, Milutinović (D) was the President of the Republic of Serbia; Šainović (D) was a Deputy Prime Minister of the FRY as well as the head of the Joint Command, which had authority over the Yugoslav Army (VJ) and Serbian forces known as "MUP" forces deployed in Kosovo; Ojdanić (D) was the Chief of the General Staff of the VJ; Pavković (D) was the Commander of the VJ 3rd Army; Lazarević (D) was the Commander of the VJ Priština Corps; and Lukić (D) was the Head of the Serbian Ministry of Interior Staff for Kosovo, referred to as the MUP Staff. Allegedly, each of the accused exercised command authority and/or effective control over VJ and MUP forces involved in the commission of the alleged crimes. They were also accused of having planned, instigated, ordered, or otherwise to have aided and abetted the crimes. During this period, NATO forces began an aerial bombing campaign against targets in the FRY in an attempt to end an armed conflict between the FRY and Serbian forces and the Kosovo Liberation Army (KLA). During the bombing, around 700,000 Kosovo Albanians left their homes and crossed the borders into Albania and Macedonia. Witnesses for the Prosecution (P) indicated this was a result primarily of the violent and coercive actions of the FRY and Serbian forces. Witnesses for the Defendants (D), however, denied any organized expulsion of the Kosovo Albanians. Other reasons people left the area were that they were instructed to do so by the KLA; they wanted to avoid combat; and they wanted to avoid NATO bombing that was close to their homes. Nevertheless, none of the Kosovo Albanians who testified cited the NATO bombing as among the reasons for their departure. Furthermore, even though the NATO bombings struck targets in the FRY, people did not leave the bombed areas in the massive numbers that fled Kosovo. The MUP attempted to conceal the killing of Kosovo Albanians by transporting the bodies of those murdered to other areas of Serbia. There was evidence of numerous events in numerous municipalities and sites involving the burning of houses, the firing of weapons, killing, sexual abuse, and other acts of violence committed by police and military forces aimed at the Kosovo Albanians, who were rounded up and ordered to leave, or who were put on buses and deported. Witnesses

Continued on next page.

from the VJ and MUP described their own participation in the killing or expulsion of Kosovo Albanians. The Trial Chamber assessed the evidence and rendered its judgment, of which it provided a summary.

ISSUE: Will government officials accused of engaging in a joint criminal enterprise and instigating and aiding and abetting war crimes and crimes against humanity be convicted only where there is sufficient compelling evidence of their participation in such an enterprise and crimes?

HOLDING AND DECISION: (Bonomy, J.) Yes. Government officials accused of engaging in a joint criminal enterprise and instigating and aiding and abetting war crimes and crimes against humanity will be convicted only where there is sufficient compelling evidence of their participation in such an enterprise and crimes. It was generally proved that the alleged crimes were committed by VJ and MUP forces in many of the locations alleged in the indictment. However, there were a number of allegations that were not proved on the facts, or did not satisfy one or more of the requisite legal elements. It was proved that there was a broad campaign by the forces against Kosovo Albanian civilians involving the alleged crimes, and, although in some instances there was not convincing evidence that in certain sites all named victims were in fact among the dead, the killing of a significant group of people by VJ and/or MUP forces occurred as alleged. It was the deliberate actions of the forces that caused the departure of at least 700,000 Kosovo Albanians from Kosovo in the short period at issue.

Milutinović (D), as Serbia's President, did not have direct individual control over the VJ, a federal institution. His formal role in relation to the VJ was as an ex officio member of the Supreme Defence Council (SDC), which comprised FRY President Slobodan Milošević, along with the Presidents of Serbia and Montenegro, and made strategic decisions with respect to the VJ. However, the alleged common criminal plan was not formulated at the SDC sessions. While he had oversight of the Serbian Government Ministries, he did not have extensive interactions with MUP, nor did he have de facto powers over it. Also no adverse inferences can be drawn against him on the basis of decrees he made during the relevant period. Šainović (D), as head of the Joint Command, was an active participant in its meetings (as were Pavković (D) and Lukić (D), and, on occasion, Lazarević (D)) and issued instructions that resulted in military orders coordinating the activities of VJ and MUP. He was very well informed of events in Kosovo during the relevant period and was aware that criminal acts had been committed by the forces, but failed to use his extensive authority in Kosovo to put a stop to such conduct. Ojdanić (D), as the Chief of the General Staff of the VJ, exercised both de facto and de jure command and control over all units and organs of the VJ. He did not, however, have direct control over the MUP forces. He was an active participant in SDC meetings. He issued orders for the VJ to carry out operations in Kosovo,

including in support of MUP. He also mobilized extra VJ units for deployment in Kosovo during the time the majority of crimes took place. He was well informed of the situation in Kosovo, and although, in response to reports of criminal conduct, he issued orders for adherence to international humanitarian law, mobilized the military justice system, and dispatched senior officers from the Security Administration to investigate, he nevertheless continued to order the VJ to participate in military operations with the MUP in Kosovo. Pavković (D) had a central role in the planning and implementation of the activities of the VJ in Kosovo, in coordination with the MUP. He was involved in the arming of non-Albanian civilians and simultaneously disarming Kosovo Albanians. Despite being informed of the excessive or indiscriminate use of force by his units, he continued to engage them. Through his presence in Joint Command and other meetings, the regular VJ reporting system, and his tours of VJ units deployed across Kosovo, he had a detailed knowledge and understanding of the situation on the ground and the activities of his and the MUP forces. This knowledge extended to the commission of crimes by both the VJ and MUP, including the forcible displacement of Kosovo Albanians, murder, and sexual assaults. In fact, even though he knew about criminal acts committed by VJ members in Kosovo, he sometimes under-reported and minimized the serious criminal wrongdoing in his reports. Although he issued some orders calling for adherence to international humanitarian law in the course of these operations, these do not appear to have been genuine measures to limit the commission of crimes in Kosovo. Lazarević (D) also knew that criminal acts were being committed against civilians and their property by VJ and MUP forces and knew this resulted in displacing a significant number of civilians. He significantly participated in the planning and execution of joint VJ and MUP operations in Kosovo during the relevant period, including in places where crimes were found to have been committed. He continued to do so, despite his knowledge of the commission of crimes. He was not, however, aware of high-level political decisions that generally took place in Belgrade. Lukić (D), as head of the MUP Staff for Kosovo, had significant authority over the MUP forces answering to the MUP Staff—which had a significant role in planning, organizing, controlling, and directing MUP forces in Kosovo. The MUP Staff planned and coordinated operations with the VJ, and served as a link to MUP headquarters. Lukić (D) was perceived to be the commander of MUP forces in Kosovo, and he regularly attended and participated in meetings of the Joint Command and other high-level meetings, including in Belgrade. Thus, he was the de facto commander of MUP forces in Kosovo, and the link between the actions of the MUP on the ground in Kosovo and the overarching policies and plans decided in Belgrade. He had a detailed knowledge of events in Kosovo,

Continued on next page.

including allegations of criminal conduct by MUP personnel there. The evidence does not, however, prove that he was involved in the concealment of those crimes through the clandestine transportation of civilian bodies from Kosovo to other parts of Serbia.

As to the joint criminal enterprise set forth in the indictment, proof that there was a common purpose to modify the ethnic balance in Kosovo to ensure continued control by the FRY and Serbian authorities is the evidence establishing a widespread campaign of violence and other crimes directed at Kosovo Albanians and the ensuing massive displacement of that population. This campaign was conducted in an organized manner, utilizing significant state resources. Numerous witnesses also testified that they were directed to leave Kosovo, and that their identification papers were taken from them and never returned. Other evidence that supports this common purpose is that non-Albanian civilians were armed; a breakdown in negotiations to end the Kosovo crisis; and the concealment of the bodies of murdered Kosovo Albanians in other parts of Serbia. The evidence does not support the inference that murder, sexual assault, or the destruction or damage of religious property was within the common purpose, so that with regards to each of the accused, the issue is whether these crimes were reasonably foreseeable in the execution of the common purpose. Satisfied that there was such a common purpose among high-level officials in the FRY and Serbia who were in a position to execute it through the various forces under their control, the Chamber has analyzed whether or not each of the accused participated voluntarily in the joint criminal enterprise, made a significant contribution to it, and shared the intent to commit the crimes or underlying offences that were the object of the enterprise. The result of such analysis is that Milutinović (D) is not guilty. Šainović (D), Pavković (D), and Lukić (D) are guilty of all five counts of the indictment and are sentenced to serve 22 years in prison. Ojdanić (D) and Lazarević (D) are guilty of counts 1 and 2, by aiding and abetting acts falling under Article 7(1), and are sentenced to 15 years in prison.

▎ ANALYSIS

While war crimes and crimes against humanity are inevitably committed by individuals, they rarely commit such crimes for their own profit. Instead, such crimes are often caused by collective entities supported by a state apparatus. For international criminal tribunals to be able to place responsibility for such crimes on the leaders of the institutions that have supported such crimes, there must be a legal theory that links the leaders to the acts that they themselves have not committed. That theory, as in this case, is a theory of conspiracy. Previously, the International Military Tribunal (IMT) at Nuremberg following World War II used a remarkably innovative and highly controversial conspiracy theory that revolved around the concept of "criminal organization." In this case, the International Criminal Tribunal for the Former Yugoslavia (I.C.T.Y.) used a similarly innovative and equally controversial conspiracy theory that revolves around the concept of "joint criminal enterprise," which had a common purpose, was well-organized, had the support of the state, and used state resources.

■══■

Quicknotes

CONSPIRACY Concerted action by two or more persons to accomplish some unlawful purpose.

INDICTMENT A formal written accusation made by a prosecutor and issued by a grand jury, charging an individual with a criminal offense.

■══■

The Law of the Sea

Quick Reference Rules of Law

Corfu Channel Case
(United Kingdom v. Albania)

Warships (P) v. Territorial waters (D)

I.C.J., 1949 I.C.J. 4.

NATURE OF CASE: Proceeding before the International Court of Justice.

FACT SUMMARY: The United Kingdom (P) claimed that it had a right to send its warships through straits used for international navigation.

🏛 RULE OF LAW
The test of whether a channel should be considered as belonging to the class of international highways through which passage cannot be prohibited by a coastal state in time of peace is its geographical situation connecting two parts of the high seas and not the fact of its being used for international navigation.

FACTS: British warships (P) sailing through the North Corfu Channel were fired on by Albanian (D) forces. The United Kingdom (P) protested to the Albanian government (D) which asserted that foreign ships had no right to pass through Albanian territorial waters without prior notification to, and the permission of, Albanian authorities. The United Kingdom (P) claimed that in time of peace states can send their ships for innocent purposes through straits used for international navigation. Albania (D) claimed this channel did not belong to the class of international highways through which a right of passage exists because it was used almost exclusively for local traffic. That channel had also been in dispute because Greece and Albania had both claimed bordering territory and Albania was afraid of Greek incursions.

ISSUE: Is the test of whether a channel should be considered as belonging to the class of international highways through which passage cannot be prohibited by a coastal state in time of peace its geographical situation connecting two parts of the high seas and not the fact of its being used for international navigation?

HOLDING AND DECISION: [Judge not stated in casebook excerpt.] Yes. The test of whether a channel should be considered as belonging to the class of international highways through which passage cannot be prohibited by a coastal state in time of peace is its geographical situation connecting two parts of the high seas and not the fact of its being used for international navigation. The North Corfu Channel should be considered as belonging to the class of international highways through which passage cannot be prohibited by a coastal state in time of peace. In light of the state of war with Greece, Albania would have been justified in issuing regulations in respect of the passage of warships through the strait, but not in prohibiting such passage.

▶ ANALYSIS

The U.N. Convention on the Law of the Sea was passed in 1982. It provides that all states, whether coastal or land-locked, enjoy the right of innocent passage through the territorial sea. The territorial sea was held to exist up to a limit not exceeding 12 nautical miles from the coast.

■━■

Quicknotes

TERRITORIAL SEA That portion of the sea that is three miles off a nation's coast and over which that nation has jurisdiction.

■━■

The "Hoshinmaru" Case
(Japan v. Russian Federation)

Sovereign state (P) v. Sovereign state (D)

Int'l Trib. for the Law of the Sea, ITLOS Case No. 14, Judgment (2007).

NATURE OF CASE: Application before the International Tribunal for the Law of the Sea for release of a ship and its crew.

FACT SUMMARY: The "Hoshinmaru," a Japanese-registered ship, was detained, along with its crew, by the Russian Federation (D), which claimed the "Hoshinmaru" had violated a fishing license issued by the Russian Federation (D). Japan (P) applied for the ship's release.

🏛 RULE OF LAW
The amount of security to be posted by a nation seeking the release of a fishing vessel flying its flag that has committed a reporting offense in the context of an otherwise satisfactory cooperative framework must reflect the seriousness of the offense and the degree of cooperation between the detaining nation and the nation seeking release.

FACTS: The "Hoshinmaru" is a fishing ship registered in Japan (P), and its crew is comprised of Japanese nationals. The ship had obtained a fishing license from the Russian Federation (D) that permitted it to fish certain amounts of specified fish in the waters of the exclusive economic zone of the Russian Federation (D), including 101.8 tons of sockeye salmon and 161.8 tons of chum salmon. While fishing in the exclusive economic zone, the ship was boarded by Russian Federation (D) inspectors, who discovered that sockeye salmon were being kept under the chum salmon and that the ship's master had declared 20 tons of sockeye salmon as the cheaper chum salmon. This constituted an offense, since part of the sockeye salmon catch was being concealed and data in the fishing log and vessel report was misleading. Accordingly, the Russian Federation (D) detained the ship and its crew. Japan (P) applied to the International Tribunal for the Law of the Sea for release of the ship and its crew. As part of its judgment, the Tribunal determined the amount of the bond or other financial security that Japan (P) would have to post to secure such release.

ISSUE: Must the amount of security to be posted by a nation seeking the release of a fishing vessel flying its flag that has committed a reporting offense in the context of an otherwise satisfactory cooperative framework reflect the seriousness of the offense and the degree of cooperation between the detaining nation and the nation seeking release?

HOLDING AND DECISION: [Judge not stated in casebook excerpt.] Yes. The amount of security to be posted by a nation seeking the release of a fishing vessel

flying its flag that has committed a reporting offense in the context of an otherwise satisfactory cooperative framework must reflect the seriousness of the offense and the degree of cooperation between the detaining nation and the nation seeking release. To determine the appropriate amount, nature, and form of the bond or other financial security to be posted, the Tribunal must apply the rules set forth in the Convention and other rules of international law not incompatible with the Convention. The offense committed is considered by the Russian Federation (D) to be very serious, since if the substitution of one fish for another had not been detected by the inspectors, the 20 tons of sockeye would have been stolen and taken illegally out of the exclusive economic zone. Thus, according to the Russian Federation (D), this is a classic case of illegal, unreported, and unregulated fishing and justifies a bond of 22,000,000 rubles. Japan (P), on the other hand, asserts that the offense is not fishing without a license or overfishing, but falsely recording the catch that the vessel was entitled to take under its license. Also, since the amount of sockeye salmon on board the vessel was well within the license limit, the sockeye salmon stock could not be deemed damaged or endangered. Both sovereigns cooperate closely in respect of fishing in the exclusive economic zone and have an institutional framework for managing and conserving fish, which includes rules for such management and conservation. Japan (P) has indicated that it will continue to endeavor to ensure that crews of vessels flying its flag respect such rules and other local laws and regulations. Although the offense at issue is a transgression within an otherwise satisfactory cooperative framework, it should not be considered a minor or purely technical offense. Monitoring of catches, which requires accurate reporting, is one of the most essential means of managing marine living resources. Not only is it the right of the Russian Federation (D) to apply and implement such measures but the provisions of article 61, paragraph 2, of the Convention should also be taken into consideration to ensure through proper conservation and management measures that the maintenance of the living resources in the exclusive economic zone is not endangered by over-exploitation. Therefore, on the basis of these considerations, the amount of security to be posted by Japan (P) should be 10,000,000 rubles, paid to the bank account indicated by the Russian Federation (D), or in the form of a bank guarantee.

Continued on next page.

▶ ANALYSIS

The Convention at issue in this case is the United Nations Convention on the Law of the Sea (LOS Convention). The LOS Convention, Article 73(2), provides that "Arrested vessels and their crews shall be promptly released upon the posting of reasonable bond or other security." As in this case, the reasonableness of the security to be posted by the flag state seeking prompt release takes into account the depletion of marine life and should serve to deter the plundering of the living resources of the sea. Given available technology, in addition to requiring a bond or other financial security, other sanctions a tribunal could order might include having a satellite tracking device on the detained vessel.

■■■

Quicknotes

INTERNATIONAL LAW The body of law applicable to dealings between nations.

SOVEREIGN A state or entity with independent authority to govern its affairs.

■■■

United States v. Flores

Government (P) v. Alleged murderer (D)

289 U.S. 137 (1933).

NATURE OF CASE: Appeal from dismissal of criminal charges.

FACT SUMMARY: The court held that it lacked jurisdiction over a crime committed overseas.

⚖ RULE OF LAW
The United States (P) may define and punish offenses committed by its own citizens on its own vessels while within foreign waters where the local sovereign has not asserted its jurisdiction.

FACTS: Flores (D), a U.S. citizen, allegedly murdered another U.S. citizen while on an American vessel at anchor in the Belgian Congo. When Flores (D) was charged in Philadelphia, the district court sustained a demurrer to the indictment and discharged Flores (D) on the grounds that the court lacked jurisdiction. The United States (P) appealed.

ISSUE: May the United States (P) define and punish offenses committed by its own citizens on its own vessels while within foreign waters where the local sovereign has not asserted its jurisdiction?

HOLDING AND DECISION: (Stone, J.) Yes. The United States (P) may define and punish offenses committed by its own citizens on its own vessels while within foreign waters where the local sovereign has not asserted its jurisdiction. A merchant vessel is deemed to be a part of the territory of the sovereignty whose flag it flies and does not lose that character when in navigable waters within the territorial limits of another sovereignty. It is the duty of the U.S. courts to apply to offenses committed by its citizens on vessels flying its own flag, its own statutes, interpreted in the light of recognized principles of international law. Reversed and remanded.

▶ ANALYSIS

The Court held that the indictment charged an offense within the admiralty and maritime jurisdiction of the United States. If the local authorities also claim jurisdiction, the local authorities would have jurisdiction in the case of a serious crime. The doctrine of concurrent jurisdiction is based on principles of international comity.

Quicknotes

COMITY A rule pursuant to which courts in one state give deference to the statutes and judicial decisions of another.

CONCURRENT JURISDICTION Authority by two or more different courts over the subject matter of a proceeding so that the case may be heard and determined by either.

DEMURRER The assertion that the opposing party's pleadings are insufficient and that the demurring party should not be made to answer.

MARITIME LAW That area of law pertaining to navigable waters.

TREATY An agreement between two or more nations for the benefit of the general public.

Wildenhus's Case

Belgian consul (P) v. American authorities (D)

120 U.S. 1 (1887).

NATURE OF CASE: Appeal from denial of habeas corpus.

FACT SUMMARY: The Belgian consul (P) sought to have Wildenhus, a Belgian national, released to Belgian authorities after he was arrested in New Jersey for killing another Belgian crew member while onboard a Belgian vessel moored in Jersey City.

🏛 RULE OF LAW
Disorders that disturb only the peace of the ship or those on board are to be dealt with exclusively by the sovereignty of the home of the ship, but those that disturb the public peace may be suppressed or punished by the proper authorities of the local jurisdiction.

FACTS: Wildenhus, a Belgian national, allegedly killed another Belgian crew member while their ship was in port in New Jersey. After Wildenhus's arrest, the Belgian consul (P) applied for a writ of habeas corpus, citing a treaty granting exclusive charge to consuls for the internal order of the merchant vessels of their nation. The circuit court refused to release Wildenhus and the consul (P) appealed.

ISSUE: Are disorders that disturb only the peace of the ship or those on board to be dealt with exclusively by the sovereignty of the home of the ship, but those that disturb the public peace suppressed or punished by the proper authorities of the local jurisdiction?

HOLDING AND DECISION: (Waite, C.J.) Yes. Disorders that disturb only the peace of the ship or those on board are to be dealt with exclusively by the sovereignty of the home of the ship, but those that disturb the public peace may be suppressed or punished by the proper authorities of the local jurisdiction. Felonious homicide is a subject for the local jurisdiction. If the authorities are proceeding with the case in a regular way, the consul has no right to interfere. Affirmed.

▌ANALYSIS

The Court discussed the many treaties governing consuls' authority. Most adhere to the principle that a ship is subject to local criminal jurisdiction. The local police and judicial authorities usually decide whether a particular incident disturbs the peace of the port.

Quicknotes

HABEAS CORPUS A proceeding in which a defendant brings a writ to compel a judicial determination of whether he is lawfully being held in custody.

JURISDICTION The authority of a court to hear and declare judgment in respect to a particular matter.

Spector v. Norwegian Cruise Line Ltd.

Disabled individual (P) v. Cruise line with foreign-flag vessels (D)

545 U.S. 119 (2005).

NATURE OF CASE: Appeal from dismissal of class action seeking declaratory and injunctive relief under Title III of the Americans with Disabilities Act (ADA).

FACT SUMMARY: Disabled individuals (P) and their companions (P) who purchased tickets for round-trip cruises from a U.S. port, brought a class action seeking declaratory and injunctive relief against Norwegian Cruise Line Ltd. (NCL) (D) under Title III of the ADA, which prohibits discrimination based on disability.

🏛 RULE OF LAW
Title III of the Americans with Disabilities Act is applicable to foreign-flag cruise ships in U.S. waters, except insofar as it regulates a vessel's internal affairs.

FACTS: NCL (D), a Bermuda Corporation with a principal place of business in Miami, Florida, operated cruise ships that departed from, and returned to, ports in the United States. Although the cruises were operated by a company based in the U.S., served predominantly U.S. residents, and were in most respects U.S.-centered ventures, almost all of NCL's (D) vessels were registered in other countries. Disabled individuals (P) and their companions (P) who purchased tickets for round-trip cruises from a U.S. port aboard NCL (D) vessels registered in the Bahamas, brought a class action seeking declaratory and injunctive relief against NCL (D) under Title III of the ADA, which prohibits discrimination based on disability. The court of appeals dismissed the claim, finding that general statutes, such as the ADA, do not apply to foreign-flag vessels in U.S. territory absent a clear indication of congressional intent to the contrary. The U.S. Supreme Court granted certiorari.

ISSUE: Is Title III of the ADA applicable to foreign-flag cruise ships in U.S. waters, except insofar as it regulates a vessel's internal affairs?

HOLDING AND DECISION: (Kennedy, J.) Yes. Title III of the ADA is applicable to foreign-flag cruise ships in U.S. waters, except insofar as it regulates a vessel's internal affairs. General statutes are presumed to apply to conduct that takes place aboard a foreign-flag vessel in U.S. territory if the interests of the United States or its citizens, rather than interests internal to the ship, are at stake. A narrow exception to this presumption, based on international comity, is that absent a clear statement of congressional intent, general statutes do not apply to foreign-flag vessels as to matters involving internal order and discipline of the vessel. What is covered by "internal affairs" is difficult to define with precision, and it is unclear whether the relevant category of activities is limited to matters that affect only the ship's internal order when there is no effect on U.S. interests, or whether the clear-statement rule is applicable if the predominant effect of the statute is on a foreign ship's internal affairs but the statute also promotes the welfare of U.S. residents or territory. Notwithstanding this ambiguity, the guiding principles are that the clear-statement rule will be applied to promote international comity and when the territorial sovereign is not interested in matters that do not bear on the peace of the port. Plainly, most of the Title III violations alleged—that NCL (D) required disabled passengers (P) to pay higher fares and special surcharges; maintained evacuation programs and equipment in locations not accessible to them; required them, but not other passengers, to waive any potential medical liability and to travel with companions; reserved the right to remove them from ships if they endangered other passengers' comfort; and, more generally, failed to make reasonable modifications necessary to ensure their full enjoyment of the services offered—have nothing to do with a ship's internal affairs. However, the allegations concerning physical barriers to access on board—e.g., the assertion that most of NCL's (D) cabins, including the most attractive ones in the most desirable locations, are not accessible to disabled passengers (P)—would appear to involve requirements that might be construed as relating to internal ship affairs. Title III requires barrier removal only if it is "readily achievable," so that barrier removal would not be required if doing so brought a ship into noncompliance with international legal obligations or threatened shipboard safety. Moreover, the clear-statement rule would most likely come into play if Title III were read to require permanent and significant structural modifications to foreign vessels. Otherwise, Title III is applicable to NCL's (D) foreign-flag cruise ships. Reversed and remanded.

DISSENT: (Scalia, J.) The clear-statement rule comes into play when a law would interfere with the regulation of a ship's internal order, and is designed to promote international comity and avoid international discord. It does not apply where the pervasive regulation of the internal order of a ship is not present. Under Title III, the structural modifications needed for compliance with its barrier-removal provisions clearly would affect the ship's internal order, as these would alter core physical aspects of the ship, some of which might relate to safety, which under international law traditionally has been the province of the ship's flag state. Such modifications would conflict with the International Convention for the Safety of Life at Sea (SOLAS), and similar inconsistencies might exist between

Continued on next page.

Title III's structural requirements and the disability laws of other countries. Accordingly, the ADA should not apply to foreign-flag cruise ships in U.S. waters.

▶ *ANALYSIS*

The clear-statement rule is an implied limitation on a statute's otherwise unambiguous general terms, and operates much like other implied limitation rules, which avoid applications of otherwise unambiguous statutes that would intrude on sensitive domains in a way that Congress is unlikely to have intended had it considered the matter. The Court in this case avoids an all-or-nothing approach to the rule, under which a statute is altogether inapplicable if but one of its specific applications trenches on the domain protected by a clear-statement rule. Such an approach would convert the clear-statement rule from a principle of interpretive caution into a trap for an unwary Congress, requiring nullification of the entire statute, or of some arbitrary set of applications larger than the domain the rule protects.

■■■■

Quicknotes

CERTIORARI A discretionary writ issued by a superior court to an inferior court in order to review the lower court's decisions; the Supreme Court's writ ordering such review.

CLASS ACTION A suit commenced by a representative on behalf of an ascertainable group that is too large to appear in court, who shares a commonality of interests and who will benefit from a successful result.

COMITY A rule pursuant to which courts in one state give deference to the statutes and judicial decisions of the court of another state.

INJUNCTIVE RELIEF A court order issued as a remedy, requiring a person to do, or prohibiting that person from doing, a specific act.

■■■■

CHAPTER 18

International Environmental Law

Quick Reference Rules of Law

Trail Smelter Arbitration (United States v. Canada)

Government (P) v. Government (D)

Arbitral Trib., 3 U.N. Rep. Int'l Arb. Awards 1905 (1941).

NATURE OF CASE: Action for damages for air pollution.

FACT SUMMARY: The United States (P) brought this action against Canada (D) seeking damages and an injunction for air pollution, in the state of Washington, by the Trail Smelter, a Canadian corporation located in Canada (D).

🏛 **RULE OF LAW**
A state owes, at all times, a duty to protect other states against injurious acts by individuals from within its jurisdiction.

FACTS: Since 1906, the Trail Smelter, located in British Columbia, was owned and operated by a Canadian corporation. From 1925, at least, to 1937, damage occurred in the state of Washington, resulting from the sulfur dioxide from Trail Smelter. The United States (P) brought an action for damages against Canada (D) and also sought an injunction against further air pollution by Trail Smelter.

ISSUE: Does a state owe, at all times, a duty to protect other states against injurious acts by individuals from within its jurisdiction?

HOLDING AND DECISION: Yes. A state owes, at all times, a duty to protect other states against injurious acts by individuals from within its jurisdiction. Under the principles of international law, as well as the law of the United States (P), no state has the right to use or permit the use of the territory in a manner as to cause injury by fumes in or to the territory of another or the properties or persons therein. Considering the facts of the case, this tribunal holds that Canada (D) is responsible in international law for the conduct of the Trail Smelter. It is, therefore, the duty of the government of Canada (D) to see to it that Trail Smelter's conduct should be in conformity with the obligations of Canada (D) under international law as herein determined. So long as the present conditions of air pollution exist in Washington, the Trail Smelter shall be required to refrain from causing any damage through fumes. The indemnity for damage should be fixed by the governments of the United States (P) and Canada (D) pursuant to Article III of the convention existing between the two nations. Lastly, since this tribunal is of the opinion that damage may occur in the future unless the operations of the smelter shall be subject to some control, a regime or measure of control shall be applied to the operations of the smelter.

▶ **ANALYSIS**

It is interesting to note that no international tribunal has ever held a state responsible for pollution of the sea or held that there exists a duty to desist from polluting the seas. The international regulation of pollution is just beginning, and the regulation must always be balanced against freedom of the seas guaranteed under general and long-established rules of international law.

■■■

Quicknotes

DAMAGES Monetary compensation that may be awarded by the court to a party who has sustained injury or loss to his person, property or rights due to another party's unlawful act, omission, or negligence.

INDEMNITY The duty of a party to compensate another for damages sustained.

INJUNCTION A court order requiring a person to do, or prohibiting that person from doing, a specific act.

JURISDICTION The authority of a court to hear and declare judgment in respect to a particular matter.

■■■

Legality of the Threat or Use of Nuclear Weapons

[Parties not identified.]

I.C.J., 1996 I.C.J. 226.

NATURE OF CASE: Advisory opinion relating to environmental law issues raised by the threat or use of nuclear weapons.

FACT SUMMARY: Certain states argued that any use of nuclear weapons would be unlawful by reference to existing norms relating to the safeguarding and protection of the environment.

🏛 RULE OF LAW
International law relating to the protection and safeguarding of the environment does not specifically prohibit the use of nuclear weapons.

FACTS: [Facts not stated in casebook excerpt.]

ISSUE: Do treaties relating to the protection of the environment specifically prohibit the use of nuclear weapons by states?

HOLDING AND DECISION: [Judge not stated in casebook excerpt.] No. Environmental treaties are not intended to deprive states of the exercise of the right to self-defense under international law. Nevertheless, states must take environmental considerations into account when assessing what is necessary and proportionate in the pursuit of legitimate military objectives. Respect for the environment is one of the elements that go into assessing whether an action is in conformity with the principles of necessity and proportionality.

▶ ANALYSIS

Wartime conduct detrimental to the environment has been considered by the U.N. Compensation Commission (U.N.C.C.) hearing claims against Iraq growing out of the 1990–1991 invasion of Kuwait.

■══■

Quicknotes

ADVISORY OPINION A decision rendered at the request of an interested party of how the court would rule should the particular issue arise.

ENVIRONMENTAL LAW A body of federal law passed in 1970 that protects the environment against public and private actions that harm the ecosystem.

■══■

Gabčíkovo-Nagymaros Project
(Hungary/Slovakia)

Treaty partner (P) v. New nation (D)

I.C.J., 1997 I.C.J. 7.

NATURE OF CASE: Proceeding before the International Court of Justice.

FACT SUMMARY: Hungary (P) claimed that it could terminate a treaty for the construction of a system of dams and other works on the Danube River for reasons of ecological necessity and fundamentally changed circumstances.

RULE OF LAW
The general obligation of states to ensure that activities within their jurisdiction and control respect the environment of other states or of areas beyond national control is now a part of the corpus of international law relating to the environment.

FACTS: Hungary (P) had signed a treaty in 1977 for construction of a series of dams along the Danube. When disputes arose, Slovakia (D) and Hungary (P) submitted the matter to the I.C.J. for resolution.

ISSUE: Is the general obligation of states to ensure that activities within their jurisdiction and control respect the environment of other states or of areas beyond national control now a part of the corpus of international law relating to the environment?

HOLDING AND DECISION: [Judge not stated in casebook excerpt.] Yes. The general obligation of states to ensure that activities within their jurisdiction and control respect the environment of other states or of areas beyond national control is now a part of the corpus of international law relating to the environment. The need to reconcile economic development with protection of the environment is aptly expressed in the concept of sustainable development. The parties must negotiate to implement the terms of the agreement.

▶ ANALYSIS

The Court asserted that there must be both economic development and environmental protection. The I.C.J. established a Chamber on Environmental Matters in 1993. The Court found here that neither party could unilaterally revoke the treaty.

Quicknotes

ENVIRONMENTAL LAW A body of federal law passed in 1970 that protects the environment against public and private actions that harm the ecosystem.

TREATY An agreement between two or more nations for the benefit of the general public.

State Succession

Quick Reference Rules of Law

Application of the Convention on the Prevention and Punishment of the Crime of Genocide
(Croatia v. Serbia)

Sovereign state (P) v. Sovereign state (D)

I.C.J., www.icj-cij.org (2008).

NATURE OF CASE: Application before the International Court of Justice for alleged violations of the Genocide Convention of 1948.

FACT SUMMARY: Croatia (P) contended that the Federal Republic of Yugoslavia (FRY), which became "Serbia and Montenegro" and then just "Serbia" (D), had violated the Genocide Convention of 1948 (Convention). Serbia (D) objected to the Court's jurisdiction by claiming that the FRY, as successor to the Socialist Federal Republic of Yugoslavia (SFRY)—which had adhered to the Convention—did not become bound to the Convention upon dissolution of the SFRY because it was not the continuator state.

🏛 RULE OF LAW
A state that unequivocally declares it will be bound by a predecessor state's legal obligations and that consistently conducts itself in accord with such a declaration will be bound as a party to a Convention to which its predecessor was bound.

FACTS: In 1999, Croatia (P) sued in the I.C.J. the Federal Republic of Yugoslavia (FRY), which became "Serbia and Montenegro" and then just "Serbia" (D), contending that it had violated the Genocide Convention of 1948 (Convention) by directly engaging in or encouraging acts of "ethnic cleansing" of Croats in parts of Croatia (P). Croatia (P) also argued that the Court had jurisdiction pursuant to Article IX of the Convention, which provides the Court with jurisdiction over disputes relating to a state's responsibility under the Convention. Serbia (D) objected to the Court's jurisdiction, contending that the FRY, as successor to the Socialist Federal Republic of Yugoslavia (SFRY), had not become bound to the Convention upon the SFRY's dissolution since the FRY was not the continuator state. To this, Croatia (P) pointed to the FRY's declaration in 1992 that it would "strictly abide" by all the SFRY's commitments, and a Diplomatic Note (Note) to that effect. Serbia (D) argued that such a broad declaration was insufficient to bring about succession of the treaty, and that a declaration specifically identifying the treaty to be continued was necessary. The Court rendered its judgment.

ISSUE: Will a state that unequivocally declares it will be bound by a predecessor state's legal obligations and that consistently conducts itself in accord with such a declaration be bound as a party to a Convention to which its predecessor was bound?

HOLDING AND DECISION: [Judge not stated in casebook excerpt.] Yes. A state that unequivocally declares it will be bound by a predecessor state's legal obligations and that consistently conducts itself in accord with such a declaration will be bound as a party to a Convention to which its predecessor was bound. There is a distinction between the legal nature of ratification of, or accession to, a treaty, and the process by which a State becomes bound by a treaty as a successor State or remains bound as a continuing State. Accession or ratification is an act of will on the part of the State manifesting an intention to undertake new obligations and to acquire new rights in terms of the treaty. Such manifestation is made in a formal writing as per the terms of the treaty itself. In the case of succession or continuation, the manifestation of the act of will of the State, which relates to an already existing set of circumstances and amounts to a recognition by the State of certain legal consequences flowing from those circumstances, does not have to be so formal, and any form of confirmatory notification will suffice. This notion is codified in Article 2(g) of the 1978 Vienna Convention on Succession of States in respect of Treaties, which defines a "notification of succession" as meaning "in relation to a multilateral treaty, any notification, however framed or named, made by a successor State expressing its consent to be considered as bound by the treaty." International law also does not prescribe any specific form for a State to express a claim of continuity. Here, the FRY clearly expressed an intent to be bound by the Convention when it claimed it was the SFRY's continuator state and declared it would be bound by the SFRY's commitments, but the FRY also did not repudiate this position when it turned out it was only one of the SFRY's several successor states. Thus, the FRY's declaration had the effect of a notification of succession to treaties, as there was no indication in the declaration that the commitment undertaken was conditional on being accepted as the continuator state. Moreover, Serbia's (D) conduct after the declaration makes clear it regarded itself as bound by the Convention. In another case, brought by Bosnia and Herzegovina in 1993, only a year after the declaration and Note, the FRY did not challenge the claim that it was a party to the Convention. The Court in that case found that both parties, including the FRY, were parties to the Convention, citing the FRY's declaration and Note. In that case, too, the FRY acknowledged that it had itself continued the rights and duties

Continued on next page.

under the Convention established by the SFRY. Additionally, in 1999, the FRY cited the Convention as title of jurisdiction in proceedings it brought against NATO member states. Thus, between 1992 and 1999, when Croatia (P) instituted its suit, neither the FRY nor any other state questioned that the FRY was a party to the Convention. When the FRY became a member of the United Nations in 2000, it also did not withdraw its declaration or Note of 1992. Thus, the declaration and Note will be given the effect they had on their face—i.e., that the FRY would be bound by the legal obligations of a party in respect of all multilateral conventions to which the SFRY had been a party at the time of its dissolution. Having made no reservations to such a commitment, the FRY (Serbia (D)) is bound by the Convention, including Article IX, which endows the Court with jurisdiction to hear cases brought under the Convention against parties thereto.

▶ *ANALYSIS*

The 1978 Vienna Convention on Succession of States in respect of Treaties will not bind a state that makes it clear that it does not consider itself bound by treaties to which a predecessor state was a party. If the state later decides to become a party to a certain treaty, it will have to do so by accession through a formal writing required by the treaty, not by succession.

■==■

Quicknotes

JURISDICTION The authority of a court to hear and declare judgment in respect to a particular matter.

RATIFICATION Affirmation of a prior action taken by either the individual himself or by an agent on behalf of the principal, which is then treated as if it had been initially authorized by the principal.

TREATY An agreement between two or more nations for the benefit of the general public.

■==■

Gabčíkovo-Nagymaros Project
(Hungary/Slovakia)

Treaty partner (P) v. New nation (D)

Int'l Ct. of Justice, 1997 I.C.J. 7 (1997).

NATURE OF CASE: Proceeding before the International Court of Justice.

FACT SUMMARY: [For facts, see the briefs for this case in Chapters 3, 8, and 18.]

🏛 RULE OF LAW
A successor state will be bound to a bilateral treaty that is territorial in character and that expressly acknowledges the interests of third states.

FACTS: [For facts, see the briefs for this case in Chapters 3, 8, and 18.]

ISSUE: Will a successor state be bound to a bilateral treaty that is territorial in character and that expressly acknowledges the interests of third states?

HOLDING AND DECISION: [Judge not stated in casebook excerpt.] Yes. A successor state will be bound to a bilateral treaty that is territorial in character and that expressly acknowledges the interests of third states. The issue here is whether Slovakia (D), as a successor state to Czechoslovakia, is party to the 1977 Treaty entered into between Hungary (P) and Czechoslovakia. Hungary (P) claims that because one of the parties to the bilateral treaty "disappeared" (i.e., Czechoslovakia), the treaty ceased to be in force upon Czechoslovakia's dissolution. Hungary (P) asserts that there is no rule of international law that provides for automatic succession to bilateral treaties on the disappearance of a party, and that for a bilateral treaty to continue, both the original party and the successor state must expressly agree to such continuation—which did not occur here. Hungary (P) further asserts that the 1978 Vienna Convention on Succession of States in respect of Treaties (Convention), Article 34, which provides for a rule of automatic succession to all treaties, has never been accepted as a statement of general international law. According to Hungary (P), the 1977 Treaty did not create rights or obligations related to boundaries or that were territorial in nature, so that even if the Convention or its principles are applicable and provide that such rights or obligations are unaffected by succession, the 1977 Treaty is no longer in force. Instead, Hungary (P) maintains that the 1977 Treaty is simply a joint venture, and nothing more. Slovakia (D), on the other hand, contends that the 1977 Treaty remains in force because there is a general rule of international law of continuity that applies in the case of dissolution, and because the 1977 Treaty attaches to territory and contains provisions relating to a boundary. Slovakia (D) asserts that Article 12 of the Convention

codifies customary international law and that, therefore, the 1977 Treaty comes within its scope because it sets forth a specific territorial regime that operates in the interest of all Danube riparian states, and therefore is a dispositive treaty, creating rights in rem, independently of the legal personality of its original signatories. Here, it is unnecessary for the Court to determine whether Article 34 of the Convention reflects the state of customary international law. Instead, a determination that the 1977 Treaty is territorial in character is dispositive of the issue at bar. An examination of this Treaty confirms that, aside from its undoubted nature as a joint investment, its major elements were the proposed construction and joint operation of a large, integrated, and indivisible complex of structures and installations on specific parts of the respective territories of Hungary (P) and Czechoslovakia along the Danube. The 1977 Treaty also established the navigational regime for an important sector of an international waterway, and included the relocation of a main international shipping lane. Thus, it created a situation in which the interests of other users of the Danube were affected. Furthermore, the interests of third States were expressly acknowledged in the 1977 Treaty, whereby the parties undertook to ensure "uninterrupted and safe navigation on the international fairway" in accordance with their obligations under the 1948 Convention concerning the Regime of Navigation on the Danube. The International Law Commission has identified "treaties of a territorial character" as being regarded both in traditional doctrine and modern opinion as unaffected by a succession of states, and the Convention reflects this principle. Moreover, the Commission has noted that treaties concerning waterways, water rights, or navigation on rivers are commonly regarded as territorial treaties. Article 12, in providing only, without reference to the treaty itself, that rights and obligations of a territorial character established by a treaty are unaffected by a succession of states, appears to support Hungary's (P) position, rather than Slovakia's (D), but this formulation was devised to take account of the fact that, in many cases, treaties that had established boundaries or territorial regimes were no longer in force, so that those that remained in force would nonetheless bind a successor state. Based on all these factors, the 1977 Treaty is a treaty that establishes a territorial regime within the meaning of Article 12 of the Convention, creating rights and obligations attaching to the parts of the Danube to which it relates. Accordingly, the 1977 Treaty cannot be

Continued on next page.

affected by a succession of states, and Slovakia (D) is bound thereto.

▶ *ANALYSIS*

Article 12(3) of the Convention provides: "The provisions of the present article do not apply to treaty obligations of the predecessor State providing for the establishment of foreign military bases on the territory to which the succession of States relates." Thus, had the treaty at issue related to military bases, rather than an international waterway, Slovakia (D) would not have been bound to the treaty as a successor state. This provision makes clear that military bases, which arguably could relate to territory and constitute part of a territorial regime, are not intended to be covered by the other provisions of Article 12 relating to "Other Territorial Regimes."

■══■

Quicknotes

IN REM An action against property.

RIPARIAN RIGHT The right of an owner of real property to the use of water naturally flowing through his land.

TREATY An agreement between two or more nations for the benefit of the general public.

■══■

Glossary

Common Latin Words and Phrases Encountered in the Law

A FORTIORI: Because one fact exists or has been proven, therefore a second fact that is related to the first fact must also exist.

A PRIORI: From the cause to the effect. A term of logic used to denote that when one generally accepted truth is shown to be a cause, another particular effect must necessarily follow.

AB INITIO: From the beginning; a condition which has existed throughout, as in a marriage which was void ab initio.

ACTUS REUS: The wrongful act; in criminal law, such action sufficient to trigger criminal liability.

AD VALOREM: According to value; an ad valorem tax is imposed upon an item located within the taxing jurisdiction calculated by the value of such item.

AMICUS CURIAE: Friend of the court. Its most common usage takes the form of an amicus curiae brief, filed by a person who is not a party to an action but is nonetheless allowed to offer an argument supporting his legal interests.

ARGUENDO: In arguing. A statement, possibly hypothetical, made for the purpose of argument, is one made arguendo.

BILL QUIA TIMET: A bill to quiet title (establish ownership) to real property.

BONA FIDE: True, honest, or genuine. May refer to a person's legal position based on good faith or lacking notice of fraud (such as a bona fide purchaser for value) or to the authenticity of a particular document (such as a bona fide last will and testament).

CAUSA MORTIS: With approaching death in mind. A gift causa mortis is a gift given by a party who feels certain that death is imminent.

CAVEAT EMPTOR: Let the buyer beware. This maxim is reflected in the rule of law that a buyer purchases at his own risk because it is his responsibility to examine, judge, test, and otherwise inspect what he is buying.

CERTIORARI: A writ of review. Petitions for review of a case by the United States Supreme Court are most often done by means of a writ of certiorari.

CONTRA: On the other hand. Opposite. Contrary to.

CORAM NOBIS: Before us; writs of error directed to the court that originally rendered the judgment.

CORAM VOBIS: Before you; writs of error directed by an appellate court to a lower court to correct a factual error.

CORPUS DELICTI: The body of the crime; the requisite elements of a crime amounting to objective proof that a crime has been committed.

CUM TESTAMENTO ANNEXO, ADMINISTRATOR (ADMINISTRATOR C.T.A.): With will annexed; an administrator c.t.a. settles an estate pursuant to a will in which he is not appointed.

DE BONIS NON, ADMINISTRATOR (ADMINISTRATOR D.B.N.): Of goods not administered; an administrator d.b.n. settles a partially settled estate.

DE FACTO: In fact; in reality; actually. Existing in fact but not officially approved or engendered.

DE JURE: By right; lawful. Describes a condition that is legitimate "as a matter of law," in contrast to the term "de facto," which connotes something existing in fact but not legally sanctioned or authorized. For example, de facto segregation refers to segregation brought about by housing patterns, etc., whereas de jure segregation refers to segregation created by law.

DE MINIMIS: Of minimal importance; insignificant; a trifle; not worth bothering about.

DE NOVO: Anew; a second time; afresh. A trial de novo is a new trial held at the appellate level as if the case originated there and the trial at a lower level had not taken place.

DICTA: Generally used as an abbreviated form of obiter dicta, a term describing those portions of a judicial opinion incidental or not necessary to resolution of the specific question before the court. Such nonessential statements and remarks are not considered to be binding precedent.

DUCES TECUM: Refers to a particular type of writ or subpoena requesting a party or organization to produce certain documents in their possession.

EN BANC: Full bench. Where a court sits with all justices present rather than the usual quorum.

EX PARTE: For one side or one party only. An ex parte proceeding is one undertaken for the benefit of only one party, without notice to, or an appearance by, an adverse party.

EX POST FACTO: After the fact. An ex post facto law is a law that retroactively changes the consequences of a prior act.

EX REL.: Abbreviated form of the term "ex relatione," meaning upon relation or information. When the state brings an action in which it has no interest against an individual at the instigation of one who has a private interest in the matter.

FORUM NON CONVENIENS: Inconvenient forum. Although a court may have jurisdiction over the case, the action should be tried in a more conveniently located court, one to which parties and witnesses may more easily travel, for example.

GUARDIAN AD LITEM: A guardian of an infant as to litigation, appointed to represent the infant and pursue his/her rights.

HABEAS CORPUS: You have the body. The modern writ of habeas corpus is a writ directing that a person (body) being detained (such as a prisoner) be brought before the court so that the legality of his detention can be judicially ascertained.

IN CAMERA: In private, in chambers. When a hearing is held before a judge in his chambers or when all spectators are excluded from the courtroom.

IN FORMA PAUPERIS: In the manner of a pauper. A party who proceeds in forma pauperis because of his poverty is one who is allowed to bring suit without liability for costs.

INFRA: Below, under. A word referring the reader to a later part of a book. (The opposite of supra.)

IN LOCO PARENTIS: In the place of a parent.

IN PARI DELICTO: Equally wrong; a court of equity will not grant requested relief to an applicant who is in pari delicto, or as much at fault in the transactions giving rise to the controversy as is the opponent of the applicant.

IN PARI MATERIA: On like subject matter or upon the same matter. Statutes relating to the same person or things are said to be in pari materia. It is a general rule of statutory construction that such statutes should be construed together, i.e., looked at as if they together constituted one law.

IN PERSONAM: Against the person. Jurisdiction over the person of an individual.

IN RE: In the matter of. Used to designate a proceeding involving an estate or other property.

IN REM: A term that signifies an action against the res, or thing. An action in rem is basically one that is taken directly against property, as distinguished from an action in personam, i.e., against the person.

INTER ALIA: Among other things. Used to show that the whole of a statement, pleading, list, statute, etc., has not been set forth in its entirety.

INTER PARTES: Between the parties. May refer to contracts, conveyances or other transactions having legal significance.

INTER VIVOS: Between the living. An inter vivos gift is a gift made by a living grantor, as distinguished from bequests contained in a will, which pass upon the death of the testator.

IPSO FACTO: By the mere fact itself.

JUS: Law or the entire body of law.

LEX LOCI: The law of the place; the notion that the rights of parties to a legal proceeding are governed by the law of the place where those rights arose.

MALUM IN SE: Evil or wrong in and of itself; inherently wrong. This term describes an act that is wrong by its very nature, as opposed to one which would not be wrong but for the fact that there is a specific legal prohibition against it (malum prohibitum).

MALUM PROHIBITUM: Wrong because prohibited, but not inherently evil. Used to describe something that is wrong because it is expressly forbidden by law but that is not in and of itself evil, e.g., speeding.

MANDAMUS: We command. A writ directing an official to take a certain action.

MENS REA: A guilty mind; a criminal intent. A term used to signify the mental state that accompanies a crime or other prohibited act. Some crimes require only a general mens rea (general intent to do the prohibited act), but others, like assault with intent to murder, require the existence of a specific mens rea.

MODUS OPERANDI: Method of operating; generally refers to the manner or style of a criminal in committing crimes, admissible in appropriate cases as evidence of the identity of a defendant.

NEXUS: A connection to.

NISI PRIUS: A court of first impression. A nisi prius court is one where issues of fact are tried before a judge or jury.

N.O.V. (NON OBSTANTE VEREDICTO): Notwithstanding the verdict. A judgment n.o.v. is a judgment given in favor of one party despite the fact that a verdict was returned in favor of the other party, the justification being that the verdict either had no reasonable support in fact or was contrary to law.

NUNC PRO TUNC: Now for then. This phrase refers to actions that may be taken and will then have full retroactive effect.

PENDENTE LITE: Pending the suit; pending litigation under way.

PER CAPITA: By head; beneficiaries of an estate, if they take in equal shares, take per capita.

PER CURIAM: By the court; signifies an opinion ostensibly written "by the whole court" and with no identified author.

PER SE: By itself, in itself; inherently.

PER STIRPES: By representation. Used primarily in the law of wills to describe the method of distribution where a person, generally because of death, is unable to take that which is left to him by the will of another, and therefore his heirs divide such property between them rather than take under the will individually.

PRIMA FACIE: On its face, at first sight. A prima facie case is one that is sufficient on its face, meaning that the evidence supporting it is adequate to establish the case until contradicted or overcome by other evidence.

PRO TANTO: For so much; as far as it goes. Often used in eminent domain cases when a property owner receives partial payment for his land without prejudice to his right to bring suit for the full amount he claims his land to be worth.

QUANTUM MERUIT: As much as he deserves. Refers to recovery based on the doctrine of unjust enrichment in those cases in which a party has rendered valuable services or furnished materials that were accepted and enjoyed by another under circumstances that would reasonably notify the recipient that the rendering party expected to be paid. In essence, the law implies a contract to pay the reasonable value of the services or materials furnished.

QUASI: Almost like; as if; nearly. This term is essentially used to signify that one subject or thing is almost analogous to another but that material differences between them do exist. For example, a quasi-criminal proceeding is one that is not strictly criminal but shares enough of the same characteristics to require some of the same safeguards (e.g., procedural due process must be followed in a parole hearing).

QUID PRO QUO: Something for something. In contract law, the consideration, something of value, passed between the parties to render the contract binding.

RES GESTAE: Things done; in evidence law, this principle justifies the admission of a statement that would otherwise be hearsay when it is made so closely to the event in question as to be said to be a part of it, or with such spontaneity as not to have the possibility of falsehood.

RES IPSA LOQUITUR: The thing speaks for itself. This doctrine gives rise to a rebuttable presumption of negligence when the instrumentality causing the injury was within the exclusive control of the defendant, and the injury was one that does not normally occur unless a person has been negligent.

RES JUDICATA: A matter adjudged. Doctrine which provides that once a court of competent jurisdiction has rendered a final judgment or decree on the merits, that judgment or decree is conclusive upon the parties to the case and prevents them from engaging in any other litigation on the points and issues determined therein.

RESPONDEAT SUPERIOR: Let the master reply. This doctrine holds the master liable for the wrongful acts of his servant (or the principal for his agent) in those cases in which the servant (or agent) was acting within the scope of his authority at the time of the injury.

STARE DECISIS: To stand by or adhere to that which has been decided. The common law doctrine of stare decisis attempts to give security and certainty to the law by following the policy that once a principle of law as applicable to a certain set of facts has been set forth in a decision, it forms a precedent which will subsequently be followed, even though a different decision might be made were it the first time the question had arisen. Of course, stare decisis is not an inviolable principle and is departed from in instances where there is good cause (e.g., considerations of public policy led the Supreme Court to disregard prior decisions sanctioning segregation).

SUPRA: Above. A word referring a reader to an earlier part of a book.

ULTRA VIRES: Beyond the power. This phrase is most commonly used to refer to actions taken by a corporation that are beyond the power or legal authority of the corporation.

Addendum of French Derivatives

IN PAIS: Not pursuant to legal proceedings.

CHATTEL: Tangible personal property.

CY PRES: Doctrine permitting courts to apply trust funds to purposes not expressed in the trust but necessary to carry out the settlor's intent.

PER AUTRE VIE: For another's life; during another's life. In property law, an estate may be granted that will terminate upon the death of someone other than the grantee.

PROFIT A PRENDRE: A license to remove minerals or other produce from land.

VOIR DIRE: Process of questioning jurors as to their predispositions about the case or parties to a proceeding in order to identify those jurors displaying bias or prejudice.

Casenote Legal Briefs